VINCE

THE AUTOBIOGRAPHY OF
VINCE HILAIRE

VINCE

VINCE HILAIRE
AND TOM MASLONA

\Bb\
Biteback Publishing

First published in Great Britain in 2018 by
Biteback Publishing Ltd
Westminster Tower
3 Albert Embankment
London SE1 7SP
Copyright © Vince Hilaire and Tom Maslona 2018

Vince Hilaire and Tom Maslona have asserted their rights under the Copyright, Designs and Patents Act 1988 to be identified as the authors of this work.

All rights reserved. No part of this publication may be reproduced, stored in a retrieval system or transmitted, in any form or by any means, without the publisher's prior permission in writing.

This book is sold subject to the condition that it shall not, by way of trade or otherwise, be lent, resold, hired out or otherwise circulated without the publisher's prior consent in any form of binding or cover other than that in which it is published and without a similar condition, including this condition, being imposed on the subsequent purchaser.

Every reasonable effort has been made to trace copyright holders of material reproduced in this book, but if any have been inadvertently overlooked the publisher would be glad to hear from them.

ISBN 978-1-78590-362-5

10 9 8 7 6 5 4 3 2 1

A CIP catalogue record for this book is available from the British Library.

Set in Minion Pro and Futura

Printed and bound in Great Britain by
CPI Group (UK) Ltd, Croydon CR0 4YY

CONTENTS

Foreword by Kenny Sansom   vii

Chapter 1	Reflections	1
Chapter 2	Home	17
Chapter 3	Starting Football	29
Chapter 4	Early Days at Palace	43
Chapter 5	Breaking Through at Palace	57
Chapter 6	We're All Footballers	69
Chapter 7	Venners	83
Chapter 8	The Break-Up	97
Chapter 9	Managerial Merry-Go-Round	111
Chapter 10	Leaving Palace	131
	Billy Gilbert on Vince	149
Chapter 11	England and Moving On	155
Chapter 12	The Gremlins	169
Chapter 13	Alan Ball	185
Chapter 14	Kevin Dillon and Kevin O'Callaghan	207
Chapter 15	Promotion, Relegation and Some Pompey Legends	217

Chapter 16	The Cast of Gremlins	231
	Alan Knight on Vince	247
Chapter 17	The Gaffers	251
Chapter 18	Staying Sane	271
	Ian Baird on Vince	289
Chapter 19	The End	295
Chapter 20	Just Vince	305

Career Statistics	315
Acknowledgements	319

FOREWORD
BY KENNY SANSOM

My memories of Vince are all really good ones. He was a great lad, a great team player; he had great team spirit and was an all-round top man.

Vince is a couple of years younger than me and I can remember him joining Palace and being a lively young lad. He just loved being a footballer and being a part of the team. He was a little comedian and every day he'd have a smile on his face. He had great character.

That character helped him because he used to get stick from fans of other clubs, but I'm not sure he took that much notice. He almost had the attitude that they could do what they wanted. Vince was laid back and more concerned with his football than anything else, so he didn't allow himself to get put off by their abuse. We were playing sport at a high level and he'd keep a smile on his face whatever was being said to him, and that says a lot about him.

To be honest, Vince got enough stick from his own players. He'd try and beat too many players at times – he'd tell you that. He'd beat three players and then cross it behind the goal and we'd tear our hair out and tell him just to beat one and cross it into the box. He used to get a lot of mickey taken out of him for that. Ian Walsh and Dave Swindlehurst used to get the hump and have a go at him. But, to be fair to Vince, he did practise his crossing, and then he'd go on a run and hit great crosses in.

I can only really speak about football, although I imagine that it's the same for all sports, but people are always remembered for the bad things that they do. It's the same in life. People are quick to say, 'You did really well but…' Vince took the stick but he kept going and never stopped working. He was a tremendous team player; he really worked hard for the team.

I think it's only now, looking back with hindsight, that we can appreciate how good that Palace side was. We had a team that was similar to the one Manchester United had under Ferguson with Giggs, the Neville brothers, Beckham, Scholes and Butt in it. They had six or seven boys that came through from the Youth team to the First team and we had exactly the same thing at Palace.

The team spirit we had at that time at Palace was as good as I've ever known in football. When Leicester won the Premier League, they reminded me of our side because we had a similar camaraderie about us. It's such a shame that Palace side didn't stay together because we'll never know how good we could have been, but I feel sure that we could have got into Europe at least.

People say that when I left it all fell apart but, the truth is, I didn't want to go. I spoke to Terry Venables on the Monday at the training ground and agreed a new contract. I then came in on the Tuesday and, as I walked past his office, he called out:

FOREWORD BY KENNY SANSOM

'Ken, don't get changed. Drive over to Arsenal as they want to sign you.' I didn't have a dad; Venners was my boss and mentor, so I did what he said. I got in my car and drove over there and signed for Arsenal. Venners always says that I wanted to leave but he's a fibber. He's a crafty Cockney and he's kept that story going.

Going to Arsenal was great, don't get me wrong, but I didn't want to go. Palace was where I started and I'd had a fantastic few years there with friends and some great teammates. Palace, at that time, was the kind of place where anyone who signed settled in within five minutes. The team spirit was that good and Vince was a key part of that, with his brilliant sense of humour.

When he was playing, he just wanted to be involved all the time, but Vince wasn't one of the lads that liked a pint and a bird – he kept himself to himself. Off the pitch he was a totally different character to the person that played on the pitch. He was a bit naive. He would come in for games wearing a black suit with brown socks. I'd ask him what the hell he was doing and he'd tell me that he had to get changed in the dark. I urged him to turn the light on in future.

Vince tells a story that whenever we played against each other after I left Palace, I used to approach him in the tunnel and check whether my shorts had a big enough pocket for him to fit into. The truth is, whenever you play against someone you know, you want to win. It becomes even more important for you to do well. Winning was what it was all about but, when the game was over, you'd have a drink together – well, maybe, a lemonade.

VINCE

I feel honoured to have been asked to write the foreword to his book, and I wish Vince every success.

Kenny Sansom
February 2018

CHAPTER 1

REFLECTIONS

I wouldn't have been a professional footballer if I hadn't gone to Leyton Orient and watched Laurie Cunningham play. I was about fourteen at the time and I used to go there with Maurice Newman, the manager of the Sunday team I played for, Beaumont. At times, I didn't even watch Laurie. I'd stand and look at the reaction of the people around me watching Laurie. The sense of anticipation when he got the ball or was near the ball was unbelievable. I knew straight away that I was watching someone special.

I'd seen top footballers playing on TV, but it was different being at a match and watching one perform live, and seeing the power that Laurie had. He was exciting. He was so different to the rest of his teammates. As far as I was concerned, Orient only had two players: John Jackson – the goalkeeper – and Laurie Cunningham. Jacko would catch it and boot it towards Laurie and then he would take over. It was incredible to watch.

Orient had quite a good team then, and reached the FA Cup semi-final in 1978. They had another good player, Peter Kitchen. He was the first footballer that I ever spoke to at length because he lodged with Maurice Newman. Though he was a professional footballer and Orient's top scorer for a couple of years, I soon realised that he was just an ordinary guy. I wasn't the most confident and outgoing person, but this interaction made me understand that becoming a footballer was an attainable goal. People back then told me that I could make it as a footballer, but it was only through watching Laurie and talking to Peter that I realised I really could do it.

Laurie Cunningham inspired me. I hoped that one day people would believe that when I got the ball, I too could make something wonderful happen. I wanted supporters to feel that same sense of excitement and anticipation whenever I had the ball, and Laurie gave me that desire. He enthralled and inspired people; it was an incredible gift.

Later on, when I got into the England Under-21s, we travelled to Romania and the full England squad were playing out there too. Laurie was in the senior side and, as much as I wanted to, I didn't get the opportunity to meet up with him and thank him and tell him what he meant to me.

He died a few years later and it's only recently that they've put a statue of him up at Orient. The word 'great' is used far too often in football, but Laurie really was great. As was Bobby Moore, who coached me at Palace. In addition to being a great footballer, Bobby was a humble, lovely man. I can't speak highly enough of Laurie and Bobby. They've got something else in common too: neither of them was truly appreciated until after they died. This saddens me. We should celebrate people while they are still with us.

I often look back on my career. I know that a lot of the older players suffer from depression, and if you look back with regret then it certainly can make you melancholy. If I wanted to delve deeply into remembering some of the issues that I suffered from during my career, such as racism, then it would make me depressed too. It would also hurt if I thought about players who achieved more than me when they weren't as good as I was, so I tend to try to look back at games that were memorable for me and, even more importantly, at things that made me laugh.

As far as I'm concerned, the more you can think about things that make you smile, the younger you'll feel. If you constantly look back on things with regret, then you age faster. Footballers are the best people in the world at finding things to laugh about, even if others think they're insensitive; they divorce themselves from reality. I can remember being at Stoke in the treatment room and I was talking about the fact that the Gulf War looked like it was going to end, and one of the lads didn't even know that there was a war on!

I don't regret missing out on the chance to earn the money that the players do now. The only thing that I do miss in football is the humour amongst the players. I think that you're a lucky person if you can go to work and find twenty or so like-minded people you can laugh and joke with every day. I packed in early – my career was finished at thirty-two – but I started at sixteen, so I had sixteen years as a professional, and I wouldn't change any of it. I always say to people that my time at Portsmouth made me grow as a man and Palace helped me to grow as a footballer, but I had to experience all of the things that I did in my career to become the person that I am today.

Writing this book has made me reflect on my life and my career and wonder how good I really was as a player. If I was more consistent, I think that my ability level would have seen me floating between the top division and the Championship. In all honesty, I don't think I would have been a top player in the Premier League and I'm not sure I would have been the top player in the Championship, but I do know that, in any given game, I could have done something that would have made the difference between my team winning or losing. I also know that there were games where you wouldn't have noticed me.

That's a criticism that the supporters of Leeds United and Stoke City could level at me. Until you mention my name, people would forget that I played for those teams, because I didn't pull up any trees while I was there. But I'd hope that people would remember me playing for either Palace or Portsmouth, if not both – particularly the supporters of those clubs.

As a player, the older I got, the more I worried about how well I was doing. A lot of players lie to other people, but they can't lie to themselves. As the years advance, you wonder whether the reason you're doing badly is because of your age or because you can't hack it any more. When you're younger, you have a bad game but then you forget about it in a couple of days whereas, as an older player, a couple of days later I'd still be thinking about it and desperately hoping that I didn't play that badly again, because if I did, I'd be convinced there was something wrong.

A lot of the criticism levelled at me during my career was for being inconsistent. People used to say that I'd play well one week then I'd have a couple of bad games and I used to think, 'Well, if I play well in every single game, or 350 of the 400-odd games that I played in, then I'd have medals galore.' It doesn't work like that. You try to play as well as you can in as many matches as you can but, sometimes, playing well to me might not be playing well to the people in the stands, even if I'd been following instructions. I might have been playing in a position or in a way that the manager asked me to and the fans don't know about.

Supporters don't think that players can hear the things they're shouting, but you can and there are times when you think, 'I can't wait for this whistle to blow because I am having the biggest nightmare of all time', or you do something wrong and you quickly have a look at the dugout to see if they've now got the sub warming up for you. Those memories have never left me. You tend to hear the individual voices more when things are going badly. In my case, it was often the manager that I could hear.

A fine example was Alan Ball. He could make you feel twenty feet tall, but he could also destroy you. He had that power and, when you have that, I don't think that you should abuse it, because it's not going to help players – even someone as experienced as me. There were training sessions where I stayed away from the ball because of him. Bally could make you feel like that. I'm pleased and proud to say that he took me to a lot of clubs, so I must have been doing something right, but I've seen him break people. As a player, you know when you're having a bad time; some players are just better at hiding it than others. Some say that it doesn't bother them, but that's a lie.

Despite my perceived inconsistency, I do think that I was unlucky not to get a full England cap, but caps were harder to get back then. For two years, around 1979 and 1980, I don't think that there were many players better than me in my position. After that, though, my character wasn't right. Maybe if I'd tried harder at Luton, then I could have pushed on with my career and gone on to an even bigger club because, in hindsight, there were four or five top-quality players when I went there. It might have meant me going there and being prepared to sit in the reserves and biding my time. Maybe I shouldn't have been so eager to go to Portsmouth when David Pleat called me into his office but, by then, Billy Gilbert had told me that they gave you a car at Pompey. That swung it for me.

I do know that I was a better player at Palace than I was at Pompey, and so was Billy Gilbert. People often ask me which was the best side I played for. Well, Palace always used to beat Pompey so, for that reason, and for that reason only, I think that the 1979 Palace side would beat the Portsmouth promotion side.

No, seriously, the Pompey side that I played in was a lot more experienced than the Palace side that won Division Two. Two-thirds of that Palace team were kids. John Burridge was the oldest, along with Steve Kember, but if you took them out of it then there was no one in that side who was even close to thirty. Even though we were young, all of us Palace players were experienced in terms of the number of games we'd played. We'd all been in the team for at least three years, and we were certainly good enough.

The Pompey side was experienced too, but not as young and, player for player, the Palace team would have shaded it anyway. We had Kenny Swain at right back at Portsmouth and he'd won the European Cup at Villa, but I would always have had Paul 'Fish' Hinshelwood over him because Fish was more of an athlete, had a goal threat and really put his foot in. Billy Gilbert was obviously in both sides and you had Noel Blake at Pompey who was intimidating, but Jimmy Cannon could do the lot. He could play nowadays; he's what a lot of top clubs are looking for in their centre-halves. Even to this day, I couldn't tell you whether Jimmy was right or left footed and the nearest that I've seen to Jim in terms of his distribution from the back was John Terry. Then, Kenny Sansom was far and away the best full back this country has produced in sixty years.

In midfield, Micky Kennedy and Kevin Dillon were good. Mick was as hard as they come, but Peter Nicholas was as hard as him and could do the other bits as well. Nico first got into the Palace team as a centre-back, which shows his versatility, and he also had a couple of good years at Arsenal, which shows his quality. That Palace side had more quality generally. There wasn't a lot to choose between Jerry Murphy and Kevin Dillon, although I would say that Murph didn't score as many goals as he should have done for his ability, whereas Kevin scored goals from a distance.

So I'm very proud to have played for both sides and it was an honour for me to be voted into Pompey's Hall of Fame recently. I'm not being modest, but there have been so many better players than me that have played for Portsmouth and haven't been held in such esteem. I just hope that the people who came to watch when I played knew that I gave everything I could for the football club.

If I'm honest, that's the slight difference between Portsmouth and Palace for me: I let Palace down a bit in the last couple of years I was there. Not in terms of effort but, at Palace, I was a much better player and, even though I was only twenty-four, I should have taken a lot more responsibility in games and helped other players out instead of only showing them the old flying winger once in every four matches. At Portsmouth, Bally wouldn't allow me to let games pass me by and I certainly couldn't do that in the early days at Palace under Terry Venables. John Cartwright – my old Youth coach – would go to a lot of the games, and he used to talk to Venners about how to get the best out of me.

Under Alan Ball, you couldn't let games drift by whether you were playing well or not and I had to contribute physically as well as creatively. I like to think that's what was reflected in getting the Hall of Fame award at Portsmouth. Portsmouth is a very working-class city, which I like. It reminds me of the East End; if you give everything, which should be a prerequisite, then people there will respond to you.

Since retiring, Palace have asked me on numerous occasions to do matchday hospitality there, and I did it for a while. It's easier for me to do the hospitality at Pompey, but they looked after me so well at Palace and I enjoyed it there. I loved getting up early to go to Palace and chatting to people about sport. I'll talk about football, cricket and tennis all day long, if you let me.

I enjoy conversations about how football has changed, too. I never say that it was better or harder in my day; I just say that it was different. You can't compare eras, and I think it's wrong to. Look at someone like Jimmy Greaves. Every Tottenham supporter over the age of fifty will tell you that he's the greatest goalscorer they've ever seen, but kids today would watch film of him on TV and think that he couldn't run and laugh at the pitches too.

If you're going to try and compare eras then I think you have to take into account rule changes. The only games that were live on TV in my day were the European finals and the FA Cup Finals. When Liverpool went away from home, their whole game consisted of their defenders getting the ball and passing it between themselves and then giving it straight back to the keeper and they'd do it again and again to quieten the crowd. Jimmy Greaves would have scored another 100-odd goals in his career, and so would Gary Lineker, if they'd played nowadays, because they were predators and they would have preyed upon the fact that the goalkeeper could no longer pick up a back-pass. It's the same in cricket. How many players really were out lbw? DRS has changed the way we look at things. Shane Warne would have taken a thousand wickets!

When I'm talking about football, people ask me if I miss running out in front of the crowds, but the truth is, I don't. It sounds so clichéd but, even now, the thing I truly miss is the banter that goes on in the dressing rooms and pubs. It was just brilliant. With the money involved now, however, I don't believe it would be anywhere near as good as it was, because I don't imagine that players go out and meet up in the pub any more. The best player in England years ago was George Best and I bet he socialised with most of his teammates. It does you good if you can socialise with your teammates away from the training ground, but I'd be surprised if, in a high-profile modern-day team, there are six or seven players who could say they are close mates. I don't think I'd enjoy the game as much today, because I'd still want to be buddies with everyone.

I did an interview with *The Times* a few years ago and they asked me to compare the Pompey side that I got promoted with to the one that won the FA Cup in 2008. They'd heard that we'd gone on the piss for a week after we'd gone up and I was at pains to make clear that we weren't unprofessional – we simply had different demands on us. If a player like George Best had the same training and attitude as the players in this era, then he would still, no doubt, be one of the best players in Europe, but I'm not sure if he could handle the discipline that players have these days. Teams today stay together overnight before virtually every away game, and for a lot of home games too, so that the football staff can ensure that they're getting the right sleep and eating the right foods, and it's a completely different environment, carefully monitored and controlled. Sport is evolving.

When I played, right up until the mid-'80s, Fridays at football clubs were a joke; we'd come in for ten minutes and just play a bit of five-a-side. When I was at Pompey, our Fridays consisted of having a warm-up, going into the gym, getting into a little circle and keeping the ball away from the person in the middle of the circle for twenty minutes. I thoroughly enjoyed it, but that was it; that was our day finished.

Things have changed so much now: tactics are discussed, diets are monitored, you stay overnight and you eat what they tell you to eat. Whereas at Pompey in my day, it was the circle, Micky Channon going off to whatever racecourse he had to be at, and then the rest of us heading into the Pompey pub for sausage, eggs, bacon and chips, and playing a bit of pool before heading home. We'd then turn up the next day at 1.30 or 1.45 p.m. for the game or, in Micky Channon's case, 2.30 p.m. Nowadays, you get to the ground at 11.30 a.m. To be fair, some clubs did that then and it was considered revolutionary, but now it's the norm. For night games we thought it was outrageous having to turn up at 4 p.m. The coaching staff would tell us that we were going to have a bit of a loosener and something to eat, and we'd all think, 'I could do that at home.'

The game itself has also changed. In my day, you could make big tackles and someone like Billy Gilbert could make four or five bad ones before he'd even be spoken to, and then he'd have to commit another four or five before he was given a yellow card, but now you can't make four or five bad tackles in the whole game. I don't think I could play now. It's not down to fitness. I'd naturally get fitter through training, but it would be more difficult for me to change the way I think about the game. I'd cope technically and in terms of fitness, but not in terms of my mind. It's too regimented now. The majority of my games were either played on the right or left wing but, in all of the games that I played, I never thought that I had to stay there and that I couldn't influence a game in a different part of the pitch.

Now, however, coaches would be looking at me, telling me that I was meant to be a right-winger and would tell me to go back there. It's now only the top, top players who can play without discipline and influence the game without hurting the team. I always used to like playing just off the front two where Paul Merson used to play but only Terry Venables would encourage me to do that and allow me to get on the ball as much as possible.

I tried to stay in football for a while after I stopped playing. I loved coaching at Havant & Waterlooville to start with and the players really responded to me initially, but I didn't realise how hard it would be for players to play at that level with full-time jobs. I was there with Billy Gilbert and he coped with it a lot better than I did. He was more calculated, whereas I think I'd been around Bally for too long and was too emotional.

I often get asked, even now, what the difference is between a non-league player and a good professional player. You could argue that it's speed, consistency, skill or strength and some might say that it's fitness because professionals train every day but, to me, there's only one thing that separates a pro from a non-league player: the professional will listen. Non-league players might well have the same amount of ability, but they'll get distracted and think they know better. Pros realise that they have got to listen in order to learn, and then they work out whether what's being said to them can help them or not.

I didn't call what I did at Havant coaching; I called it giving the players the benefit of my experience in the game, but I found it really hard. In the pro game, if you have a go at someone, he might not agree with you, but he'll listen. For example, a manager may criticise a professional player for bringing a ball down in the wrong area when he'd been told not to and the pro will hold his hands up and say, 'Fair enough.' He might get upset but, by Monday, he'll have forgotten about it and be ready to go again. The non-league player will take it personally and won't like you from that point on, no matter what you say to him after that.

A lot of the lads that I didn't get on with at Havant bump into me now and they admit that they didn't understand at the time that what I was saying to them was for the team's good. They've also admitted that sometimes they didn't listen to me because I'd had a go at them the week before. Therein lies the problem. The non-league player doesn't realise that you're having a go at the footballer; they think that you're having a go at the person, when you're not.

If I disliked every player or manager who'd ever had a go at me, then I wouldn't like anyone. So frustration was one of the reasons why I gave up. I also didn't like the fact that when I went out after a game, the only ones who came out with me were the ones I hadn't criticised, and had been the best players. The other players just didn't understand that after you point something out in football, the slate should be wiped clean the next time you see them. Instead, for them, it lingered.

My only active involvement in football these days is doing the hospitality on matchdays at Pompey. I stayed in Portsmouth after my career finished, in part because I grew up as a man down here. Every opportunity was available for me to go back to the East End but, if I'm being honest, I still had that footballing mentality in my head and, much as I hate saying it, when you're a footballer, you get more things done for you and it's a bit of a rude awakening when you go into the real world and have to do everything for yourself – even paying bills. I hate myself for saying it, but because I had that mentality – which I don't have any more, I hasten to add – it just made it easier for me to stay in Portsmouth when I finished playing.

I try to console myself with the idea that people in Portsmouth made it easier for me because of the way I was as a footballer but also how I was as a person. I never ever thought that I was special because I was a footballer. I was different, but not special. As I got older, I made even more of a point of showing that I was just an ordinary person, and that's why I could go out after games without getting any hassle. You should never forget where you're from.

My family is here too. I know that I wasn't really up to scratch as a dad because, honestly, I didn't know how to be a dad, so I was always just Vince. I'm a lot better grandad to Albie than I was a dad, because it was only as I got older that I realised how much other people relied on me. It wasn't that I was being selfish, and it may be a footballer's mentality, but people would point out to me that I was a father, but I was acting as if nothing had changed.

With being a professional footballer often comes immaturity. How many other professions have people who pay your bills for you or look after your passport or arrange for a psychologist to discuss any problems you think you may have? I'm proud of how my two daughters have turned out, but that's despite me. I'm still making it up to them now. There is always something more that a parent thinks that they could have done for their children. If you've done it properly, then your kids will make sure that you're alright and they'll pick up the phone to check on you and, fortunately, that does happen to me.

One thing that never changes is that you only learn as you get older. With age comes experience. I've said that I try not to regret anything that I've done in my life but that experience has allowed me to reflect. I've changed as I've aged and I'd like to think that I've become more aware of the needs of others.

CHAPTER 2

HOME

My parents were first-generation immigrants from a small, French-speaking island called Dominica and they came over in the 1950s when lots of people from that area were asked to come to England by the Conservative government. I don't think that my dad had much of a childhood. I always remember him telling me about the first time that he saw snow. He was getting the train across Europe to get to the port and he asked the conductor what the white stuff on the hills was.

I was brought up in a family where my parents spoke French to each other. I don't speak French, but I used to get scolded in French at home, so I do understand the language, as a friend of mine, Pete, found out. There used to be a market in Palmerston Road in Portsmouth, and a guy came up to him and started speaking French and Pete wanted to ignore him but I told him that the guy just wanted to know what sort of fish he had and how much they were.

The great thing about my mum and dad was that they put the kids first. My siblings and I never wanted for anything, even though there were a lot of us. We were taught the value of right and wrong. My parents were strict Catholics and they didn't think anything about giving us a clout if we stepped out of line. We were a very religious family and I was a regular churchgoer even beyond the time that I became a pro. Respect played a big part in our lives and you had to look after what you had and make it last as long as possible.

My dad loved to be surrounded by kids. There was nothing untoward; he was just like the Pied Piper. Every Asian kid in the area used to pop round to see him. Maybe they confused his Christian name, Alie, with Ali? He used to buy them sweets and ice lollies and was really cheerful with other kids, but very strict with us. Knowing the difference between right and wrong was a very big deal to him. Occasionally, we'd get a slap, but it didn't happen often.

I remember taking four shillings off the sideboard one day on the way to school – it was just lying there, telling me to pick it up. That was a lot of money to someone who was getting two pennies for pocket money. I took it, but I couldn't bring myself to spend it; I don't know why to this day, because if it was fear then I wouldn't have taken the money in the first place. I put it back a little later knowing that my mum had been looking for those four shillings all morning and that my dad had got home earlier than normal and had been helping her. When I put it back, my mum knew it was me straight away as I was the only one in the room at the time and she was genuinely frightened for me because of what she thought my dad might do. Thankfully, he just hollered at me.

Apart from that, I never gave myself the opportunity to get into trouble. I knew a lot of lads who got into a lot of trouble though, which they tend to do in the East End. One of them, Peter, who played for Beaumont with me, was a good footballer, and he befriended me. I joined the team at around twelve and Peter had already been smoking for around two years. Peter asked me if he could come over to mine. I went out and got some comics and I came back and opened the door and, bearing in mind how strictly I'd been brought up, the first thing I heard was him asking, 'And can you blow smoke rings like this, Mrs Hilaire?' My mum was looking at me in amazement. I was sitting there thinking that I was dead because my mum was going to think that I smoked too, but she just laughed.

Smoking had never interested me. My mum and dad had smoked and, when I was about seven or eight, I was watching TV and my mum offered me a puff on her cigarette. It was the first time that I'd ever put a cigarette in my mouth and I coughed for ages. I've never minded other people smoking but, since then, I've never ever wanted to smoke myself. It was a good way to stop people from smoking. Peter ended up as a real unsavoury character and managed Nigel Benn before they fell out. They were the sort of people I grew up with.

I got on with my parents. There was only one problem child in the family and that was my sister. She could be neurotic when she was younger. I remember my mum having a go at her for going out when she was young. We had a big house with a kitchen upstairs and she ran into it and we didn't see her for about an hour. Then, my brother John came down and shouted, 'You better come upstairs, quickly. Vivienne's got her head in the oven!' She was trying to gas herself because our mum had reprimanded her. She forgot to put the gas on, though.

I've got two brothers and a sister. My sister is the eldest. I love her and I hope she loves me, but I didn't grow up being close with her like I did with my brothers. All of the sport that I played was with my two brothers and we played a hell of a lot of cricket in the back garden. We lived in a massive house that my dad bought for under £3,000. He'd been a fisherman in Dominica and, like every other fisherman, he was the greatest one there was. My dad tried to turn his hand to everything, but he didn't play cricket with us. As I found out myself when I retired, it's much easier to talk about how good you were and convince people that way. My dad used to show us his fingers and say that he'd broken this one or that one fielding at cricket.

Although he didn't play with us, my dad loved watching and listening to the cricket. We used to listen to the radio together when we were younger. Because of the way my dad was treated when he first came over, whenever England played, he wanted them to lose. It was murder when the West Indians came over to play England. You wouldn't hear the end of it if an umpire gave a West Indian out lbw. You've never heard anything like it. I look back now and I think, 'Dad, you didn't even see it. We used to listen on the radio! How did you know where the ball pitched?'

When England played the West Indies at cricket in recent years, my dad would still want the West Indies to win and there was no one more upset than him about the decline of their cricket team. You can go all the way back to the 1940s and 1950s and the one thing that the West Indies had, sport-wise, that they could compete with the rest of the world in, would be cricket. It was a game that people there identified as their own.

It was sacrilege to ask my dad how old he was. He was a bit mysterious, but he was a funny man, my dad. He worked at Ford's in Dagenham for twenty-odd years and he didn't have it easy. He hated whatever government was in power and said that they were crooks. In fact, if he didn't agree with something then he'd say that they were on the fiddle.

My dad must have had about seventeen driving tests before he passed and I remember him coming back having failed but he didn't throw tantrums, he just went up the betting shop. He took his anger out on Lester Piggott. One of the things that he used to say to us was that Lester Piggott was a crook too and it seemed that whenever he put good money on him, he lost. Then, famously, Lester spent a few months in jail so he was walking around saying, 'I was right but no one listened to me.' He only ever bet what he could afford to lose but my mum wasn't too amused that he spent most of his life in there.

When he did eventually pass his test he had a 3.5 litre Rover – a second hand one. He used to go and pick my mum up; she had about eighteen jobs at the same time. She worked at Watneys and Trebors and was a cleaner too. When she worked at Trebors, we never wanted for sweets. We were probably the only kids that were fed up of them. After that, she worked at Watneys and it was a good thing that I wasn't a big drinker as a kid.

He was an upstanding man, my dad, but he didn't mind doing a few deals. We lived quite near the docks in the East End. It's a very similar place to Portsmouth, as it happens. Lot of Pursers used to come off the ships and he had a particular friend who we used to see two or three times a year – he was a French guy, so he tended to only speak with my dad – and my dad used to buy watches and get decent deals from him.

My parents left England when they retired and went back to the West Indies but, despite the fact that they had a big house on the beach front, ten years later they came back here because they missed London so much. My mum turned her attention from hating England and English people to loving it, and she now says that there aren't enough English people in the country.

It's an old adage and a cliché but you don't realise what you've got until it's gone and it's true. As much as the Caribbean is a lovely place to live – they had a bungalow on the beach and wanted for nothing and the weather was great – they didn't realise how much the London way of life had become ingrained in them. Subconsciously, they'd turned into East Enders.

I got on great with my parents. They were still together up until my dad's death in 2017 – still arguing with each other just the way they did when I was a kid. My mum is still in east London and she's seen a change there now but she doesn't think that it's for the best. She can't stop moaning about it. When they went back to the Caribbean they yearned for England and, now my mum talks about how much better things were in London previously. My mum is older but she doesn't think that London is as friendly a place as it was when we were growing up as kids. That may be because we all look back on our past with rose-tinted spectacles, but I'm not sure.

SCHOOL

Where I lived, if someone didn't like you the very first thing that they didn't like about you was you. That's always stayed with me. No one made any bones about you being black or from Africa or West Indian. They told you they just didn't like you as a person. They didn't turn to their friends and say, 'Oh, he's a black bastard. I don't like him' or 'That wog'. So, in the end, because it was open and in your face, it didn't worry you. I was lucky because where I grew up most of the people were open and honest.

I went to a Catholic primary school. The schools in that area were, for want of a better word, like zoos and, towards the end of my last year at primary school, I heard a rumour about the secondary school around the corner from me, which was called St Bonaventure's. We all had to tick which school we wanted to go to, and St Bonaventure's had produced a lot of professional footballers, but people were saying that they wouldn't go there because the older boys flushed the first years' heads down the toilet and whacked them around the heads too. That worried me, so I put it down as my second choice. I put a school called Rokeby down as first choice – and this was a big mistake. Rokeby was in Stratford, but I didn't know that it was one of the roughest schools in the area and I didn't find that out until the start of the next year. Of around 100 or so kids that I grew up with from the ages of six to eleven, only one other was going to Rokeby and I wasn't particularly close to him so I thought, 'Here we go'.

My dad said to me that I had to step up and make something of my life now that I was going to secondary school, so my mum promptly went out and bought me a briefcase. That was the worst thing that could have happened because they were so unfashionable and I immediately became a target for the other kids. I didn't know anyone and there were only a few other lads with briefcases and one of them was Mukesh Mandelia, a Kenyan Asian, so I made friends with him. This was about the time when Idi Amin got rid of a load of Asians from Uganda so a lot of Asians came over here. They either got out or lost their lives. It was me, Mukesh and a couple of other kids that decided to be pally with me because they brought briefcases to school as well. We were the briefcase kids and went around together.

Because Mukesh was my first friend at Rokeby, I used to walk home or get the bus with him. It was after a couple of years there that I got my first taste of racism. London then was nothing like it is now because now you'll find schools in London which are well over 70 per cent ethnic. London was the most cosmopolitan place in England then but it would still have been only about 20 per cent minority ethnic which was obviously a lot less.

At that point, there was something very popular amongst the older teenagers called 'Paki-bashing'. I don't even like using the word but that's what it was called amongst them. I often tell this story because it shows how people's minds work but I've never forgiven myself for it. We were about fourteen at the time and I used to sit next to Mukesh in the majority of lessons and we'd put our briefcases down and have a laugh and a joke; we shared a love of the same things. It was around the time of the Kung-Fu phenomenon and he was the first person that I saw an X-rated film with.

Break time came along and Mukesh went off and I was with a couple of other lads. After break, Mukesh came in to the classroom a couple of minutes late and he sat down next to me but he had the biggest eye you've ever seen and his nose was smashed round his face. Everyone looked at him and I asked him what had happened and he told me that the skinheads from another form came and found him and gave him a good kicking and they told him that they were going to keep doing it. I asked him to give me a couple of seconds and I moved seats and I didn't sit next to him for the rest of the half-term. I didn't like myself for it but it had to be done.

At the time, I was just starting to make a name for myself at school for being Mr Popular. I didn't like it but, when I thought that I had got to a certain level of popularity, I started to be his friend again and no one touched him because of me. It's sad and I did reproach myself every night but the only thing that kept me going was that I kept feeling my nose and eyes and thought, 'Well, I'm still good looking.' The bullies left me alone when they saw that I wasn't hanging around with Mukesh any more and I put my own welfare first. I think that Mukesh understood, although he did keep asking me why I kept getting the bus home rather than walking with him and also why was I now hanging around with the Caucasian kids.

I was good at school; I passed my 11-plus and I got a few O-levels in subjects that interested me like English, History and Maths. School was important to me. I was a popular boy there but it was nothing to do with sport – far from it – because I didn't even get into my school football team until I was eleven or twelve.

I loved watching sport – anything with a ball involved. I was obsessed with the TV. We had a slot TV with a timer and had to put money into the back of it. I used to listen to a lot of cricket on the radio too. A lot of my humour comes from the cricket commentators like John Arlott and Brian Johnston. John Arlott had a great voice and those commentators should get a lot of credit because they used to have to make you visualise what was going on and paint pictures in your head. These men played a huge role in cementing a lifelong love of sport in me.

We moved house and my dad thought that he could turn his hand to anything and said that he'd patio the garden. It was probably the worst bit of patio you've ever seen in your life. It was like crazy paving except he didn't mean it to be. You walked into our garden and you were lucky if you walked for thirty yards and didn't break your ankle. I'd just got into the school cricket team because that was my first love, and me and my brothers played cricket out there. We bowled on the crazy paving and, if you've ever played on uneven surfaces, then it teaches you to get into line properly and that's what it taught me. It helped me to get into the right position to deal with the ball during a game.

We started off with bits of wood for bats because we couldn't afford proper ones and we'd play for hours, in the rain, with a tennis ball. Then we'd go over to Wanstead Flats and then West Ham Park and it was nearly as dangerous as the garden as the wickets there were uncovered and dogs used to go on them.

Sometimes things are so uncomplicated. Clubs have got their academies now but, at the end of the day, if you've got the right technique in any sport then you've got half a chance. You can get pampered too much. Look at the way I learned to play cricket. When we played it was a case of playing double wicket which means you were paired off and if your partner was out then you were out too. To save time, we'd only use one pad each so I used to get side on because I was worried that if I missed the ball then I'd break my leg. In cricket they'll tell you to get your foot as close to the ball as you can and that's how I learned.

I played County standard cricket for Essex Schools for three or four years, which was quite a feat for someone from a state school in the East End. When I was at school, the headmaster, Mr Scott, was one down from God and one of the reasons why I became popular was that it got back to him that one of the pupils was good at cricket. He asked to see me and told me that he'd been getting good reports from the PE Department and had heard that I'd been called up by Newham District, so he said that I could clean his bat once a week and he'd look at my timetable to arrange a time that I could do it. He told me that if I ever got called up by Essex then I could have the bat. He stuck to his word and I scored a couple of 50s for them, which he was delighted about.

CHAPTER 3

STARTING FOOTBALL

I was the same as any other kid my age; we used to watch *Match of the Day* on a Saturday night. It was the dribblers that caught my eye: players like George Best and Charlie Cooke at Chelsea. Celtic were on a few times and I liked Jimmy Johnstone too. I also liked the showmen like Rodney Marsh; they were the players that made the biggest impression on me. West Ham and Leeds were my favourite teams then. I liked the Leeds socks because they used to have their numbers on them.

I always wanted to go to watch West Ham but it only happened once as a kid. I'd never been to a football match before; I must have been about eleven and one of the lads that I played with used to talk about standing on the North Bank at West Ham. He always used to ask me to come up there with him so we went one Saturday and we got there at about 12.30 p.m. These kids that I went with told me to watch the rush when the gates opened to get in but I didn't know what they were talking about.

All of a sudden, we heard the gate open to the first turnstile on the North Bank and the crush knocked me to the side. Out of the corner of my eye, I saw a couple of blokes who seemed really old but, looking back, must only have been about nineteen or twenty and they winked at each other. They could see that I was a bit frightened and I lost the lads that I was with – even though they were probably only a couple of yards in front of me. I looked at these lads again and they nudged each other and I thought, 'Not for me' so I turned on my heels and went home as fast as I could. I was frightened to death and I vowed that I'd never go to West Ham again and I didn't until I played there for Palace.

I first got spotted playing football in the playground by a man called Maurice Newman, who was a combination of Sergeant Bilko and Arthur Daley along with the Penguin in the Batman films. He was a complete and utter wide boy but, what a man, and, without him, I'd have never kicked a ball in pro football. Maurice was having a chat with the best footballer at Rokeby School who happened to have the greatest name ever – Ossie Tutu. Ossie had just signed on for Orient and was now playing in the Youth team with Laurie Cunningham and Glenn Roeder. I was just kicking around in the playground and Maurice spotted me and asked me, in a real Cockney accent, if I played for anyone. I didn't so he asked me if I wanted to play for him on a Sunday for Beaumont.

Maurice was a scout at Orient and he used to say, 'Look son, you do well for me and I might get you down to Orient. I know George Petchey!' I told my dad that I was going to start playing on Sundays but he told me that I wasn't going anywhere if it meant missing church. Maurice assured me not to worry and, because he was such a wide boy and my dad was so gullible, he convinced him to let me play. My dad fell in love with Maurice and if Maurice had told him that the sky was green, then it was. I still had to go to church, but I just went at the earlier time of 8 a.m. which meant that I could then go and play football afterwards.

We used to get picked up in a transit and we had goals with nets! This was the life! We started signing players like Billy Hurley, who played for England Schoolboys; I still think that he had the hardest shot that I've ever seen – he used to beat goalies from sixty yards. Billy ended up playing a few games for Orient but drifted out of the game.

I wouldn't have become a professional footballer without Beaumont. Maurice used to come and pick me up and, one day, he told me that he'd take me down to Orient as he wanted to see George Petchey. I stood in the corner of the dressing room and, all of a sudden, the door opened and I trod on someone's big toe and it happened to be Laurie Cunningham's. He was the first footballer that I'd come into contact with and I'd trodden on his foot. Maurice told me off and I learned a valuable lesson that day. Feet are the tools of a footballer's trade and you need to look after them and I was always very conscious of that afterwards. Despite that inauspicious start, I realised that this was the life that I wanted. Laurie and Glenn Roeder were only Youth team players at Orient then and I wanted to be like them.

As a young kid, I knew that I had an aptitude for cricket but I never knew that I had an aptitude for football as well. The only time getting selected for a team ever took my breath away – and I'm including England B and England Under-21s in this – was when I got selected for Newham District, because I thought,

'How can I be good enough for them? They've got people like Nicky Morgan and Henry Hughton playing for them and Alan Curbishley's brother!' When they told me that I'd been selected to go to training, I couldn't believe it. I'm not the most confident person so if I don't believe that I'm good enough to do something, then I won't do it. I was thirteen and I'd only been playing football for the school and for Beaumont for a little while at the time.

I was thinking all week about how I was going to get out of the trial because I always liked to feel comfortable in my own environment. Newham trained at a place called Beckton Playing Fields near the sewers by Canning Town and I got on the bus to go but, when I got to the entrance, I saw in front of me the biggest rat I've ever seen; it must have been about eight feet in length – it was probably only about eight inches. I thought that it was a sign, so I didn't go in. The rat wasn't moving; it looked me square in the eyes so I went home. I'd only been at Beaumont for a couple of weeks and didn't think that I was anywhere near good enough for the District team, so I was just looking for any excuse and the rat gave me one.

I got a phone call from them later on and they offered to give me one more chance. I didn't tell them about the rat; I told them that I'd missed my bus! I played in a training session and I didn't speak but I must have shown the teacher – Mr Goodwin, it was – something, so he said that I'd start as sub in a game against Basildon, but that he'd put me on in centre midfield at some point. I played there for Beaumont too because Ossie Tutu had now gone to Orient. We won that first game 11–0 and I came on at 2–0 up. I made a few assists but we were nine goals better in the second half, so that was my turning point in terms of believing that I was good enough to play at that level.

In my second or third game, Paul Curbishley came up and told me that he was a full back that liked to get forward and overlap and get crosses in and that he liked playing with forwards that held the ball up. I was fourteen years old and I couldn't believe that these lads were talking football tactics to me when all I ever thought about was just going out to play. Anyway, Mr Goodwin heard this and told me that Paul liked to think that he was a manager but that he'd got everything out of a book and from watching his brother play. His brother, Alan, was a couple of years older and had just started to establish himself as a precocious talent at West Ham, so that made Paul seem better than he was. Bless him, he was a fairly good player, but he didn't quite have what it takes to get to the next level.

I became quite established at Newham. I'd been there about a year and a half when Henry Hughton – who later played for Palace – said that two brothers had turned up at his school, St Bonaventure's. One of them came up with Henry to Newham, but he had just left Nigeria and couldn't speak a word of English. He was John Chiedozie, who went on to play for Spurs. He had the biggest thighs that I'd ever seen. It was a shame that he came up with Henry Hughton, because Henry barely opened his mouth either.

I'd been to primary school with Henry and Chrissy Hughton before they went to St Bonaventure's. The only time Henry ever spoke was about banana sandwiches. That was all he ever had. I asked Cheddar – John Chiedozie – if he was a good player and he said, 'Maybe.' I replied, 'Maybe?' and he said, 'Maybe, yes.' That was all the English that he spoke. He was one of the first players to wear tights. We went out and trained and John was lightning-quick and had the most powerful shot so Mr Goodwin said that he'd have him in the team. John used to rub tubes and tubes of Deep Heat into his legs just to stay warm – two or three tubes of it. No wonder no one wanted to mark him; he stank.

There were about seven of that team that went on to have good careers; Peter Hucker, who went on to play for QPR for years and played in the Cup Final, was amongst them. It was a shame because, with the team we had, we thought we were going to win the English Schools trophy, but we got knocked out up at Sheffield and were robbed.

Maurice Newman had always thought that you only ever found one good player, but he now figured that I was the new Ossie Tutu! Maurice loved me; he thought I was Mr Beaumont. I could do no wrong, as far as he was concerned. Teddy Sheringham and Jimmy Carter ended up playing for Beaumont later and I used to coach them when I was fifteen. Maurice told them: 'Boys, I'm going to bring you the next superstar of football and he's going to coach you.' My brother played in the same side and I used to go to their training sessions and Maurice would tell me to juggle a football 100 times. I'd do it and then Maurice would look at the Beaumont players and say, 'You could be like that one day. Right, Vince, you can go now.'

As soon as Maurice saw I had brothers, he took them to

Beaumont until he saw that they weren't as good and then he didn't take much interest in them. But, to be fair to him, he got them both into pro clubs: Julian was at Ipswich for three years and John was at Millwall for two and then Maurice took over a non-league club, Woodford Town, and that's basically what finished my oldest brother off. He said that it killed him because every game he played he'd hear the shout: 'Johnny, come off. I've seen enough.' Maurice didn't know the effect he had on John. His comments really affected him and, in the end, he lost confidence. He finished him with football. I went down and coached a couple of sessions there and juggled a ball for them too!

VINCE DOCUMENTARY

Maurice told Malcolm Allison at Palace that I was the best player that he was ever likely to see and Malcolm watched me play once and said that he might be right, and I signed for them soon afterwards. Malcolm then said that Thames Television had got in touch with him and wanted to make a documentary about one of his young players, and he chose me.

The trouble is, the documentary was so boring. The TV company asked me if I did anything interesting, but I told them that I just watched telly and played football and cricket. They asked me when my next cricket match was, and I was due to play for Essex against Kent. The thing is, I didn't talk to the cricket lot about my football. They knew that I played, but I was quite happy not mixing the two. The people playing cricket didn't know the standard I played at because most of them were from private schools. They used to say, 'Oh, that's a jolly good catch you've taken,' and there were only two or three of us from state schools and we'd be like, 'Yeah, alright mate.' Football wasn't something that interested them.

I had the phone call the day before and the TV company told me that they'd booked the film crew and that they were going to come down to Sittingbourne for the game against Kent; there were six or seven of them. They said that it was going to cost them quite a bit of money so I'd better make sure that I got some runs.

I had to tell the other players and the teacher that there was going to be a film crew filming me and they were all asking me why. The crew asked if we could win the toss and bat first so they could get back to London but we didn't and we were in the field for most of the day, so it was costing them even more money. At the end of the Kent innings we were clapping the opposition off and all of the players, even theirs, were all looking at me. The director came up and said, 'Right, we've been here four hours, Vince, and it's cost us £600 so you'd better, better, get some runs.'

I was batting at number five and the boys were starting to ask questions and the pressure was on. We lost the first wicket and I started padding up and my hands were shaking. It had gone round the ground and even the umpires knew why the film crew were there. When I was in, all the players were laughing and joking as I took my guard. Their bowler came in to bowl and, because I was so nervous, I played and missed and the ball hit my pad and everyone appealed for my wicket – everyone – and I thought, 'This is it.' I looked at the umpire and he just burst out laughing because he knew what was going on and he said, 'Not out'. The fear in me when that ball hit my pads was intense; I thought they were going to slaughter me. I ended up scoring thirty-seven or thirty-eight and was in for just under an hour, but the way they edited it, it looked like I'd hit about 150. Every shot I hit to the fielders, they made it look like I was hitting runs.

The TV people kept asking me what else I did so they came to film me do athletics. I did the 100m, 200m and the 400m. The thing is, this was the school sports day, so I knew I was going to win; it wasn't like the district event. The boys I was up against had probably only ever seen an athletics track on the TV. In fact, one of the boys who finished second in one of my races was running in his school shoes, but I was really going for it as I thought that I'd better put on a show. They told me that they didn't quite get the shot they needed in the 100m, so I had to go for it in the 400m too and, if you've ever run that, it's really physically tough. I ended up winning it by about 100 metres and, afterwards, I went into the changing rooms and I was sick as a dog – and I still had the 200m to go.

Even after all of that, they told me that they still hadn't got the shot they needed, so they also asked me to get in the relay team. The next thing I remember was throwing up in the changing rooms and when I came out there was no one left in the stadium. They'd abandoned a fifteen-year-old kid, who could have been having a heart attack, lying on his own in the changing room. Five events I ended up doing and they used about ten seconds' footage!

MOVING ON

When I first started playing football, I had boots that had been bought at a jumble sale, but then my mum went and bought me a pair of Top Dog Continental football boots from Woolworths and they were the worst pair of boots I've ever seen. They were a size 9 and I'm a size 6 even now. After that, I existed on hand-outs from the pros but, to be fair to my mum, I don't think she knew the level I played football at until I was about twenty-five. She took absolutely no notice of what I was doing in football. I'd say, 'We've got an FA Cup quarter final today, Mum' and then she'd ask me later how we got on and I'd tell her that we'd lost and she'd say, 'Oh, well. Someone has got to lose. Are you eating here today?'

My dad liked the little perks that came my way with the football but I think he only came to watch me twice in my whole career. In my mum's case, she was too busy working and she didn't have the time. I preferred it like that, to be honest, because my dad would try to talk to me about football, but it would embarrass me – for him, it was always the goalkeeper's fault, no matter which team I played for and no matter what had happened on the pitch.

I was in the first team at Palace when I finally ended up moving out of my mum's home. I'd said in passing to Peter Nicholas, because he was talking about moving, that I'd have a look at his flat and he told me that he'd have a word with one of the Palace directors about it. Prior to that, Terry Venables had had a talk with all of us young players and told us that a good investment to make was in bricks and mortar. I was still living at home so it wasn't at the forefront of my thinking – my career was. I wasn't even saving the money I was earning, although Palace had sorted out a pension for me.

After my conversation with Nico, for about half a season after every home game, one of the directors, would say to me, 'Vince, can you sign this?' and this went on for about six weeks before it stopped and then, sometime later, Peter Nicholas asked me if I was going to move into the flat. I asked him, 'What flat?' because I didn't even realise that I had bought it off him. I'd had it for about four or five months. I was only eighteen!

I'd started seeing a girl called Christine – I hadn't told her that she was my first girlfriend because that could have scuppered it – and I asked her if she'd move in with me and she agreed. It was in south Croydon – a one-bedroom luxury flat. It wasn't bad. I told my mum that I was moving out and, looking back, there was a bit of delight in her face. Let me put it this way: she didn't put up a fight for me to stay. The three brothers were still living at home so she was probably relieved that one of them was moving out. She didn't even realise that I'd bought the flat either. The club had been taking the money out of my wages and had been using it for the deposit and the mortgage, which was great; I didn't even miss the money as I was on about £110 a week.

After I moved out, and up to the present day, I tried to see my parents as often as I could, especially as my dad wasn't in the best of health before he died. I still go back to London for three or four days every couple of months. One of my brothers and my sister live very near to my mum, and my other brother lives out towards Ipswich. We're quite close, even though we're now scattered across the country – particularly me and my brothers. As I've said, I wasn't close with my sister when I was growing up, fundamentally because I didn't see a lot of her, but we get on well now. You've also got to remember that it must have been really difficult for her because she had three brothers who were all into films, sport and TV and, obviously, she wasn't.

When I ended up establishing myself at Palace, if my brothers weren't playing for their school or district sides – because they were decent players in their own right – then they'd always come to Palace to watch me, and my sister wasn't involved in that. There was no envy from my brothers towards me. They were brilliant about my success. If anything, they got more out of it than I did.

For a large part of my career, up until I joined Portsmouth, I would play the game, get into my car, rent a film, and then me and my brothers would spent the majority of the evening at home, whether I lived there or not. We'd discuss the game, stay at my mum's, and then get the newspaper in the morning and read the football reports.

Julian cherishes what I've done, but he never looked up to me. He never had to. He's proud of what I did. I'm lucky with my two brothers because they always understood sport. My other brother, John, is still, at fifty, getting excellent times in the various marathons that he runs; if I had been as dedicated to fitness as he is, then I'd have been a much better player. Julian was more talented than me and could try his hand at any ball sport. People often ask me what my proudest moments have been and I can honestly say that one of them was the only time that I ever played in the same cricket team as my two brothers. We all played at a decent level at school but, because we were different age groups, apart from that one time, we never got the opportunity to play cricket or football together other than when we played in the park or the back garden.

Ultimately, I think my name actually worked against Julian. He signed Schoolboy forms for Ipswich, but everyone knew who I was and so people expected to see a lot of what I did in Julian. Me getting my breaks in football was as much to do with Crystal Palace as my ability, so, in that respect, he was unlucky. My other brother, John, signed Schoolboy forms for Millwall. They weren't mugs. John and Julian might have gone on themselves if I hadn't had so much success so quickly and, to that end, the documentary didn't help as it just put added pressure on my siblings. You have to have the breaks and I was lucky enough to get them, but they weren't.

CHAPTER 4

EARLY DAYS AT PALACE

SIGNING FOR PALACE

The Assistant Chief Scout at Palace was called Arnie Warren and he was good friends with Maurice Newman so he said that he'd have a look at me and he then reported back to Malcolm Allison and told him that he might have found a good player. Little did I know then that Malcolm's big plan was to do with Palace what Matt Busby had done at Man United with the Busby Babes. As a result, the older pros at Palace resented the Schoolboys because we were getting treated better than they were. He was putting some of us up in three- or four-star hotels, which wasn't really necessary but he wanted us looked after.

People couldn't understand how a Third Division club could attract the best fifteen- or sixteen-year-olds in the country. They wondered what Palace had that clubs like Manchester United didn't have, but it was the mere fact that Malcolm promised us that when we were good enough we'd have first shot at the first team because he told us, 'I've got rubbish here.' In fact, as Schoolboys we actually used to play the first team in training.

Loads of clubs were offering financial inducements to players to get them to sign for them. I'm not saying that Palace were doing that but, around that time, I started wearing a leather trenchcoat which was worth about £40, which was an extortionate amount of money back then. The real reason I signed for Palace was because I knew that I'd get a chance quicker at a club like Palace than I would at the others, and also because of the way they looked after the Schoolboys. No club could compete with it and that's why we were getting all the top players, like Kenny Sansom, who everyone was after, people who played for England Schoolboys, lads from Manchester, and even Peter Nicholas from Newport.

JOHN CARTWRIGHT & PALACE YOUTH

Even before Malcolm Allison signed us all as kids, he wanted like-minded people to work alongside him. That's why he got John Cartwright who, even now, is the best coach that I ever worked with. Malcolm had met John at West Ham when they were players there and he also became good mates with Terry Venables and brought him to Palace too. I think that Terry is perhaps the most innovative thinker that football has ever seen.

It makes me laugh that when Chelsea had such a bad start to the 2016–17 season, Antonio Conte was lauded for switching to three at the back, which led to them winning the League. If people cast their minds back to Euro '96, England played that same system under Venables, got to the semi-finals and they probably should have won that tournament. Twenty years before that, in 1976, Venables was an advocate of playing out from the back and told his centre-halves that they didn't have to just head and kick it, they could get the ball down and play – and yet Palace were a Third Division team back then.

Big Mal knew that it was all very well having innovative thinkers, but he couldn't have him and the other coaches putting points across to players who were set in their ways, so, consequently, he signed young players who had ability. He then hoped that they could take on board the ideas that were fed to them.

Palace used to invite every schoolboy that they wanted from around the country down to the club; they talked to them like adults and laid out their plans for them and the club. They did a great job of selling Palace to people. It was always over a cup of tea and a bacon sandwich at the café called Solly's at the top of the ground, which we all lived in for the entire duration of our time at Palace. The first team would come back from training and they would meet there too, so you'd be sitting there with your bacon sandwich eating with all of them.

At the beginning, I trained with Palace on a Thursday night and then went back to play for my County or District side on a Saturday and then went back to Palace on the following Thursday. If you had holidays or a week off from school, you'd train all week and that's when they'd put you up in a three- or four-star hotel.

John Cartwright had been at West Ham as a player. Anyone that was at West Ham in the '60s walked, talked and acted the same. They tended to be a bit flash and had a strut. All of the young players at Palace loved John Cartwright because he had that confident air about him, but the other coaches resented him for it a bit.

John had the biggest influence on me as a footballer in my career. He used to pick me and Jerry Murphy up from outside the café by Mile End Station, which was where the Krays used to eat, and then, when we got through the Blackwall Tunnel, he'd pick Billy Gilbert up too. Between the ages of fourteen to sixteen, we were privileged because he brainwashed us – whether we liked it or not – about the way that he thought that football should be played. He told us that the reason why he hadn't made it as a top player was because he was a coward, so one of the things that he made sure of was that me and Jerry Murphy could look after ourselves no matter how small we were. I never pulled out of a tackle, and that was because of him. He taught us how to tackle and how to protect ourselves, telling us that he didn't do it and that there were a few players just like him at West Ham, and that's why they didn't win many away games.

John only ever talked to us about football, but he used to get frustrated because we'd switch off sometimes. Jerry would be preening himself ready to go out and Billy would be in another world. John was quite young for a coach – about thirty-two or thirty-three – and he used to look in the mirror and see us laughing and joking with each other and he knew that we weren't taking any notice of him. One day, he said something quite profound that stuck with me and I remembered it much later. He said, 'You three never think that you'll get to thirty-two, do you?' and we just burst out laughing because we couldn't imagine getting that old.

I used to look up to Murph then because he was a bit of a guru to me with regard to clothes and fashion. Every Friday, we would go into a record store opposite Mile End Station and buy 12" vinyl records. I was heavily into Motown, but Murph introduced me to other types of soul music, which I then thought was the coolest music I'd heard. He'd take me to a clothes shop called Kooks in Walthamstow and got me into fashion too.

Much later on, I remember picking him up from home and he had on a new pair of shoes that he said had cost him £200. That's probably the equivalent of about £2,000 nowadays, and he begged me not to let the other lads know how much they were worth. I couldn't keep quiet. The other players tore into him and Murph was fuming at me. Swindy reckoned that Murph's shoes were worth more than the flat he'd just bought.

I do remember him playing a trick on me around that time. The club got me a new pair of boots; they were a size too small, but I wanted to wear them the next day. I used to stay at Murph's house before some games and he told me that the only thing that I could do to help was to go to sleep in my boots and that he'd done it before and it worked for him. I went to bed that night in these boots and my feet were throbbing. I had about half an hour's sleep, got up, took my boots off and I don't think that I got the feeling back in my toes until Tuesday and I had a nightmare in the game. The story soon got around because Murph told everyone.

John Cartwright takes a lot of credit for the way that we

played football because he was so heavily into the technical side of the game. A lot of our education as young players involved talking. John was always talking to us, but it was difficult for us as teenagers in the mid-1970s to be told not to watch *Match of the Day* because we wouldn't learn much from those players. We were told to watch the great players from abroad instead, and to buy *World Soccer* magazine. We'd do sessions at Palace as young kids where we were taught to copy great players' technique from around the world.

As an example, all of the players at Palace at that time shielded the ball the same way because there was a fellow playing outside right for Italy called Franco Causio, and John was really impressed with him. For three days after Italy beat England in Rome at a World Cup qualifier in 1976, we were taught to get the ball and shield it like Causio. We did it for days and it helped me as I wasn't very big, but I soon realised that my size didn't matter because if you received the ball and shielded it in the right way, a defender could never get the ball.

Another example of that was when we played Spurs in a pre-season friendly and Ossie Ardiles was playing. (I remember it vividly because Peter Taylor was at Spurs then but he was injured and watching the game from the side, and whenever the referee blew the whistle and awarded anything against Spurs, he was loudly teaching Ricky Villa suitable swear words to say.) That game was played behind closed doors at the training ground and John Cartwright told us all to watch Ardiles because he was slight but he protected the ball so well. He showed us how Ardiles used his arm to create distance between himself and the ball and these things were introduced to us and became part of our armoury.

It wasn't just the attacking players that they focused on either. Billy Gilbert was taught to jump for the ball and to protect himself but not to give a foul away and Kenny Sansom learned the hooked tackle at Palace. Terry Venables and John Cartwright also taught us that if a player was stupid enough to make a rash tackle in the penalty box then we were to take advantage of it. They wanted us to widen our knowledge all the time. It was like going to school. Thursday nights at Palace under John Cartwright was an education.

It was easy for us at Palace for a couple of years because we had all the best players and we knew that we were going to win. We were winning some games 12–0. Our Youth team won everything. We got to the Youth Cup semi-final as fifteen-year-olds against eighteen-year-olds and we then won the competition in the following two years. We beat Everton in 1977 over two legs – Terry Fenwick got the winner – and the following year we beat Aston Villa at Highbury and Terry Fenwick got the winner in that one as well.

At the time, we knew how good we were as a group of players and we all expected to turn pro for one reason and one reason only: we were complimented all the time. You show me someone who doesn't like to be complimented and I'll show you a liar. The younger you are when you get complimented then the more confidence that gives you. A lot of people mistake confidence for arrogance, but if someone is confident, it simply means they have a belief in themselves and in where they are going to get to. That was instilled in us by Malcolm Allison. Big Mal had a dream and he wanted a team of young players who all played in the way that he thought football should be played. He believed that his way was the best way of playing, and he only wanted like-minded people around him.

But we never sat down as a group of lads, even when we won the FA Youth Cup twice, and agreed that if we all stayed together and stayed focused then we could end up in Division One and have a chance of winning the League. There are times when confidence leads to arrogance but, at that point, we didn't succumb to it. Initially, we wouldn't let ourselves be put up there to be shot down but we were young and we didn't have any life experience Sadly, much later, our confidence did turn to arrogance and it proved to be the end of us as a team.

At that time, Kenny Sansom was absolutely the stand-out player in the group. I can't put my finger on exactly what it was about him but he was just a great footballer. He was quick, strong, never distracted and the most confident player I've ever seen. I played against him on a couple of occasions later on in my career and the first thing that he'd say to me before we'd even kicked off was that he hadn't checked yet whether the pockets in his shorts were big enough for me to fit into. I used to get deflated straight away because I knew that I wouldn't get a kick in the game.

While Kenny was confident, I was still such a quiet lad but, if you played for a London club, then you either sink or swim straight away and Kenny made sure that he swam. He was an inspiration for me and I tried to follow his lead to make sure that I swam too. The only person at Palace who made it uncomfortable for me was a guy who played on the wing called Peter Johnson, who was a bitter man. I remember travelling down to Bournemouth very early on in my career for a reserve game, and he was angry that he was in the reserves. His face didn't fit and he was out of the picture and he could see all these kids coming through and he resented it.

We were playing cards and I thought that it was going to be a laugh and a joke, but Peter told me to pack it in because I was with the big boys now. No one said anything but Kenny Sansom – who was only sixteen at the time – looked at him and said, 'The big boys? Where do you think you are? You're in the reserves!' I couldn't believe that Kenny would talk to him like that. Peter had played a lot of first team games and Kenny hadn't even played in the first team yet, but he was that sure of himself that he gave it back to him.

The one stand-out memory for me with Kenny was when we played a game against Sunderland. It was the only time that I played with or against Kenny, or even watched him, that he got given the runaround. It was by Bobby Kerr and Kenny was distraught and he made a point of never allowing it to happen again. The confidence that he had at sixteen or seventeen was unbelievable. He was upset if someone that he was up against even got a cross in. We saw him get into the first team and it gave us all confidence and the belief that we could get there too and, when we did, and he was surrounded by all of us young players, he just became even more of a leader.

Peter Nicholas was also in that Youth side, as were Billy

Gilbert, Jerry Murphy, Kenny Sansom and Terry Fenwick. Palace signed Fenwick and he was a good player but he was very, very shy and got homesick. So Palace being Palace, and being ruthless and clever and prepared to go to any lengths to keep a young player, they told him to bring his brother down with him as they said that they'd heard he was a good player as well. His brother could only ever have had a kick around in the playground, but he came down for about a year and a half and he helped Terry settle in. Terry ended up managing a few clubs and had a great career, but he barely spoke back then. But we all grew up together so we knew each other's quirks and we had a bond for a long time. But, while we had a lot of success, we didn't learn how to handle adversity and, later on, that's where the problems came.

I remember once, when we trained as Schoolboys, John Cartwright took us all to a factory because he wasn't happy with our effort and he thought that we were cutting corners so he wanted us to see what it was like to really graft. But we weren't interested. We were asking each other why we were there and what films were on that afternoon. Though it's the norm now, it was unique then for kids to be looked after in the way that we were, and it wound the older players up big time. There were players at the club like Peter Taylor, who was a really good footballer and got capped by England in the Third Division, and we used to get pampered more than him even though he was the shining light at Palace and could do no wrong.

To sum up how highly Malcolm thought of us, Kenny had only played in four or five reserve games and the rest of us were only just into the Youth team yet Malcolm was dabbling with the idea of putting a couple of us Schoolboys into the squad for the 1976 FA Cup semi-final against Southampton. In the end, he thought better of it, but that's the esteem in which he held us. We were fifteen or sixteen.

While Malcolm rated us, his assistant at the time was a frightening guy called Frank Lord, who didn't agree with how Malcolm treated us. He was a very emotional and enthusiastic man but he thought we were too spoiled. Him and Ernie Walley, the reserve team manager, hated it. Ernie was hard graft and none of us wanted to be anywhere near the reserves because of him. We wanted to be with John Cartwright, where the emphasis was on skill.

Frank saw things as black and white, but he only ever had a go at us when Malcolm wasn't around because he knew Malcolm wouldn't want to see anyone having a go at his golden boys. One day, the first team had finished training so Frank stayed behind and was doing some finishing with a couple of the goalkeepers. We'd just finished our session, which probably consisted of seeing how many times we could keep the ball up, with a focus solely on technique. John Cartwright told us to go in and have some lunch and put our feet up. We thought Palace was the greatest club in the world.

I was having a little jolly walk back to the dressing room and I heard Frank Lord call me over. I didn't know this then, but it was his stock question to every footballer: he asked me if I'd kick my mother to score a goal. I went, 'Erm' and, as soon as I did that, he hit me round the back of the head and told me that I was no good to him. He said that he'd kick his mother, his gran, his wife and his kids to score a goal, and exclaimed, 'That's why I'm Frank Lord!' I turned to go, but he told me to line up eight balls on the six-yard line, a yard apart. They were only six yards from goal and the goalkeepers weren't even there but he said, 'Watch this!' and he proceeded to hit these eight balls into the back of the net. Any four-year-old could do that but he turned around and said again, 'And that's why I'm Frank Lord! I'm ruthless!' I didn't know what he was trying to teach me. I told John Cartwright but he just said, 'That's what we're up against.'

I ended up signing as an apprentice at sixteen but I didn't clean boots or the changing rooms. That was the norm for most apprentices at 99 per cent of clubs, but Malcolm Allison had a meeting with us and told us that we weren't there to learn how to sweep dressing rooms or how to clean boots; he told us that we were there to learn how to be professional footballers and learn to play football the right way. Malcolm told us that was why he'd employed someone to clean the boots and dressing rooms.

This antagonised the older pros because they'd had to do those jobs when they were apprentices, making sure the boots were clean and the kit was laid out. After that, they'd train and then tidy everything up and then, if they were lucky, squeeze in an hour or so of college. Our apprenticeship was to roll in at 10 a.m. at the same time as the pros, train and then have lunch and then either go home or buy some records or play pool, so we never had to face hardship or adversity. The option of college was there, but none of us thought that we needed an education because we'd been told that we'd become professional footballers. We'd been at school already!

We formed a clique. There were the younger ones and the older ones and, while it didn't affect anything that went on on the pitch, we were juvenile and they were men. I went on my first ever pre-season trip when I went to Holland at sixteen with the first team along with Kenny Sansom and Ian Walsh. I knew that the only reason I went was because of the deal done with Thames TV when they were following me around and filming me for the documentary, but it was hard for the experienced players to take. They used to look at me and think that I hadn't done anything in my career and yet I had a TV crew following me around.

In my first game over there, we played a Dutch Third Division team and we battered them something like 8–2. I was only fifteen, so I just tried to get through the game without making a mistake; I wasn't interested in trying anything too tricky, but I spent twenty of the forty-five minutes on my backside after I'd passed the ball or shot, because I kept slipping over. I was so nervous.

Venables came in at half time, and this shows how clever he was because he could tell that I was nervous. He was having a go at everyone and he turned around to me and asked what was up with me. I had a name at the club as a good cricketer. When the club had a game, I took charge of it and, even at my age, I was telling experienced pros where to stand on the field. So he said, 'If you can tell players what to do when you're playing cricket, then you can tell them what to do when you're playing football.

VINCE

You've got to take responsibility otherwise you're not going to get on in the game.' He then asked me why I was looking at my boots but I'd forgotten to tighten the studs and had lost about three of them so he told me to sort them out.

CHAPTER 5

BREAKING THROUGH AT PALACE

Malcolm was responsible for getting all the players to the club that got Palace promoted to Division One in 1979, but the majority of our footballing education was provided by Venables and John Cartwright. John was an extension of Venables. To me, the Youth team coach is such an important job because they mould players at that level and affect the way they think about the game. Someone like Brian Kidd was always in demand as a coach but not as a manager. They're two completely different roles and some personalities are able to speak to kids differently to pros. You couldn't have Sir Alex Ferguson taking a Youth team because those kids would probably be broken by the time they were sixteen. People think that Venables would be different but Venners liked working with talent. You could build on talent; you can't give someone talent.

Someone like Allan Harris, who was our Youth team manager before John Cartwright and eventually became Venables' assistant, had a completely different philosophy to John. When we got into the Youth team for the first time, Allan Harris was the coach. He didn't have the same technical ability as John

Cartwright but what he did instil in us was a win-at-all-costs mentality and, even with my size, I learned how to look after myself.

He wouldn't stand on ceremony, Allan. He was one of those people who would use the saying, 'You have to earn the right to play.' If a team made it physical, and their desire was greater than yours, you'd lose even if you had more ability than them, so you had to match their desire, and he instilled that in us. He was good with regard to winding us up and letting us know that we had to win the battle before we got the right to play. I suppose when you come from the Harris family where Ron Harris is your brother, then you're going to want to compete.

When the TV company was doing the documentary on me, we were about fifteen years old and Palace arranged a game against the Saudi Arabian Under-21 team. In those days, the Saudis weren't a great side. We played them at the training ground but Allan told them that he wanted them to go easy and not kick lumps out of us because we were only young boys. But from the very first whistle, they started booting us. That was the worst thing they could have done, because it spurred the borderline lunatics like Billy Gilbert and Peter Nicholas to respond.

There were a couple of free-for-alls during the game. With about twenty minutes to go, Allan Harris and Ernie Walley asked the ref to call it off as someone was going to get hurt but, by then, it was too late – some of our boys had scented blood because of what he'd taught us. If you ever get hold of the documentary, you'll see the Saudis go into their dressing room, but what you don't see is that Billy ran off and got a corner flag and was carrying it around like a spear, Terry Fenwick picked up a cone, and the cowards amongst us, like me, all went and stood by Ernie Walley because he was so hard! Once they'd hit a couple, we had our two coaches' backs against the door trying to keep the Saudis out of our room. An international incident was narrowly avoided!

So, even at fifteen, we were playing against men, and even though they were kicking lumps out of us, we didn't back down. That summed up what we were about and we kept that spirit for three or four years. That was the most spirited side I played in, even though it was a kids' team, really. We'd grown up together and, at one point later on, there were about nine of us from the Youth team playing in the first team together.

Sometimes the players used to ask each other what Allan did because tactically he said very little. I remember Venners always liked to finish a session with a bit of running – doggies or shuttles, as they are known. There were four lines of cones that we had to run to but we were a cone short and the other ones were on the other side of the training ground. Venners said that he couldn't be arsed to go over to get them so, without thinking, I called out – and a couple of players punched me in the kidneys for it – 'Allan, why don't you be the last cone?' Allan didn't take any offence at all and he went, 'Yep, with this group, I'll be the last cone.' Billy whispered, 'So that's what he does…' and we couldn't contain our laughter. Allan didn't know, but for about a year after that we used to call him 'The Cone'.

We did like Allan, though. He'd known us for so long that it helped us when he became Venables' assistant manager, though that didn't mean that it was easy for us youngsters to make the step up to first-team level. Venables had his hands full trying to get the first team promoted, and John Cartwright was doing all he could for us at Youth level but, in between, there was the reserves and they were run by probably the most terrifying man known to the human race: Ernie Walley. None of us wanted to train with the reserves because Ernie was old school. Whereas John would tell us to get a ball out of the bag to warm up, Ernie used to tell us all to lift weights or we'd go to Crystal Palace Sports Centre to run.

Ernie Walley was totally unimpressed by our reputations. Because of the way he treated us and the fear we had of him, we were actually motivated to get out of the reserves and stay out of there. Looking back on it, I wonder whether Terry Venables was actually being very clever and keeping him there deliberately so that our fear of him would motivate us to avoid being dropped at all costs! Ernie was completely different to all of the other coaches at Palace. Every other coach would focus on the technical side of the game for 80 per cent of the time, whereas Ernie would focus on the physical side for 99 per cent of his sessions.

Venables was technical with his coaching in general, but he used to leave me alone and wouldn't get too technical with me. On the training ground, he'd go off and talk to another group of players and he'd send me off to go and chip some balls about on my own because I didn't know what he was talking about. People used to say defenders were stupid but they weren't. It was the defenders who would get all the technical information about holding the line and things like that, while me and Jerry just used to stand there and look at each other. We didn't have a clue what Venables was on about. He just told us two to go out and play.

After Venables had done all his technical stuff, Allan Harris would come in and go, 'So, if you get tight with him, Billy (Gilbert), hit him and let him know you're there.' And then he'd say to Peter Nicholas: 'Nico, once he's gone down, check that the linesman can't see you and, if he can't, stamp on him!' Nico loved Allan because he was an assassin.

So that was Allan's technical advice! He used to tell us, 'If he gets it, give him a couple of whacks to let him know you're there and, if that don't work, whack him again' or 'Look them in the eye and compete and, if they want to fight, fight them. If they want to play, still fight them.' We used to laugh.

It was no secret that Allan's favourite players were Billy Gilbert, Peter Nicholas, Terry Fenwick and Steve Kember because they loved that side of the game. With respect to Allan, he used to like working with them because they didn't need technical coaching. His coaching talk to me was, 'Vince, when you get the ball, take them on.' I used to say, 'And?' but he'd just repeat it. It was good for me, I suppose. Sometimes a player doesn't need coaching. Venables liked Allan because he used to agree with him – Allan didn't complicate matters. Venners did the complicated stuff but Allan would be the first one there if the coaches had a row, and the players loved him for it.

In turn, Billy and Nico really responded to Allan Harris. In one of my first games as an apprentice at Palace, Nico and Billy were playing together at the back against Ipswich. It was the first time that I ever saw Billy hurt someone and, while it was an accident, the fella got stretchered off the field having convulsions after hitting Billy with the side of his head.

I was feeling a bit sick watching the guy having convulsions yet Billy was completely unfazed and Nico was just standing there watching it with his hands on his hips. Ipswich had two good players playing for them up front that day called David Geddes and Alan Brazil. It wasn't Geddes or Brazil who got hurt, but, after that incident, those two never went near Billy for the rest of the game.

I remember going on a pre-season tour to Norway and we were playing Viking Stavanger and it was Venables' intention to give all of his players a game. We were winning quite comfortably; there was no reason for anyone to get excited or upset, it was a gentle stroll, so Venables made his substitutions and took me off too. I sat down next to the manager and, all of a sudden, Nico tried to read a pass and got there slightly late and fouled one of their players. It wasn't too bad. Nico put his hands up in the air and started walking backwards to his position and, as he was doing it, he trod on the windpipe of the fella who was still down on the ground and did a little tap dance. Venners just turned round to me and said, 'Do you think he meant to do that? Is he that ruthless? He'll do for me!'

Nico was a hard man but he could be away with the fairies. We were in the bath one day at Palace when he said that he was going to sell his motor. He told us that he was a bit worried about the mileage, though, as it was a bit high. Jim Cannon said that if he wanted to trade it in and the mileage was high, it might be more trouble than it's worth but he said, 'I tell you what you should do. Leave it until late, but go out at night, jump in your car, stick it in reverse and go round the block in reverse a couple of hundred times. It'll knock the clock backwards.' There was a few seconds silence. We were all looking at each other but Nico was thinking about it. Eventually, he's gone, 'Er, no, I can't be bothered to do that...' We were in hysterics. He actually thought it was an option.

ADULATION AND DEBUT

I eventually made my full debut against Millwall at The Den in south London. It was quite an intimidating place to play although I didn't really think about that until later. You've got to remember that I was seventeen then. Terry Venables, whose word was law to me, just told me to go out and play and said that we had players out there who would look after me.

It was the first game of the 1977–78 season and I played up front with a big centre-forward called Steve Perrin. Venables had a masterstroke and put the usual centre-forward, Dave Swindlehurst, on the wing – he wasn't too happy about that – and played me up front with George Graham behind. We won the game and I scored, and I remember thinking that not only was this brilliant but that it was easy too. I thought, 'I could get thirty goals in a season! I can do this all the time.' That's honestly what I thought – that I would get at least thirty goals – but I didn't score again until the following year.

One of my teammates that day was Rachid Harkouk. What a player he was. He was the first maverick footballer at Palace. Rachid was what I call a playground player; he was wild. We called him 'Spider'. I loved him because he didn't conform; he paved the way for me, really. He played the way he wanted to, without a care in the world, regardless of what he was asked to do.

Spider was as mad off the field as he was on it. One day after training, Murph and I were about to walk to Thornton Heath to get the train home when Rachid asked us if we wanted a lift. He asked if we'd ever been to Harrods, as he was on his way up there. Murph had been a couple of times, but I hadn't. We parked close by and Spider told us that he'd meet us back at the motor in forty-five minutes. When we came back, he asked if either of us wanted to buy a watch. When we said no, he asked if we wanted to buy some aftershave instead. I'm not accusing him of anything but I will say that he had a Crombie coat at the time that was two sizes too big for him.

Playing with Rachid was a highlight, but the greatest feeling I had was scoring my first goal at Selhurst Park. It actually felt better than my goal at Millwall because I'd become a little bit of a favourite with the fans by then, being a young kid and all, but, for the life of me, I couldn't ever get near the goal. We played Burnley and I hit a shot and it rebounded back to me so I hit it again and, for a split second, time stood still before I realised that I'd scored. I went for it. I turned to run and, the next thing I knew, Dave Swindlehurst grabbed me round the throat telling me to calm down. It was a good thing that he kept hold of me because I would have run straight out of the ground and I wouldn't have stopped.

I remember Billy Gilbert doing the same thing when we played at West Ham. He scored from about forty yards and just turned around and ran and I caught him and shouted, 'Where are you going?' because he was running towards the wrong end! It's a feeling that you can't explain when you score but, at seventeen, I was gone.

It started very well for me that season. In those times, they played the first two legs of the League Cup before the season started and we played Brentford and beat them easily. We'd started well and I thought that being a pro footballer was the easiest thing in the world and that we were going to get promoted that season. We then played Hull City at home, whose player-manager was Billy Bremner. We got beaten 1–0; I didn't play well and I couldn't figure out why.

Venables was one of those managers who didn't like talking after games; he preferred to wait until Monday. He'd tell us to go away and have a think about the game before we went over it. I never thought about the game at all. I was seventeen and in the first team so I went out and got the *News of the World* and the *Sunday People* to see what marks they'd given me and it was a six and a five. I thought, 'But they don't know anything about the game. I'm in the first team!'

So we had this meeting and Venables was going round asking the players their opinion on the game. I was hoping that he wouldn't ask me for mine but he turned to me and said, 'What about you, Vince? What did you think?' He told me that

I looked a bit lethargic. I figured that must be what he thought so I agreed that I was a bit tired. Then he told me to have a blow for a few games, which taught me not to agree with him in the future. I remember vividly: Dave Swindlehurst, who had a bit of a problem with me when I got into the first team, was happy that I got dropped and Venners put him back into the middle.

I was still so young and had so little life experience at that time. Back then, I used to go home with a Kentucky Fried Chicken to be with my girlfriend and watch *Dallas* and that was my typical Saturday night. Her name was Christine and she was my first girlfriend. Christine worked at the football club and I was so shy that it helped that I could just talk to her about the games. I did feel a little left out sometimes listening to people like Billy Gilbert and Jerry Murphy talking about what they'd been up to at the weekends. Jerry was a playboy from about the age of eleven. I remember coming in one Monday morning and I asked if anyone had seen *Match of the Day* on Saturday night and they all started laughing. Billy said that he'd turned it on but then he'd been rolling around on the carpet with someone.

Unlike those two, I didn't have any vices and it's sad but, at that age, I didn't really have close friends either. After I'd passed my driving test, on a Saturday night at about midnight, I used to drive up to Ilford and pass people at bus stops and have a chuckle to myself because they were waiting in the cold and I'd be in my car with my music blaring and the heating turned up. I thought it was great. But one day, I reversed into a road that was a 'No Entry' and I got spotted and pulled over and got told that I had to produce my documents. I was so young and naive that

I didn't take it seriously. I was a professional footballer; I didn't adhere to rules – so I didn't bother producing them.

Some while later, a letter came through my door informing me that I had a court appearance and, as we all did when anything went wrong at Palace, I went to see Arnie Warren. He asked me when I was due in court and said that he'd get it sorted out so Arnie, my dad and I turned up at court together. Just prior to going into the court they'd asked me for my driving licence and my insurance, but my dad had handed over his own insurance. I told him that it was his and not mine but he'd thought that if he was insured then that meant that the car was insured no matter who drove it. Arnie looked at the heavens and told us to keep quiet because we weren't in there because of the insurance.

The court was intimidating and I was overawed by the whole situation. I stood up in front of the magistrates and they read out the charge: I'd reversed down a one-way street. The magistrate conferred and then said that they knew that I was a new driver but that I had to read the signs carefully. Then he asked me if there was anything that I wanted to say, which is when people normally say sorry, but, because I was overawed, I blurted out, 'I didn't know my dad never insured me. I just didn't know.' I turned around to the gallery and Arnie had his head in his hands while my dad didn't have a clue what was going on. The magistrate was staring at me and the policeman had to get up and explain what I'd just said. They had intended to fine me £25, but instead they banned me from driving for three months. You could say that I had some growing up to do.

Cars continued to expose me. The lads knew a guy called Ron Brewer – a massive Palace fan – who used to work on their motors for them. We used to eat in Solly's café and we'd mix with the fans in there. I came in one day and asked Jimmy Cannon whether he knew anyone who could do re-sprays, and he told me that Ron would do it for me. He was a big guy, always in his overalls, and he loved the fact that he used to know all the players. I was a bit intimidated but he offered to help so he took my car away. When I collected the car from him, it was night-time so I didn't notice that anything was amiss but, when I drove it in the next day and the lads saw it, they started pissing themselves laughing. He'd sprayed it in two different shades of blue.

Ron charged me £200 which, back then, was a fortune. I couldn't believe how much it cost. But I gave Billy an envelope with the money in it and asked him to give it to Ron when he went to the café that day. Unbeknown to me, Jimmy Cannon got hold of the envelope and took the money out of it and Solly, the café owner, wrote a note and folded it and put it back in. He'd written on it, 'If you think I'm giving you £200 for the worst fucking re-spray in the world you've got another think coming. You can go and do one.'

Ron came in and asked Solly whether I'd left an envelope for him and he ordered ham, egg and chips and sat down with it. The boys were all in there and were discreetly watching while Ron read the letter and all of a sudden he shouted out, 'The little black bastard!' I didn't know anything about it.

CHAPTER 6

WE'RE ALL FOOTBALLERS

I wasn't the first black player to play for the club. Just after I signed, Palace had a young black boy called Mark Lindsay break into the first team. He was a hardworking player but was nothing to shout about. Even at Schoolboy level at Palace, the black faces were few and far between. Later on, there was another lad called Mark Annon and a lot was expected of him. He could have been a good player but, again, it probably didn't help him that I got in the team so early because people automatically thought that as another black player he would be like me. Tony Sealy joined in the year that we got promoted and he ended up being a good mate of mine. He actually used to joke with me that it was good to see another black player as he didn't see any where he was from down on the south coast.

The first time that I encountered racism when I was at Palace was when I went on my first pre-season trip to Jersey at the age of fifteen. It was actually the first time that I came across racism towards me outside of school. I came down for breakfast and as I was walking down a long corridor back to my room to collect my boots, I saw two elderly ladies walking towards me. As I walked past them, I said 'Good morning' and then, when they were about two or three paces past me, I heard one of the ladies say, 'That's the first one I've seen.' The way they referred to me, you'd have thought that I wasn't even a member of the human race. I'm sure they didn't mean it like that, but that's the way it felt. It was so matter-of-fact. I went straight to the boys and told them and they thought it was hilarious. Not one of them said that it was out of order, though. That was the first time that I was aware of being a black footballer – or should I say 'coloured'.

The first bit of abuse that I got as a young footballer on the pitch was in a reserve game at Bournemouth, and it was from three or four kids making monkey noises and calling me 'Blackie'. I was a bit taken aback but you've got to remember that I was from a rough part of London and I'd been on the end of racial slurs and I'd seen graffiti about black people, so it wasn't something that shocked me. The only thing that it gave me was strength of character to withstand it.

The first time an opposition player made reference to my colour was on my debut, at the age of seventeen, at Lincoln City, and that player went on to manage a few clubs. We had a corner and he turned around to his teammate and said, 'Who's marking Midnight?' I didn't know who he meant, but I looked around and it dawned on me that I was 'Midnight' because I was the only black player on the field. I was so caught up with making my debut that it didn't affect me, but the one that really got to me was in my second game against Port Vale. I was sitting in the dug-out and, for no reason whatsoever, a lad with glasses on put his head round the side and shouted at me from a foot away, 'You black bastard!' – and no one did or said anything.

I also have a clear recollection of playing Forest, who were the European Cup holders, at Palace. It was a full house. I picked the ball up and went on a mazy run and, from nowhere, after beating a couple of players, I was scythed to the floor by one of their defenders. He did the typical thing that hard-men did: the immediate apology to the referee, the 'I didn't touch him' line, then he did the bit where he called the ref by his name, which would always impress them. Then he said, 'The wee man was just too quick for me' and bent down and picked me up and dusted me down. He then patted me on the head, the ref turned away and he said, 'And there's more of that to come, nigger', and he pulled my hair. I jumped up and chased after him for a few yards and the ref blew up and booked me.

We were just easy targets. A programme called *Roots* came out around that time which didn't do black players any favours. I think all of the dozen or so black players that were playing at the time were called Kunta Kinte. Some people would chant 'Kunta' and then others would go 'Kinte' and then you'd get 'Roots, Roots, Roots!' I first heard that directed towards me at Port Vale. Looking back, that was quite mild because I then had bananas thrown at me in the late '70s and the early '80s, and that even happened to me at West Ham where I was from.

Soon after we got promoted, we went up to Liverpool. Venables liked his teams to go out and warm up and get a feel of the pitch and get used to the atmosphere. But, by this stage, I didn't really want to go out. I thought that I'd rather suffer the abuse when the game started, because at least I'd have the match to take my mind off it. Playing at Anfield was supposed to be one of the pinnacles of a pro footballer's career, but I did everything I could not to catch Venables' eye so I could avoid warming up. He noticed me and said that I'd better warm up because not every young player could cope with playing at Anfield. It just so happened that everyone else in the team had gone out. He told me the atmosphere was brilliant and that the Kop was full up already and I just thought, 'Oh, my God!' and I knew that I just had to get it out of the way.

I ran onto the pitch expecting the familiar sound of boos but there was nothing much and I remember thinking, 'I've got away with it. Maybe these are the best supporters in the land,' and then I heard a lone voice shout, 'Day-o, day-o' and the rest of the Kop sang, 'Daylight come and he wan' go home'. I had one kick of the ball and ran back down the tunnel.

The worst ever, though, was at Leeds when I was there with Palace and went to take a corner – the game was on the TV – and their fans sang, 'Nigger, nigger, nigger, pull the trigger'. Alan Ball thought that the worst racism he'd ever heard was when me and Noel Blake went up to Leeds with Portsmouth but it was nowhere near as bad as when I went there with Palace. Terry Connor was playing for Leeds at the time, and yet they loved him, for some reason. I still can't fathom out what was going through their heads. Even when I was playing for Leeds, people would be chanting, 'Sieg Heil!'

Despite all that, I used to love playing away because I'd get stick from away fans and then I'd do something and get a grudging round of applause. It's better than 40,000 people cheering you on at home because they are your own supporters. Grudging respect from people that abused you was the best feeling in the world and that was why I always preferred playing away from home, because I wanted to rub their noses in it. I got so much more pleasure from doing well against people who disliked me. I used to talk to other black players about this and we agreed: it just made us try harder to show that what they shouted didn't bother us. We just wanted them to have to give us grudging recognition. It made you feel ten feet tall because there were thousands of people giving you stick every week. What was sad was, at that time, it was part and parcel of the game that black players were booed, but I don't just put that down to football; that was society back then. People were ignorant.

There was a stage where it got that bad that I used to look at the opposition line up to see if they also had a black player to see how much stick I was likely to get. People used to say to me that it must have hurt getting racial stick from fans who had a black player in their own team, but there were hardly any black players at the time. The West Brom boys weren't there when I was coming through: Cyrille Regis was still at Hayes when I started my career, Brendon Batson was a reserve at Arsenal and Laurie Cunningham was at Leyton Orient. Despite the scarcity of black players, I didn't see myself as a figurehead for black footballers – not one iota. I saw myself as a young footballer.

It started off when I played football that every black player would get booed. If you touched the ball, then you'd get booed again. People thought it would put us off. Then, from their booing, it progressed to monkey noises. I even met people when I went out and they'd say, 'Black bastard – no offence, Vince' and then, 'Look at that coon over there. I didn't mean you, Vince. You're one of us.' Oh, right. I'm not black then. And, is he a bastard just because he's black? And why are you apologising? You must know it's wrong. It all went through my head.

And then, as I got older, I started responding when I came to Portsmouth. I took a lot of stick when I came down to Pompey with Crystal Palace. That was actually one of the reasons why I went to Leeds United; I managed to turn the abuse around when I came down to Portsmouth and I thought I could do a similar thing up there, although it didn't quite happen.

A lot of the stuff that was said to me, people would get arrested for nowadays, but back then, people didn't think it was offensive. I do believe, though, that the majority of football supporters only see the shirt. They don't care if they hurt your feelings; they just don't care. People used to see that teams had black players in their sides so they shouted out monkey noises and when the game finished that was the end of it. Those people probably didn't walk away from grounds thinking that they were racist. But, as it progressed into the 1980s, it became political and there was a really nasty racist edge to it. You'd go to places like Leeds, Chelsea and even my home club, West Ham, and people would be giving out National Front leaflets. They were frightening places to go to then.

I never got abuse at Palace, though, but it's funny because, when you want to be a footballer, one of the things that spurs you on is imagining what it would be like to have thousands of people singing your name and you think that it must be brilliant. I remember the first song that was sung about me at

Palace. Nowadays, the song that they sang would be considered extremely racist. It was by Boney M, who were a huge dance group in the '70s, and the Holmesdale Road End used to sing, 'We've got a brown boy on the wing, la la la la la.' I used to wave and they'd cheer but it was only later that I thought, 'Hang, on. That ain't right' and I'd wonder if they were having a pop at me, but I'm sure they weren't.

I can honestly say that I didn't play alongside anyone that I considered racist at the time. Although I used to get some comments from people at Palace that I didn't think anything of but, looking back, I'm not sure that they should have said them. As an example, I remember Billy Gilbert being in the showers and asking Jerry Murphy if he thought my dick looked like a walnut whip and that became my nickname for a couple of weeks. I was so used to being called names by crowds that what my own players had to say to me didn't affect me because they'd never take it to the level where they'd call me a black bastard, although players from other teams did.

I don't know how young black players now would react to some of the things that Allan Harris used to say to me too. He liked me because I used to have a laugh and joke with him and he would ask me every day if I'd been listening to any Ron and Reggie music instead of actually referring to it as reggae. He'd go, 'What's that all about? That Reggie music?' Allan used to tell me that I must have been one of the few black players that could take a kick and not be frightened to get stuck in because if you were a black player in the 1970s, a common accusation was that we didn't like being kicked. It was a total fallacy. That and not being able to take the cold weather. People always used to say that because we were black we must prefer the warmer weather. It was ridiculous.

Around that time, I got a team of black players together to play against Jim Cannon's side in his testimonial. It came about when we were having some food after a game once and I was sitting with Jimmy and he was wondering what opposition he could get for his game. I think he had about four testimonials since then because he played 3,000 games for Palace. I told him that there was a bit of an influx of black players coming into the game and he asked me whether I thought that I'd be able to get a team together.

I knew enough of the boys and started writing a list down and I got an agent called Richard Coomber to help me get it organised. I'd just got friendly with a few of the black lads so I started phoning round and they were all keen to play. As I've said, there weren't many black players that were in their first teams then, so you tended to speak to them. I got quite a good team together and I even got Jomo Sono, who was a South African international playing at New York Cosmos, to join us.

Looking at the side, I realised that we were a bit top heavy with forwards and that we needed a centre-back, so someone suggested Larry May, who was at Leicester City. I got hold of his number and phoned him up. I told him that I was getting a side together for Jim Cannon's testimonial and I had George Berry, Bob Hazell, Garth Crooks, Henry Hughton and Dave Bennett playing and I wondered if he'd like to take part. He said that he'd be happy to play, so I told him I'd be in touch with all of the details, and he said that was great.

Just as I was saying goodbye, he said, 'Vince, Vince, before you go, why did you ask me?' I was sitting with Richard and I turned round and covered the receiver and I said to him, 'Larry doesn't think he's black. We can't have him. He doesn't know he's black,' so I didn't put him down. I couldn't believe he'd asked why I got in touch with him; I'd just reeled off every single black player that played in the country!

In hindsight, I should have been far more sensitive of the social situation at the time. All of the black footballers suffered so much. I should have approached it far more carefully and explained that I was getting a team of black players together and asked if they'd be comfortable playing in a game like that. I just didn't stop to think about all of the difficulties that we had to face on a daily basis and I should have been more sensitive in the way I approached Larry.

It ended up being quite a good game and there was a decent crowd there. Even now, there aren't many black people that go to watch football, but when we ran out that night, about 10,000 of the crowd were black.

Shortly afterwards, a company in the Caribbean approached me and asked if I could get a team together to play in a tournament against Trinidad & Tobago and Fulham. The competition was staged in Trinidad and we were offered a two-week holiday in Tobago afterwards. I formed an All-Stars team on the same premise as for Jim Cannon's game, but we had a much better side this time. The two players that got the most attention were Garth Crooks and Chris Hughton. They'd just won the FA Cup with Tottenham when it had a much higher profile both in

England and around the world, so that was understandable, but we had other good players too.

Bob Hazell and George Berry were there. It was the first opportunity I'd had to spend any length of time with them and, if you wanted to find two black players who were vocal and happy to speak out about how much abuse they got and how oppressed they were, then they were the two that you'd pick. They were both so serious to the point that you'd have thought that they were activists. They used to disappear on matchdays in their tracksuits and wander around the shanty towns talking to the locals about how oppressed they were and telling them that they shouldn't stand for it. We used to refer to them as the revolutionaries.

We had two guys from Millwall with us: Trevor Lee and Phil Walker. They had to put up with a lot playing for Millwall, as their fans were notorious at that time. It's to their credit that they made themselves favourites with the Millwall fans because that wasn't easy for a black player. I knew from playing against Millwall how ferocious their fans could be and it wasn't a place where I relished playing. Terry Connor, from Leeds, was also in our side, as was Tony Sealy who was a teammate of mine at Palace. We also had Brian Stein and Ricky Hill, who were stars at Luton; both of them went on to play for England. It was a good side. We beat Trinidad & Tobago and drew with a full-strength Fulham team.

But the real star on that trip was a guy called Pedro Richards – God rest his soul – who played for Notts County. Trevor Benjamin, who was a teammate of his at Notts County came along too. Now Benji had the greatest Afro of any footballer that I've ever seen, but he only spoke twice on that trip and that was to say hello and goodbye to us. Pedro just ripped into him the whole time. He stole the show. He wasn't even meant to be out there. We'd had a player drop out of the squad just before we travelled and we bumped into Pedro at the airport as he was coming back from a holiday in Spain. He asked us where we were all going and, when we told him, he said that he'd come along too. He didn't have any kit or many clothes with him but he didn't care. We sorted out the paperwork and he borrowed everyone else's stuff for the duration of the trip.

For some reason, Pedro had a problem with Tony Sealy, and the feeling was mutual. One evening, he did the usual and walked up the corridor knocking on doors asking to borrow things. He came into our room and used half a bottle of Tony's aftershave on himself. After he'd emptied the bottle, he threw it down saying, 'I don't know why I used this shit; it's cat's piss' and walked out. I watched Tony's eyes following him as he left the room before he turned to me and said, 'I really hate that man so much!'

Pedro didn't care who he upset. Trevor Lee had a stutter but none of us said anything about it except for one person. We were having breakfast one morning and Trevor walked in and said, 'G-g-g-good morning.' Pedro burst out laughing and Trevor just said, 'I wondered how long it would take!'

Spending those few weeks with some of the most prominent black players from England taught me that black footballers were just like all other footballers. We laughed at, and spoke about, the same things as everyone else.

We did, though, used to talk amongst ourselves about the stick that we had to put up with in England, and what became clear was that we all expected to get abuse wherever we played. We'd focus on the different levels of hostility that we'd get. Trevor and Phil knew that if they hadn't been playing for Millwall they'd have been murdered every time they went to the Den. We all agreed that once we put a shirt on, it was like we weren't black to our own fans, but if a black player was in the opposition side then he'd get slaughtered regardless of our presence. We all hoped that it would eradicate itself but, apart from that, Brian Stein and Ricky Hill agreed with me: the best way to cope was by scoring a goal and sticking it up these people's backsides.

People are frightened of difference and I also believe that people are frightened of what they don't understand. As the years go by, I can see that if you don't like something but can't do anything about it, then you tolerate it, and I think that a lot of people have become like that in their thinking with black people. They now say, 'I don't mind the West Indians but I can't stand Muslims' and you know what? That is exactly what was said about the Polish and the West Indians before. As time goes on, people find new targets.

The Asians walk around London confidently, yet their parents were being beaten up for being Asian. There were riots up north because Asians there wouldn't stand for that shit just like the blacks in Brixton years before. Black people turned around and said, 'Fuck that,' declaring that they wouldn't stand for it any longer. The one advantage that blacks had over Asians is that, in general, they spoke the same language as the whites, so that part of it wasn't so frightening to people who didn't understand or weren't comfortable with them. And then they'd say, 'You ain't too bad. It's *them*.'

A lot of Asians I know still suffer from racism, but I do believe that, in time, people will have the same attitudes towards Asians that they now have towards blacks; they'll be more comfortable with them. And then it will be someone else. And, by that time, their attitudes towards black people will have softened even more. I think it softens because the world gets smaller and because of familiarity brought about by the TV and the radio.

I do, though, find it very worrying when I see kids coming out of school in separate groups – Asian kids together or groups of black kids together – and there's very little integration. I was brought up in a so-called racist world where stuff was written on walls but, in my day, you'd walk home with anyone. You didn't see colour as kids, but I think that kids now are more aware of colour than they were then. A lot of the stick that I got was from people who didn't understand that they were being hurtful. They thought that they were just being funny, but if you get stick now then that's different because people do understand what they are doing and they know that it's not acceptable.

CHAPTER 7

VENNERS

TERRY VENABLES AND PROMOTION

I never found out the actual reason why Malcom Allison left. I think he had visions of us walking out at Wembley in the FA Cup Final, and when that didn't happen and we lost in the semi-finals and then also lost out on promotion from the Third Division, I reckon he thought that he couldn't take the team any further and didn't have the time to wait for the kids to come through. It was a shame because I'd have liked to play a few games for him. He gave me confidence. I don't think I was the most confident person when it came to football, but Malcolm helped me with that.

Venners then came in for the next three or four years and I made my debut under him. I always remember, after Malcolm left, walking into Venables' office, and he had a big, thick black book in front of him and he said to me, 'Alright, Vince. And what did Malcolm promise you then?' He opened this book up and it had been a procession. Malcolm had promised all of us the world!

Venables was new to management; he was only in his early thirties. His masterstroke was that we'd won the FA Youth Cup twice in a row, so he made Allan Harris, who we all knew, his assistant manager. Managers have to surround themselves with good people.

Venners' team talks would be technical. Not every footballer in the country would have understood them, but the players had been brought up with similar ideas under John Cartwright, so we were used to it. Their thoughts on football were very similar to each other so when we got into the first team, we just carried on with what we were doing and Venables continued to educate us. It wasn't rocket science; he just simplified things to the extent that it seemed like genius.

Venables didn't put any restrictions on me. It used to be said about Palace that we played without fear but it's nothing to do with that. If the coach tells you to go out and enjoy it and play your normal game, then that is what you do on the park. But if a coach says to a seventeen-year-old that they don't want you to make any mistakes and they don't want you to dribble in certain areas or do other stuff then you're going to play with that in your head and it puts fear into you. The best message that you can have is for the manager to tell you not to be frightened of making mistakes because he won't get on your back and that's what he was like with me.

As you get older as a player – and I was exactly the same – you play entirely differently to how you did when you were seventeen, eighteen or nineteen. You're different physically but, more significantly, when you're younger, you're just not experienced enough to take on too many instructions. Managers put you in the team at a young age because you've got ability and they don't want to clutter that up with too much information so, like Venners, they just tell you to do what you're good at. For that reason, I used to love playing for the England sides because any time that I met up with them they just used to tell us to do what we did for our clubs. That's all they said. I used to think that I'd love to be the manager of England if that's all they had to say.

Managers can do damage to youngsters by giving them too much information. When I was a youngster in the Palace side, Venners used to tell me to go and stand on the halfway line when the opposition had a corner. That was easy for me. I'd ask him what he wanted me to do when the ball came to me but he used to just tell me to do whatever came naturally. As I've said, he used to tell me and Jerry Murphy to go and practise our skills while he'd work with the defenders and the defensive midfielders. I used to catch Jerry Murphy's eye during team talks and I'd shrug my shoulders because I didn't know what he was talking about. But, as I got older, he'd give me more specific instructions on how to receive the ball and where to go with it. These were all things that I'd have probably done naturally but now I was getting coached. And coaching is about helping players to make the right decisions.

When I was younger, I didn't think about crossing the ball because I thought that I was an entertainer and Venners barely spoke to me about final product. But, then, for two years all I did with Terry Venables was work on my crossing and being able to maximise fouls. It became natural.

Throughout my career, people used to have a go at me about my crossing, but I could bring out loads of videos of games at Palace when my crossing was excellent. The old-fashioned coaches used to tell wingers not to look up before crossing the ball and just to get it into the box and that it was up to the forwards to get onto it. Venables didn't agree with that. He thought that meant that I might cross the ball but the forwards could still be on the halfway line or I might put the ball to the far post and everyone would be at the near, so it would be a waste of an opportunity.

Venables was the only coach that I had who was very clear in his instructions about crossing the ball. His idea was that he'd coach me and tell me what he wanted me to do and then he'd go and coach the strikers and tell them exactly what he'd coached me so that we were all on the same page. Venners told me that he never wanted me to cross the ball from near the halfway line. He said that was 'hammer-throwing stuff' and that we played football at Palace. He told me to cross the ball from near the goal. He explained how to use the lines of the penalty box to help me and said that it didn't matter whether I looked up or not – the lines of the box would be there as my guide. He told me that once I got into a position at the edge of the box, all of the space would be beyond the far post because all the defenders would be near the goal guarding it. He said this meant that the space was behind them and so that's where I should aim to cross the ball. Venners then told me that our forwards would pull away beyond the far post and, by playing the ball into space, away from the defenders, that would make them favourites to win the ball. He wanted our forwards to knock it back towards our midfielders who were running on to score a goal.

He'd pick the ball up and move it further forward so that it was halfway between the edge of the penalty area and the dead ball line, explaining that I'd have normally got into that position by taking on and beating a defender, and I should then hit the ball into the corridor between the defenders and the goalkeeper. It was a channel that goalkeepers didn't like to come into to claim the ball, but the defenders didn't like it either because my run would have made them turn round and face their own goal, so all our forwards had to do was gamble on that space and, hopefully, knock it in. Defenders would be in two minds whether to stick their foot out or gamble that their keeper was coming. Venners said that he would tell our forwards that if I was ever in that position then that's where I would be aiming and they should make the run into that corridor and gamble.

He then told me what to do if I got right to the byline, so we had a system where I knew where to cross the ball depending on where I was on the pitch and the forwards were all aware of it; it wasn't just willy-nilly. Later on in my career, I had people like Howard Wilkinson who just told me to get it in the box and there was no plan but, at Palace, the wingers knew where the ball should go depending on where it was in relation to the box and so did the forwards – and it worked.

Another important factor was who you were crossing the ball to. I knew when I played with Micky Quinn that all I had to do was get the ball into the danger area and he would do the rest. But, with respect, with players like Mike Flanagan and

Kevin Mabbutt at Palace and then Alan Biley at Portsmouth, I had to get the ball in with a bit more quality to give them better chances.

One cross that I haven't mentioned was the one that ended up behind the goal in the stand. I was taught something at a very early age at Palace by a guy called Tony Hazell, who bore a remarkable resemblance to Fred Flinstone and, he won't mind me saying, played a bit like him as well. The *Evening Standard* used to have a five-a-side indoor competition in the middle of the season and it was very popular. All the clubs sent strong teams. Ours had me, George Graham, Neil Smillie and Tony Hazell in it.

This particular night I won Player of the Evening and got a magnum of champagne. They had digital scoreboards in the arena, which must have been about thirty feet up, and Tony got the ball just inside the halfway line and hit a shot that struck the board and the clock stopped working. I turned around and saw Tony replacing a divot – and we were playing on hardboard! I asked him what he was doing and he told me that it always gets you out of trouble with the fans if you do that. So I started doing it myself whenever I hit a bad cross or shot and, if it was particularly bad, then I actually used to gesture at the groundsman.

It's only when you look back on your career that you realise how much a manager does for you. Sometimes Venables took me out of games when I thought I was doing alright but he would say that I was tired and use that as an excuse rather than tell me that I wasn't playing well, which would have crushed me. At seventeen, the only opinion that counts is your manager's, and I bet it's the same for players today. If Venners told me that I was tired then I would believe him and it wouldn't knock my confidence.

Around about that time, 1976–77, I used to travel in with George Graham. Twelve years later, he won the double with Arsenal as a strict disciplinarian and Sergeant Major-type manager, but I don't remember any of that side of his character. He was the most immaculate man I've ever met and was the closest thing I saw to Sean Connery in the early Bond films. He was a funny bloke too. If he saw a nice-looking girl when we were sitting in the car, he used to press the horn, which always made the girl look up. He'd do it twice and then he'd mouth to her and ask why she was beeping her horn at him and they'd start flirting. You wouldn't think it would work, but it did!

I had just started getting into the team as a regular but, by that time, George was at the back end of his career. Venables was saying that we needed a bit more steel in the middle of the park and we needed to make our tackles, but anyone who saw George play will tell you that he was an elegant player and not a tackler. I thought it was asking a bit much, as George was a bit too long in the tooth to start putting his foot in and changing his game but, bless him, he had a go.

We played a game at Stoke, and George knew that if he didn't start toeing the line and playing how Venables wanted him to then he'd struggle to stay in the side because there were a lot of kids my age like Jerry Murphy who were pushing to get in the team. It was an away game and we won, but George made a tackle that was so late that he connected after the game was over. Venables asked George what had happened with the sending off and he said, 'He was just a bit too quick for me, Gaffer', but Venables told him not to worry as we'd won anyway.

In those days, if you got sent off you didn't miss the following game if you appealed, because they gave you a couple of weeks' grace, so a lot of clubs used that system. The next week, we played Bolton at Selhurst and they were a good side. They were top and had Frank Worthington, Alan Gowling and Neil Whatmore playing for them. Lo and behold, George got himself sent off again – two weeks running. Afterwards, we were sitting together in the dressing room and he turned to me and said, 'All the years I've played the game, you'd think I'd crack this tackling lark but I can't do it, Vinny. Do you reckon he noticed?'

The funniest memory I have about George Graham, which might make people see him in a different light, was when we played a league game against Mansfield Town. The game was on the Bank Holiday Monday and we'd trained the day before and, in those days, Barry Silkman travelled in with me and George. George was the driver and we used to meet him at Liverpool Street Station. When he dropped us off, we told him that we'd see him the next day for a lift to the game. We thought we'd told him that it was an early kick off so we were going to meet at 11.30 a.m.

I turned up and Silky was already there waiting. Silky was the original wide boy. He's an agent nowadays and he knew everyone in London. We were standing there for about half an hour and we were worried that George was cutting it fine as we had to get to the ground. We were struggling, as it was still an hour from there to get across to Selhurst Park, but we figured that he must have been stuck in traffic. We didn't know what to do but, all of a sudden, Silky spotted someone that he knew in a car and wangled a lift and we turned up about five minutes before Venables had to hand the team sheet in. Venners asked where George was and we couldn't believe he wasn't there so he just told us to get changed. We played the game but we didn't know what had happened to him and were worried that there had been a car accident.

Nothing more was said and we all went home and Silky offered to give me a lift to the next training session as we hadn't heard from George. We got to the training ground and who happened to be there but George. We went up to him and said, 'George, what the fuck happened?' He just looked at us and said:

Boys, you are not going to believe this. I did my usual and got up in the morning, put my dressing gown and slippers on and had a bit of breakfast. I was sitting there watching a bit of *Grandstand* and the Missus came in with a cup of tea and I was looking at the football results. I was dunking my biscuits and then, all of a sudden, it's come up with the Second Division half times and I saw Palace v Mansfield. I thought it was an evening kick off! I couldn't believe it. I was just starting to think that I should be getting ready and the half time score has come through. I dropped my chocolate biscuit! Who kicks off in the afternoon on a Bank Holiday?

He'd missed the game! In the space of twelve years, he went from that to being the Youth team manager at Palace, to managing

Millwall and then winning the double with Arsenal as a strict disciplinarian.

Venables took it well and didn't react; in fact, it rarely seemed as if anything fazed him. Venners was a very humorous man and always had an answer for everything, which some people resented. I always remember when we were staying at a hotel and an elderly waitress was coming round with a tray of steaks. She was breathing so heavily that she sounded asthmatic. Venables was watching her and when she got to him he said, 'I've heard of service but you actually keeping my steak cool for me by breathing on it is way beyond the call of duty.' We all burst out laughing. We couldn't believe he'd said it, but he always had a quip for everything.

He kept us very relaxed in games. In fact, the only time I saw him under pressure was when he left me out for four or five games on the promotion run in 1979 when Terry Fenwick had taken my place. Even though I wasn't happy, he was such a Svengali that I didn't say anything to him. Something came up in the papers about the chances of me leaving and going to play for Leyton Orient. They'd been the first club I'd actually gone to and I knew a lot of their players and Maurice Newman, the fella who discovered me, was still working there so, after a particular game in which I hadn't come on, I'd had enough and I decided to go and see Venners.

I went up to him and asked him if I could see him. One thing he liked about me was that I was the only player that called him 'Boss' – everyone else called him Tel. I called him Tel once and he asked me why I was calling him that and not boss! When I asked to see him, he went bright red as he thought I was going to say that I wanted to leave, but I just told him I wasn't happy being out of the team; that was it and I walked away. I bottled it, but I got back in a week or so later for the run in and we got promoted.

Burnley was the last game of the season and we still had to get a point to go up and a win to be champions. Venables took us to a local hotel to get us away from everything, but the game felt like nothing to us because there were so many young players in the team; we just couldn't understand the significance of it. The oldest player in the side after Steve Kember was John Burridge and he was only about twenty-six or twenty-seven. Budgie was one of those people who was ultra-professional and he needed to have his rest and to eat the right food. We had something to eat at lunchtime and then Venables told us to go and lie in bed.

To give some idea of what we were like as a team and what the atmosphere was like amongst us, me, Billy Gilbert and Jerry Murphy all burst into Budgie's room with a tennis ball and started playing a match there, but he just wanted to go to bed and get some rest. I remember him shouting:

> This is one of the most important games of my career! I could get my career back on track and all you lot want to do is play tennis in here. Do you not know what's going on? Look out of the window. People are going to the game now and it's only 1.30 p.m.!

We were telling him to relax and that it was only a game but he shouted, 'The leopard needs rest!' We just carried on and that showed how relaxed we were. To us, it was a nothing game; we didn't feel pressure.

A total of 51,482 people paid to get in to see the match, but I reckon there were more inside the ground. That's still the record crowd at Palace. It's quite funny. We won 2–0 and I made both goals but, after about fifteen minutes, I got a bang on the head and I have no recollection of the match. I've seen the goals on news reels but I have absolutely no memory of them. The fans were out on the pitch after the game but I never went up to the stand to celebrate, not because I was concussed, but because it just felt like any other game to me. I remember speaking to a couple of the Burnley players in the bar afterwards but I was home fairly early – that was the way I was at the time. I tried so hard to remember the game and the goals, but all I could remember was the bang on the head. I woke up the next day, saw the goals on the news, and then got ready for my first trip to the States – we had a bonding trip to Fort Lauderdale.

We didn't feel any pressure at all that season. We'd won the FA Youth Cup a couple of years before, Kenny Sansom had been talked about as being capped by the full England side, Billy had broken into the Under-21s, Murph and Nicholas were breaking into their international sides and stuff was coming to us quickly. Venners sheltered us and so the pressure didn't register. I can honestly say that all we wanted to do at that time was play football. Many times we were told to get off the training ground and go home to get some rest and yet, now, the top players boast about their skills coming from extra practice. We were told to save our legs when all we wanted to do was get a ball out. In the end that enthusiasm sort of gets kicked out of you, so it became a case of going to the betting shop or playing snooker and all the other things that people associate with players from that era.

We went on a pre-season tour to Sweden after we got promoted. Come the end of the trip, the manager said that he wanted to speak with the younger lads about our contracts when we got back to England. I remember asking Jimmy Cannon for advice and both him and Paul Hinshelwood told me to stick to my guns and not let the manager bully me over the financial side of the deal. Jim looked at me and said that he'd have a bet for any money that I'd take the first offer that Venners put to me. It became a running joke amongst the lads.

When we got back to Stansted airport, I went to the toilet and Venners followed me in and stood next to me at the cubicle. He asked me if I'd thought about my contract and asked how £110 a week suited me. I told him it sounded great and thanked him very much. He'd doubled my money, but Jim was right: I took the first thing he offered. When I came out, I told the other lads that I didn't have to go into the club the next day as I'd just negotiated my deal in the toilet. Jimmy Cannon slaughtered me. He thought I was so weak.

We trusted Venables, though, and he looked after us. He was that much of a Svengali that we didn't bother about agents. If he'd only offered me a pound raise, I was going to say yes to him. It may not seem a lot now but as a teenager in those times I was on good dough.

When I think of the way that Venners looked after us, it makes me sad to see the way that he's viewed by some Palace supporters now. I can remember when Venables returned to the club as manager under Mark Goldberg and I watched a Palace match on TV and they were interviewing the supporters, who were all having a go at Venables saying that he'd ripped the club off and drained them of money and that it had led to Palace going into administration. What made me sad was that none of them mentioned all of the good work Venables put in during his first spell at the club. He put Palace on the map and yet none of the supporters spoke about it. You read articles on Venables and he'll say that some of his best times in his career were at Palace and it's sad that people don't remember them. All they remember is this business with Goldberg. But that side that Venables helped to create could have been a truly great one and I imagine that they're some of the greatest days that Palace fans have had.

CHAPTER 8

THE BREAK-UP

VENABLES LEAVING AND PALACE BREAKING UP

When we were younger, we refused to let our confidence turn to arrogance, but a turning point came when we beat Nottingham Forest in our first season in Division One when Peter Shilton threw one into his own net. Even though we only won 1–0 with a lucky goal, we were easily the better team; they were European Champions and we'd outplayed them. Forest were going through a bit of a bad patch but they still had all of the European Cup-winning team playing – and after that game, we all thought that we could do whatever we liked. As far as we were concerned, they weren't up to much and yet they were Champions of Europe.

We were top of the league at one stage that season after we thrashed Ipswich 4–1 and a journalist called Jeff Powell travelled with us on the train up to Liverpool and was a bit taken aback by the lack of fear amongst us young players about going up to Anfield and playing against the likes of Dalglish, Hansen, Case and Souness. He wrote, 'This could well be the team of the '80s.' That statement stuck, but unfortunately we didn't live up to it.

We went to Anfield that day and Liverpool smacked our arses 3–0. We never threatened the top of the table again after that, although we still had the odd good result, and we ended up finishing thirteenth. I played all forty-two League games that year and it was probably my best season for the club. A game that a lot of Palace fans remember me for was at the end of that season when we played Liverpool in the return game at home and drew 0–0. We should have beaten them easily and they won the League that year. We tended to hold our own against the best teams. I was up against Avi Cohen and he couldn't get near me so they took him off and got Jimmy Case to mark me instead and he couldn't get near me either. We ended up finishing thirteenth and it should have been a good basis for us to go again the following year.

Terry Venables has got to take a lot of the blame for the fact that we didn't carry on progressing, because he didn't see the signs and arrest our arrogance. But he was only a young manager too and I guess that you only understand that difference between confidence and arrogance through living life – and none of us had done that. Honestly, to know how to deal with success, I think you have to have experienced failure. Then you don't want to suffer that feeling again so you keep striving to be your best. This was something that Venables didn't understand, because he hadn't experienced failure and neither had we. As soon as it started to go wrong for Venners then it started to go wrong for us too.

THE BREAK-UP

In hindsight, selling Steve Kember was a mistake. Selling him and bringing Gerry Francis in wasn't right. I'm not talking about in footballing terms because Gerry Francis was probably one of the best footballers that I've ever played with or against. He was absolutely brilliant and that's why he was one of England's youngest captains. Terry Venables thought that he was bringing in an experienced player who had captained England, was younger than Steve Kember and had more ability than him, but Gerry also had injury problems and was only twenty-six years of age himself.

Venables thought that Gerry would carry us, but he was still young and had issues of his own, and was too busy trying to get back to the level he was at previously. Keeping Steve at Palace might have been the right thing to do. Terry wanted to try and take us to the next level, but clubs rely on certain players who don't always stand out. I stood out because I was black and beat players and got the crowd excited but people didn't realise that I didn't cover a lot of ground in a game. The fans would see Jerry Murphy picking a pass out or Swindy hitting a shot from thirty yards and Kenny Sansom running down the left wing from full back but they didn't notice someone like Steve Kember or Nicky Chatterton who was an original box to box player and did the dirty work.

Nicky was the type of player who quietly went about his business and did his job, but some people thought that he was only in the side because he was the groundsman's son. Even when he arrived late in the box and scored important goals, a lot of people used to say that it was the only touch that he'd had in the game. Palace have always had flair players since Big Mal was there. He signed Don Rogers, Charlie Cooke, Peter Taylor, me and Barry Silkman and that carried through with John Salako and, now, Wilfried Zaha and Andros Townsend. Those are the people who win you games, but they aren't the ones that stop you from losing and I include myself in that. It's your Nicky Chattertons who do that.

To give another example, I played for a lot of time at Palace with Paul Hinshelwood behind me at right back. The fans used to call him 'Doris' but they didn't realise that I wouldn't have been anywhere near the same player without him because he had great stamina, was strong in the tackle, good in the air and, whenever he had the ball, the first person that he looked for was me. For a wide player, there are times when you are only in the game for small periods and, when you get the ball, the crowd expects you to do something but it's the hardest thing in football to do the simple things – especially when you're playing well.

I say that because when you're playing well, you start to think that you'll try something a bit extra and that's when it starts to go wrong. It's really difficult to stay focused and do the easy thing for an hour and a half but, for me, it wasn't that hard at Palace because for the majority of my time there I had Paul Hinshelwood playing behind me. As a result, I had the ball more than most players so I didn't feel the need to do something special all of the time because I knew that I'd be seeing a lot of the ball throughout the game.

I think that I was spoiled a little bit by people like Steve Kember, Peter Nicholas and, more than anyone, Paul Hinshelwood. We nicknamed Paul 'Fish' because he could drink the majority of people under the table and he smoked too but, for all of those vices, I would say that he would be in the top four or five players that I've ever played with in terms of fitness. There were a lot of times that Fish would play behind me, go on an overlap and pass me and I'd invariably play to the crowd and ignore him or just lose the ball. He'd pass me on the way back, after making a sixty- or seventy-yard run, and yet he never criticised me for my work rate. He looked at me as a player who could win games for the team, so I was spoiled from a very young age.

Fish could be fiery, though, and I've seen him hit people on the field. I remember a game at Blackburn Rovers in the late '70s when he did it and it makes me proud that it never came to this between us. I was playing on the left wing that day and Barry Silkman was on the right in front of Fish. Silky was quite brainy for a winger and I hope he doesn't mind me saying this but if he knew that he was going to get kicked then he'd try and swap wings. We'd swapped wings in this particular game and we were under the cosh. Silky had the ball and Fish was going on one of his marauding runs past him but Silky pulled out of a tackle and Blackburn won the ball back.

Paul had run ten or fifteen yards past him to get the ball, yet Silky was now jogging very slowly back into defence. I was still young and hadn't learned how to loaf yet and I glanced over to that wing as I was running back and, as Paul ran past Silky, he cuffed him round the head. I couldn't believe it. Silky started sprinting after Fish, Jim Cannon came across and knocked the ball out for a corner and, while we were regrouping, Silky was just about to have a go at him before Fish shouted, 'You fucking got back quick enough then, didn't you?' He'd only run back because he'd hit him round the head.

Before our second season in Division One started, Venables sold Kenny Sansom on the back of having Terry Fenwick to play at left back but Fen couldn't even kick with his left foot. He was a good player, though, and could play in any position: centre half, right back, defensive midfield but Fen was so determined to show how two-footed he was and prove that he was a left back after Kenny went, that even when he had time to use his better foot, he'd still use his left, despite the fact that he was only ever adequate with it.

It was well documented that Kenny Sansom had a gambling problem and that was actually the real reason why we had to sell him. Venables was good because he looked after Kenny like that.

I got in one morning at about 9.45 a.m. and, evidently, Kenny had got in earlier because he had a few problems that he had to talk to Venables about. I was sitting outside Venners' office with a cup of tea and Kenny came out and said, 'Thanks for that, boss. I really appreciate it.' With that, Venables saw me and asked me what I was driving. I didn't even finish the sentence before he told me that I'd just bought myself a Triumph Stag, a nice car, that was only six months old and he'd sort out the money with me.

Venners' word was law so all I said was, 'Yeah, no problems, Gaffer.' I'd just bought Kenny's car off him to get him out of the hole he was in. The thing is, I'd recently bought a Triumph Stag that was only three years old. It was quick and I'd always wanted a sports car. Billy couldn't believe it: 'So you've just bought a car three or four weeks ago. Venners then tells you that you're buying another so now you've got two Triumph Stags!' But Venables told me I was buying it, so I did.

Kenny leaving was really the end of it. None of us could believe what Venables had done and we all figured that if Kenny could go then it meant that the manager wasn't going to be around much longer either. Clive Allen came in for him from Arsenal on a swap deal and was a quality goalscorer, but none of us were pleased that we'd managed to replace Kenny with an excellent striker. There were a couple of rows that come to mind where Clive missed some chances and we got beaten and Billy Gilbert and Paul Hinshelwood basically blamed him. Clive was told in no uncertain terms by the players that he wasn't an adequate replacement for Kenny. As it turned out, he was technically the best finisher that I ever played with, but we didn't make best use of him.

On the pitch, it started to go wrong from the first game of that season. We got beaten comfortably at Liverpool but no one took too much notice because it was the first game and it wasn't an easy place to go to. In the second game, we played Spurs in a derby in front of a big crowd. They had a front pairing that was electric: Archibald and Crooks.

I'd got pretty pally with Crooksy from my England Under-21 days; he was the most articulate person in the world. We used to have a great laugh when we met up together. I used to look forward to it just to see Crooksy. He always talked about people with such disdain and his favourite comment to end any conversation was, 'I can't believe it. I just can't believe it. I can't believe what I'm hearing,' in the poshest voice you can imagine.

We were like the three musketeers: me, Crooksy and Justin Fashanu. I hadn't seen Garth for about six years after I retired and he was commentating and doing the post-match interviews for *Match of the Day* when Portsmouth played Leeds. I walked past and he saw me. The first thing that we talked about was Justin.

Garth told me that he'd met him in Atlanta when he was out there for the Olympics in 1996 and he'd asked Justin why he hadn't told the two of us that he was gay as we were so close to him. Justin told Garth that it was none of his business and asked him whether it actually mattered. Garth said that of course it didn't and then Justin told him that he didn't have to worry as he hadn't ever fancied him. Garth and I looked at each other and Crooksy said that he'd thought, 'Well, why not?' He ended up getting the last train back and we spent the whole time laughing at the old tales.

In this Spurs game, they went 1–0 up; Ardiles, Hoddle, Archibald and Villa were playing. They had a decent team. It was a derby and, although it wasn't necessarily heated, it was frenetic. I scored a good goal and equalised and this all happened in the first fifteen minutes of the game. I then got the ball and Crooksy, of all people, attempted to tackle me. He never tackled anyone and I think that's what made me snap. I just thought, 'Why's he tackling me?' The ball broke loose between us and Crooksy mistimed his tackle and caught me on the ankle. I was expecting the referee to blow for a free kick but he waved play on and I shouted out, 'You're joking! Play on?' Then, completely against my nature and for some unknown reason, I took a couple of steps towards the ref and pushed him and, before he hit the ground, he had his red card out.

It was like slow motion. All I remember in the background was Crooksy going, 'I can't believe it!' and he repeated it about four times. My head was spinning and then I kept hearing Terry Yorath saying, 'Vince, what have you done? Vince, what have you done?' I turned around to him and shouted, 'Why don't you just fucking shut up?' All the crowd were screaming but even over them I could still hear Crooksy repeating, 'I just can't believe it!' He was laughing at me. He phoned me up the next day and, in his eloquent way, said, 'Tell me I was dreaming.'

I stood at the dressing room door and apologised to Venners and the lads. We got beaten 4–2 and retribution was swift. I went up to the FA's offices at Lancaster Gate and got charged with bringing the game into disrepute and got a six-game ban and a £600 fine. That's a lot of matches to miss when you're fit and I don't think that I ever recovered that season. Venners was absolutely stunned. He just asked me what happened and I told him that I thought that I was pushing Croosky and had pushed the ref by mistake but I didn't really think that … I'd just lost it for a while. That was the beginning of the end, and we never really recovered.

We lost about three games in a row and the straw that finally broke the camel's back was when we lost away to Coventry. We got a free kick about thirty yards from goal and Clive Allen hit it and it just flew in. It was one of the best free kicks I've ever seen and the three of us that had been standing round the ball all jumped on Clive, celebrating. All of a sudden, we realised that the game was still going on. The ref thought the ball had hit the post. It actually hit the stanchion at the back of the net and came out but the ref played on. Neil Smillie used to wear contact lenses and he was the only other person on the pitch who played on too.

I ran the length of the pitch telling the ref what a nightmare he'd had and, because the game was being filmed for *The Big Match*, told him that he'd be proved a fool on telly the next day. He turned around and told me that I'd be proved a fool too because my performance was embarrassing. We lost 3–1 but the 'goal' would have put us in front. I always remember Billy Gilbert after the game saying, 'You silly c*nt, Smelly [Neil Smillie]. If you hadn't chased after the ball after it flew back out he would have given a goal. You want to check those fucking contact lenses you've got in.' The next day, on the telly, it was obvious that it had gone in, but Jimmy Hill, who was presenting the show, was the Coventry chairman and he didn't dwell on it too much.

The club then lost the plot. We'd had too much too soon and that started with the manager. People had been talking about us as the Team of the '80s and Venables as the next England manager, but we lost about three games in a row and he lost his sanity. We just didn't feel that we could arrest it. We'd had such good times at the club up until then. Ray Bloye had been the chairman when we were thought of as the Team of the '80s and we were getting anything between 27,000 and 42,000 spectators at Selhurst regularly. We'd had a blend of youth with experience but, suddenly, there was infighting amongst the players, the chairman left and then Ron Noades came in. That was when it all went wrong and we went from doing pre-seasons in Florida and Memphis to pre-season tours of Calais with eighteen to a room!

It was enough for Venables and he left not long after that and went straight to QPR. We found out he'd gone when we were away with the Under-21s. Initially, we couldn't understand why he hadn't come out to the game with us. Venables said the chairman questioned his sanity over some of the things that he was doing, like swapping Kenny Sansom for Clive Allen and bringing Paul Barron in, but I think he used that as an excuse because he couldn't see things getting better. In the end, I think he was proved right. The club's ambitions weren't growing like his and he didn't get the backing that he had before. It was basically turmoil so he just left the club to get on with it.

He went to QPR and every single player who rejoined him there enjoyed an upturn in their careers whereas all the ones who stayed, their careers took a downturn. We'd bought Mike Flanagan for a large fee. I didn't think that we'd needed him as we had Elwiss, Swindlehurst and Walsh, but Venners thought that he was a good player. He didn't have a great first season for Palace; Venners knew that he would become good, but he wasn't allowed to wait for that. Flanagan then went to QPR with Venables and did well. There were also a lot of older players at QPR, like Tony Currie, who got a lot better and found a new lease of life, which showed that Venables had motivational skills too.

Terry Fenwick followed Venners to QPR. Now, I've got great admiration for him as a player as he was very versatile, but the biggest benefit that he had, unlike players such as myself and Billy Gilbert, was that he could carry on his career under Terry Venables. He was able to continue improving under the man who knew how to get the best out of him and we didn't have that advantage.

Losing Venables happened too early in my career. There's no question about that; he was like a guru to me and the other young players at Palace. People used to consider me and Billy to be inconsistent, but I didn't miss many games when Terry Venables was our manager. As I've said, in that first season that Palace had in the top flight, I didn't miss one match and that was back when we played forty-two league games and all of the Cup games. The reason why I played in all of those games was because I was consistent.

We ended up getting relegated in that 1980–81 season. We just kept losing and couldn't turn it around. It wasn't a confidence thing; there was just so much apathy at the club that it dragged us down. Losing just became such a habit for us. People make a big thing of it now but there weren't enough winners left there. As much as Venners and John Cartwright were into the technical side of the game, Terry still got Allan Harris in as his right-hand man and Allan was all about competing. Ultimately, football is about winning. It goes back to what I was saying about Steve Kember. He wasn't as gifted as Gerry Francis, but he stuck his foot in. Peter Nicholas learned a lot from him, but then we sold Nico as well.

It was frustrating because we still had good players at the club, like myself, Jimmy Cannon, Billy Gilbert and Jerry Murphy but we went to pieces. Even the young lads like Shaun Brooks, who had got into the team, used to call it Fred Karno's Circus.

We thought that the lads who got out were so lucky, and my own heart went out of it. I'd grown up with those players. We'd been together from the age of fourteen all the way through to becoming professionals and then topping Division One. It was like being married and then getting divorced. None of us had ever spoken about leaving Palace. It's like when you're a young kid and you never think that you'll get old.

I've already said, many times, that we hadn't learned how to cope with adversity, and we just couldn't handle failure on a regular basis. When we were kids, we'd played a London Youth Cup Final as fifteen-year-olds against eighteen-year-olds and half of the opposition were first-team players at Tottenham – Hoddle, McNab, Brotherston and Walford. We got comfortably beaten in the end but, for a lot of the game, we'd held our own even though we were still schoolboys. We were all going to school the next day and they were proper professional players, so even though we got thumped 5–0 that didn't teach us about failure either.

I was looking to leave from the point that Venners left, but you can only leave if someone wants you and people only want you if you're doing the business. If I'm totally honest, before then I used to play three good games out of four, which was brilliant for a flair player but, later on at Palace, I played one good game out of four. Some people remembered the one bit of brilliance I did in a game and talked about that, but I knew that it wasn't good enough. That's what I became. I went from being a young player who got into the team and was consistent and made or scored goals regularly to being totally inconsistent.

Towards the end of that relegation season, I got a phone call from a well-known ticket tout who did all of his business at Arsenal Football Club to the extent that Arsenal would use him to sound out players to find out if they'd be interested in going there. He asked me if I fancied going to Highbury. Palace was falling apart; it was deadline day the following day, so I told him that I definitely would. In those days, there was only one deadline and that was in March, so the tout told me that he'd let Arsenal know and they'd probably put in a bid the next day.

The following day we went out to train, but I still hadn't received the call and I think the deadline for transfers was something like 5 p.m. We actually finished training early because Palace were doing deals themselves and they told us to stay by our phones in case we were wanted. I got in the car and started driving home very slowly and I planned to stop at the club first because there were no mobile phones then and I wanted to find out if anyone had been trying to get hold of me. There was no news at Selhurst, so I left and put the radio on in the car and there was still, just about, time for me to get across London if I needed to.

I put Radio 2 on and I can vividly recall the sports news coming on and they said that Crystal Palace had agreed a fee with Arsenal. At that moment, I flicked the indicator to turn the car round but the reporter said that it was for Peter Nicholas to leave Palace to go there. I pulled the car over and put my head in my hands and sat there for about ten minutes. It killed me.

CHAPTER 9

MANAGERIAL MERRY-GO-ROUND

ERNIE WALLEY

Ron Noades had taken the club over by then. He'd come from Wimbledon and, with due respect, Palace were a lot bigger club than them. They were still finding their Crazy Gang feet at that time and, looking back, a lot of his ideas were fairly small-time for players that weren't used to thinking that way. He was cost-cutting all round the club and he was doing it with players too.

Allders was a big department store in Croydon and Peter Nicholas told us that he was going to go there to buy a carpet, a fridge, a TV and stereo and loads of other furniture for the house that he was moving to. We thought that would set him back but he said that he'd gone to see the secretary, who had given him a letter which showed that Palace had an account with Allders so we could go there, order what we wanted, and they would deliver it to us. Word spread round the club like wildfire because Jimmy Cannon told us that he'd also used it and that Allders had never ever been back for the money.

I fancied some of that so I went up there and must have spent about £3,500 on white goods and furniture and Billy Gilbert did the same. None of the money ever went out of our wages until the chairman sold Palace. One by one, we were all called in by Ron Noades and told how much we owed the club. In effect, for about three or four weeks during that season, I was playing for nothing because I was paying the club back.

Noades also wasn't happy with the wages that were being paid out either or the signing-on fees we'd all got and, when he first joined, we had managers galore. Ernie Walley – the man we'd all been frightened of in the reserves – took over for a few weeks and he was the worst person who could have taken over from Venables.

I've already said that he resented the way that we were looked after by Malcolm Allison and all of us youngsters dreaded being trained by him when we were kids. Ernie had very quickly got wind of the fact that we were being pampered, so he couldn't wait to get hold of us and show us what it was really like to be a professional footballer. He was basically an Allan Harris+ and he tended to focus on physical attributes rather than technical skills.

One of my first meetings with Ernie was when I joined Crystal Palace as a Schoolboy. I was that far advanced that as a fourteen-year-old, I was training with the Youth team with boys two or three years older than me. It just so happened that, on this particular day, we were doing weights circuits. The idea was that we would be put in a group with someone who was twice our size and we would all have to try and lift the same weights. I wasn't big then and I'm still not now and these boys, being two or three years older than me, were huge.

I'd never lifted weights before so Ernie said that he'd show us how to lift them safely. He showed us how to perform a jerk with bent knees and a straight back and told us to do it in reps of five. They were quite heavy and I think that the weight that I had to lift was about my body weight. By this time, I was petrified and didn't think I'd be able to do it. I was with quite a muscular group. I managed to perform five reps but it was the longest five repetitions in my life. When I stopped, my arms were actually shaking because the weights were so heavy and I wasn't used to it.

Ernie was walking around and came to our group. He told the player who was lifting before me that he had been watching him and he'd noticed that he wasn't lifting the weights correctly so he showed him how to do it. He picked them up as if they were a feather because he was a big bloke – he was solid muscle. He then pointed at me, but my arms were still shaking after my go, and told me to do it. My arms were shaking but I knew that I couldn't tell him that I wasn't going to do it. By now, everyone had stopped because they'd heard Ernie shouting. I told myself that I just needed to do one rep because then he'd walk away to another group.

I got into position and picked the weight up and with every bit of strength I could muster, I got it to my chest and, just as I was psyching myself up to raise it above my head, he shouted, 'Look! What's he forgot? He hasn't checked the weights to make sure they're fastened.' With that, I turned the bar to look at the weight and the other one dropped down and missed my foot by inches. It would have crushed my foot and I would have been out for weeks. Everyone burst out laughing and he walked away shaking his head, and I just thought, 'Thank God!' I sat down and my arms were shaking as if I was having an epileptic fit. Needless to say, that was the last time I did weights with Ernie. That's the type of guy he was and that was why you didn't want to get dropped from the first team when he was managing the reserves. He was a tough man.

A few weeks later, we were late for training. John Cartwright phoned us to say that he couldn't give us a lift from the East End, so me and Murph had to make our own way to the club. We turned up ten or fifteen minutes late and the Youth team had already left. We bumped into the chief scout, Arnie Warren, and he said that the reserves were staying at the ground so we could train with them. Me and Jerry Murphy looked at each other in panic and we went into the away team dressing room and locked ourselves into a toilet cubicle and stayed in there for an hour and three quarters hiding from Ernie. That was how much fear we had. What a state of affairs. We only got away with it because he didn't know we were training with the reserves that day.

When Ernie was the first team manager, our warm ups were the equivalent of stuff that other clubs did in their pre-season training, and our football was more graft than craft. You have to have the two but you need to have the right balance. If you don't have skilful players then you should lean more towards the graft but we had more crafty players at the time.

I was desperate to go, but no one asked to leave the club when Ernie was the manager because we were frightened of him. He had been having a pop at me about my performances because I hadn't been playing well. I hadn't been having a particularly good time, and things were getting to me, but we then played Leicester City and the game was on *Match of the Day*. The ball came to me and I put my head down and beat three players and hit one into the top corner from about twenty-five yards. Second half, I was involved in the move that got us a penalty. We were winning the game, and I thought, 'I'm still the business. They still love me, the crowd!' And then, with twenty minutes to go, he took me off.

I remember thinking, 'You can't do that to me. I'm Vince! They love me!' but he didn't care. I ran straight down the tunnel and was sitting in the dressing room and all I could think about was that I had to leave the club to get on in my career. The boys came in but Ernie was still outside and I was going, 'I fucking can't believe it; I'm fucking out of here. Who does he think he is taking me off?' I was spewing. Jerry Murphy told me not to worry about it but I said that I was going to go and see him and he replied, 'All the best, he'll probably knock you out.' The door opened, Ernie came in, larger than life with his 52-inch chest and he's gone, 'What's your problem?' and I said, 'Nothing at all, Ernie.' And that's how it was. We were all scared to death of him.

But he lost me big-time. I didn't know what else I could do, but he told me that I hadn't been working hard enough. That's when I thought that I had to get out of the club, but he left before I could go through with it. The results under him weren't too bad and Ernie desperately wanted the job, but he was only there a few weeks. It wasn't that he didn't rate me; it's just that he thought that he could get more from me than others did. But you've got to remember who I'd played under before. Venables had told me just to go out and play but Ernie tried to change my game and it was a dodgy spell for me. After him, Big Mal came back and he'd completely changed. That was a disaster too.

MALCOLM ALLISON

Malcolm Allison was, obviously, the first manager that I had and he did look after me when I was a kid with the TV documentary. Unfortunately, that didn't turn into a TV series; the pilot episode didn't do that well! It was a shame that I didn't play for him in a league match; I only played in one pre-season friendly at fifteen against Epsom & Ewell so, unfortunately, I didn't get to spend enough time with him to understand what he was like as a person. But, even though he didn't see the success, he was definitely the man who put Palace on the map as a football club.

I knew all about Malcolm before I signed for Palace. I loved my football so I was well aware of what he'd achieved at Man City; I'd seen him on the TV panels for the 1970 World Cup and I loved the fedora hat that he wore during Palace's 1976 Cup run.

I was only a kid then and, when he spoke to me, I was incapable of listening to what he was saying because I couldn't believe that he was actually talking to me. It was like being spoken to by John Wayne. When Malcolm walked into a room, people stopped talking and, when he spoke, people listened, but they didn't hear him because he was such a major presence.

Malcolm was the first manager that I was aware of who introduced the need to eat well, have a good diet, and get enough sleep. You can find recordings of him on YouTube when he was on the TV panels at the 1970 World Cup and you should listen to what he's got to say. Brian Clough used to be on the panels with him but, if you listen to him and Brian Clough, you tell me which one talks like they would be a top manager now. You will recognise which manager relied on motivation and which one relied on tactics and quality preparation and there's only one that stands out and that's Malcolm.

You can't knock Cloughie, but he was a person who signed good players and got more out of them than others had. He didn't make them better players but he motivated them brilliantly. Malcolm was so innovative. Even in the second spell when he came back and had lost the plot, he told us that everyone had to have breakfast and not eat later on in the day. His mantra was to eat early, and nowadays all managers tell you when to eat – but he was the first to do it.

The other managers that I played under would just have a standard time for breakfast, lunch and dinner and not take into account when kick off times were, whereas Malcolm was the only one who said, 'Eat that and eat it now.' Another example was that we had a sprint and agility coach at Palace when we were fifteen, which is the norm now, but it wasn't the norm back then in 1976.

We'd all been gutted when Venners left and the chairman

knew that we all wanted to leave too so it may have been an attempt on his part to appease us by bringing Big Mal back. But he didn't seem too interested and I'm not even sure that he wanted to be there. It was too much of a grind for him; it just didn't work. Billy Gilbert had been so pleased that Mal was coming back because he'd been instrumental in making us footballers in the first place, but the first thing that Mal did when he returned was he bought someone to play in Billy's position. He then got loads of other players on trial and they all seemed to be in Billy's position too, so he lost Billy straightaway.

He was like a different man in his second spell. His word had been law when I was a kid but some of the ideas he came out with when I was older... It seemed like he'd totally lost it.

Malcolm had been clued up, but when he left Palace and went to various clubs overseas, he picked up loads of strange ideas. It was as if someone had put too many into his head and he went into overload. Some of the things he did, you had to be there to believe them. Players were just looking at him, astounded.

He had loads of revolutionary ideas. Gerry Francis had been one of the best midfielders in England and had captained his country. He was an attacking midfield player, but Malcolm turned round to Gerry and said that he was going to get him back in the England team as a sweeper. We won the first game he tried it in but then we got battered and Gerry knew it wasn't for him. But Mal kept trying to play people out of position because he claimed to see things that others couldn't see. You'd come off sometimes thinking that you'd had a nightmare and he'd be telling you how well you'd played.

Malcolm's training in his first spell had been really innovative and forward-thinking but his ideas upon his return were just weird. At most clubs, crossing and finishing sessions follow the same routine. One player gets the ball and knocks it out to a wide player who is level with them, the winger then passes it to someone by the box who returns it to them to cross the ball. By this time, the two people who started the move will have made their way into the area after a thirty-yard run and they wait for the cross and finish it. It's not strenuous; it's all about technique.

Malcolm, though, came back to the club with the idea that our crossing sessions should now consist of a group of players standing by one corner flag, and he would stand with thirty footballs in the centre circle and strike a ball towards the corner flag at the other end of the field. He would then tell one player to run the length of the pitch to get the ball and cross it while, on the other side, another player would also have to run the same distance to get into the box to receive the cross. So you were running the length of the field and you can imagine, after one cross, that was it – you were knackered.

We had a goalkeeper at that time called David Fry who was in and out of the team. Malcolm had signed him as a young kid and, in his wisdom, said that he'd been watching David but noticed that he'd lost a bit of confidence. He wanted to help him get it back so Malcolm told him that he was going to take the goalkeepers for a session to boost his confidence.

We were training but we couldn't resist looking over to see what Malcolm's idea was to get his confidence back. It consisted of Malcolm standing on the edge of the box with a load of footballs and half volleying them in Dave's direction and, every time Dave made a save, he had to shout, 'Catch!' So Malcolm would strike a ball and you'd see Dave flying through the air shouting, 'Catch!' and then throwing it back. That was Malcolm's way of getting his confidence back because he didn't want him to palm shots away; he wanted him to catch them. Needless to say, a couple of games later, Dave spilled a couple of balls that he should have just palmed away and he was promptly dropped.

Mal didn't completely take the training over, though. Ernie was still doing most of it and you can imagine what mood he was in. He'd been the manager and had that taken off him so you can guess what training was like; the running was even more vigorous.

It was a bad time to be at Palace. Loads of players got a transfer out of the club and we were congratulating them. If he didn't fancy you, Big Mal would happily give you to QPR and that was where we all wanted to go because Terry Venables was there. I fancied going anywhere, though, by that time. QPR would have been good because of Terry but it just frustrated me to see players that I'd played with do so well after leaving when I was still stuck at Palace. They all ended up getting Championship medals at QPR. Terry Fenwick got England caps after his move and played in the Cup Final and scored in it, Clive Allen played in the Cup Final and got a move to Spurs but the rest of us were stuck because Palace wanted a bit too much money for us. Malcolm managed to do some serious damage in that short period of time. We were going downhill rapidly.

After a couple of months, Malcolm was making no sense to

anyone. He told us that players always had to be ready to react and that we should even get out of our chairs in a certain way. He told us that he was going to start shouting 'Go!' at random times and that, if he did, he didn't care what we were doing, we had to react and be on our toes. He told us that if he came into a room and we saw him then there would be a possibility that he'd shout 'Go' at us.

We played a team away from home and had an overnight stay with dinner and breakfast. Malcolm didn't want us to have to eat again later in the day so he insisted that we all had to come down to eat in the morning. Some of the players hated it, but we all had to do it.

On that trip, Fen was the last one down – his hair was sticking up, he was like a zombie and he didn't want to be there. As soon as Fen walked in, Mal shouted 'Go!' but Fen just looked at the table that Mal was on and carried on walking. Mal wasn't happy, but we told him that he'd done well to get Fen out of bed, let alone to react. The worst thing about it was that the table next to him had cutlery falling all over the place and plates coming off the table because we'd all got up straight away when he shouted.

Malcolm's head had gone. Honestly, you would not believe some of the other ideas that he came up with. He told us that he'd spent a few weeks with some Russian gymnasts and that would inspire training sessions for a while but then he wouldn't turn up for days at a time.

Soon after he came back, we got drawn against Manchester City in the FA Cup in 1981. John Bond was the manager of City and it was the dream draw for Malcolm as he'd just been sacked by them. Monday morning, we asked Ernie Walley where Malcolm was but he didn't know and it was the same all week. We travelled up north on the Friday and he hadn't got in touch with the assistant manager all week to tell him who was going to be in the team so Ernie had no alternative but to travel up there with a squad of twenty-odd players, which was unheard of in those days as you'd normally take thirteen tops.

We went to the hotel and there was still no sign of Malcolm. We had the pre-match meal and we still hadn't seen him all week but when we put *On the Ball* on TV, who was on there but Malcolm. He was telling the interviewer that he was really pleased with the draw and that we'd give a good account of ourselves and that he had a few ideas that would shake City up. It would have been nice of him to tell us. He didn't come to the hotel at all but we got to the ground and briefly glimpsed him. We asked Ernie what the team was and he reckoned that as we hadn't done any work during the week that we'd have the same side as the previous Saturday, although Malcolm might change the sub.

At ten past two, Malcolm came into the dressing room and this was the first time that we'd seen him since the previous Saturday. I'd put a shirt on and Neil Smillie had done the same. Malcolm asked me what I thought I was doing and told me that I wasn't playing. I asked him if I was sub and he said no. He then told Tony Sealy to play in my position but Tony had never played there before. We had a lad called Gary Goodchild who got named as sub but Gary was surprised to be a professional footballer, let alone a sub at Man City. Mal then came out with a system of playing that we'd never even heard of and certainly hadn't worked on.

As you'd expect, we were 3–0 down before you knew it and it could have been ten. Malcolm was sitting up in the stand and Ernie was on the bench but he kept looking up at Malcolm for some guidance. In the end, Mal came down and told Gary to have a warm up. He kept running up and down, he was just so happy to be there, and the few of us that weren't involved were laughing because we knew what a joke we'd become. Gary came back and sat down and Malcolm was moaning. He said, 'Where's my cigars, Ernie? I need a smoke. It's not going too well. I probably left them up there in the bloody directors' box.' With that, Gary Goodchild's looked at us and said, 'I don't want to go on' and he showed us that he'd sat down on the cigars and flattened them. We just burst out laughing. In the end, he got on for the last few minutes and we lost 4–0. Malcolm was gone soon after.

DARIO GRADI & STEVE KEMBER

I felt sorry for a lot of the managers who came after Venables at Palace because we thought we knew it all and so we were impossible to coach and improve. Dario Gradi must have thought that every single player at Palace had a problem with his eyebrows because, at the end of every one of his sentences, every single player's head cocked, they'd raise their eyebrows and then they'd look the other way. Every single player. We'd say to each other:

'What did he say?' 'Don't know, but I'm not going to do it.' And that's how it was at that time.

The thing is, he was dealing with people who had been at the club for years and years and we were used to doing things in a certain way. From kids' age up to our early twenties, we'd only ever known one way to play and carry ourselves, so you can imagine us with these managers: 'You're talking crap!' We had a complete and utter lack of respect for what they were saying and for them in general and, if you don't have respect for your manager, then you're not going to get on. As far as we were concerned, there was only one way of playing football and that was the Venables way.

Looking back, the players were out of order because there was no respect towards the coaching staff but some of Dario's ideas and methods just didn't work with us. We had training sessions under Dario where we played matches without a ball. We thought we'd left all that behind with Malcolm. Danny Blanchflower had, apparently, done it at Chelsea and Tommy Langley told me that sometimes at Chelsea they used to have training matches with two balls because then they'd find playing with one in a match so much easier... It didn't make any sense to us.

He also used to make us do warm-ups in the positions that we played in on the pitch and we'd have to play shadow football in our own position on the pitch too. I'd be kicking imaginary balls down the line and we had centre-halves heading imaginary footballs too.

Our best young player at the time, who had come through

after us, was Steve McKenzie but Malcolm, in his wisdom, bought him for Manchester City, when he went back to manage them, for £250,000 when he hadn't even played a single game for Palace. The next best was Shaun Brooks, whose dad had played for Tottenham. Shaun ended up playing for Bournemouth and had a good career there. Even as a young teenager, he was very opinionated, which made us laugh. He reminded us of ourselves.

Brooksy, for some reason, was one of Dario's flavours of the month. Maybe because Dario thought that he could get into Shaun's head, as he possibly hadn't been poisoned by us older players from the Venables era. Dario had a reputation for working well with kids, so he put Shaun in the team and a lot of the play revolved around him and he loved it. But Brooksy then had a couple of bad games and you could see that he was struggling, so Dario left him out and just disregarded him.

Brooksy's face had been put right out and on this particular day in training we were doing a session again with an imaginary ball. We were going through the motions, which was bad but all of this imaginary ball stuff was too much. Anyway, Brooksy was strolling around the pitch and Dario saw him out of the corner of his eye and shouted, 'Shaun Brooks, I need you to enter into the spirit of things and do as I've told you, because I might be giving you a half in the next game.' Quick as you like, Brooksy turned around and shouted back, 'Wowee! A whole fucking half!' in such a sarcastic voice. And this was from an eighteen-year-old.

Dario had no respect from us but he was unfortunate because

he'd joined a club with a group of players that had been spoiled, and he wasn't the right appointment for Palace. He was basically a yes man for the chairman but he's since proved that he's far better than that and has produced a lot of good players. Dario brought in Ken Shellito as a coach; Ken had been with him at Chelsea, and he also had a reputation for bringing young players through. I liked Ken because he was a footballing man and understood us as players but he was just too quiet. He looked like he'd just come for a kick-around with the boys and then he'd wait for the manager to say we could all go home.

Because of the way that he struggled with us, Dario tried to get players to Palace that he could take a short-cut with so they were ones that he already knew. Unfortunately, a lot of those players weren't up to the job. For example, Steve Galliers, who'd done a good job at Wimbledon but was only about four feet tall, was terrier-like but lacked the necessary quality. As badly as Palace had been doing for the past three or four years, the club was used to having players with some semblance of quality. Brian Bason joined us, as did Tommy Langley. They had both done pretty well at Chelsea but neither of them did well at Palace.

Noades also paid a lot of money – probably today's equivalent of £4–5 million – on Steve Wicks to play centre half, but he didn't play for about five months because of a back injury. But the back injury was sustained because Dario brought in a British Gymnast to teach us how to vault a pommel horse! When you ask someone who's 6ft 4in. to do something that he'd never done before and then he hurts his back, who do you hold accountable for it? Then we had the chairman walking around with a badge for the last two months that Steve was out injured with 'I saw Steve Wicks play – once' on it. He wore it to half a dozen home games and it didn't do much for team morale.

We'd gone from winning FA Youth Cups, to being top of the whole league, to being called the Team of the '80s… to this. It was just amazing. Dario was very clever, though, and he realised that the longer he stayed at Palace, the more he was going to tar his own name and then he may never have got another job in football. He was still a young manager, but his reputation was taking a bit of a battering from people who had come across him at Palace, so I think that moving on was a wise thing for him to do. It takes a special kind of person to turn around a place that is an absolute shambles and, at that time, he wasn't that person.

It was hard for Dario, though. I can't lie. He came to a club with a nucleus of players that thought that they knew it all. Personally, I still hadn't come across anyone that made me think, 'That's better than what Terry Venables has taught me.'

The chairman then appointed Steve Kember, who had only recently stopped playing. Even though he had retired, he still had a footballer's mentality so he was very positive for us all the time. Palace had bought Steve back from America and he played a big part in the team that got promoted in 1979 so he was popular with the players. He was the oldest in the team at that time and he had been at Palace before, at Chelsea too and at Leicester, and we remembered him as a great player.

When we used to do our running days at Crystal Palace

Athletics track in our promotion season, Steve used to feel it a bit more than the rest of us. We used to do reps of six 200m runs or six 100m runs, and it wasn't easy. I wasn't the best at recovering from these runs but, after about three of them, I remember Steve lying on the track, staring at the sky. All the trainers kept saying, 'Come on, there's only three to do. Get air into your lungs. Don't look down.'

Steve was an experienced pro so I went up to him and asked what he was doing, as lying down was the wrong thing to do. He snapped at me, 'How long have you been in the game for? I've been playing for twelve or thirteen years and I know exactly what I'm doing. And do you know what I'm doing? I'm fucking dying, that's what I'm doing so go away!'

The players liked Steve's company because he didn't think like a manager. One of my favourite away trips was up to the northeast when we used to play Sunderland or Newcastle because there was a nightclub up there called Tuxedo Junction where we always used to go; they had telephones on every table so you could ring other people in the club, which was quite unique at that time. We'd won at Sunderland 2–1 in our promotion season and I hadn't gone out but the boys had been to this club and they absolutely raved about it. Every trip up north after that, we went there and it was brilliant.

When Steve took over we were due to play Newcastle but we had an injury crisis and we needed to get some points. I had a bad ankle and had a fitness test; it was still sore, but we were in a serious position at the time. As soon as the physio had finished with me, Steve came up and asked how it was and I told him that I was struggling and that I didn't think I'd make the game the next day. He told me that they needed me. I thought that was good of him to say but he told me that I knew my way around Tuxedo Junction better than anyone else. He was deadly serious! He was saying to me, 'You've got to remember: it's Tuxedo Junction!' so I told him I'd do my best. Then he told me that he'd take me up there even if I wasn't fit. To be honest, that's probably why Steve didn't make it as a top manager. He still had the attitude of a player and was probably too close to us.

CHAPTER 10

LEAVING PALACE

PALACE GOING DOWNHILL & QPR FA CUP TIE

The coup de gras for me was the quarter final of the FA Cup in 1982 when we got beaten at QPR in the last minute and lost 1–0. We knew that there was only one decent team left in the competition and that was Tottenham Hotspur so we all knew that if we could get past QPR then we had a good chance of getting to Wembley. Forget England caps and everything. The one thing that I always wanted to do was to play in an FA Cup Final. The one game that I always remember was in 1966, but it wasn't the World Cup Final, it was the FA Cup Final between Everton and Sheffield Wednesday. Even now, I could tell you every goalscorer from Cup Finals from 1966 onwards.

To me, the Cup Final wasn't just about the match – that was secondary. It was all about the build-up and players being interviewed on the bus going to the game and talking about their teammates. That's what it was all about. We were having a crap season in the League but we had a chance of getting to Wembley and I knew that we'd never get a better opportunity than this.

QPR played on a plastic pitch, though, and, because of that, Rangers had a great home record. As good as Venables was, and as good as some of their players were, even an idiot knew that a plastic pitch was going to help the home team far more than the away team. I can't believe QPR got away with it and I can't believe that Luton did either. It was such a big advantage. If you tried to play your ordinary game on it, which a lot of teams did, then it would never work.

They used to say those pitches helped teams that played passing football but they didn't. They helped teams that were direct. If you didn't try to take a chance on them, then you wouldn't make a mistake. What QPR did was they played on the opposition's mistakes. It was similar to tennis when one player just keeps trying to get the ball into the court but their opponent keeps going for the line. If you can keep getting it back, eventually your opponent will miss.

QPR knew how to play on it, no doubt about it. They did play with a little bit of flair, at times, but, basically, they just waited for the mistake, so we decided that day that we wouldn't make any. We didn't care how badly we played; we just weren't going to take any chances. I played probably the worst game of football I've ever played that day. If the ball came to me and I was facing the stand then I just kicked it into the stand; if I was facing forward then it went forward. I didn't try and take anyone on. I'd not felt this motivated for a game since Venables had left.

Billy Gilbert was outstanding that day. He felt the same way as I did about the Cup Final and he'd got his head straight. Billy even wore a pair of tights because if there was a slide tackle to be made then he was going to win it, which showed his intent. Jimmy Cannon did the same. We did well. We held them and held them and then they scored this goal with four or five minutes to go after a melee that you couldn't believe. It was Clive Allen who scored. The Palace fans had slaughtered him throughout the game and they'd also slaughtered him when he was with us, as they weren't happy that Venables had swapped him with Kenny. I can clearly remember Clive running towards the Palace end sticking two fingers up at our fans.

I was the most gutted I'd ever been up to that point. I'd been a pro footballer for six years or so but there was nothing that was going to lift me. It was a worse feeling than relegation because, without casting aspersions on people's ability, I knew that Palace were going down in 1981 and Portsmouth were too in 1988 with about fifteen games to go; when you do finally get relegated it's a bit of an anti-climax.

That was the very first time that I had a drink after a game. We had a wine bar at the club called Strikers' and I sat in there when we got back to Selhurst. I can even remember the drink that I had: they were called 'Zombie-killers'. A lot of people say that I didn't drink until I went to Portsmouth, but that's a bit of a myth. I didn't drink as heavily as I did at Pompey but QPR was the game that started it and took me away from being the perfect pro. I'd tasted drinks before but that was the first proper drink I had. I was just so gutted and the pain was unbelievable.

My girlfriend at the time, Christine, was having a party that evening and I told her that I'd be there as soon as I could. We had a taxi firm at the club – I think I still owe them money – and I got a cab and went to the party, but I have no recollection of being there apart from lying on her mum's bed at one point, being sick, and feeling very ill. I couldn't even move to tell anyone that I'd been sick. After about an hour, I must have got up and said goodbye to her parents and gone home. I can still remember Christine telling me over the phone that one of the bastards that had been at the party was sick in her mum's bedroom but she didn't know who it was. This is the first time I've told anyone. From that day on, whenever I had a bad result, I used to have a drink. I didn't go mad but those 'Zombie-killers' started it. They got me drunk from the feet up. Getting knocked out of that FA Cup quarter final at QPR was the crossroads for me as that started my 'drinking to forget' stage.

ALAN MULLERY

I didn't put a transfer request in; I just let my contract drift to the end. I just figured that if I didn't leave Palace then, I never would. Even when Venners was there, people were telling me that I should move on. Maybe I'd got into the team too early, because people were saying that I'd been at the club too long and it was time to go. Nowadays, even if you only have one good season at a lower level and then look like you're going to maintain it for another year then that gets you a move, but I was stuck.

The worst thing was that the players who had left from the 1979 promotion team made it more difficult for the ones who stayed at Palace because they all went on to bigger and better things and that hurt. When you finish playing, people are always quick to tell you what you could have done differently and that you should have moved at certain times in your career. I can only speak for myself. I did what I did and played the games that I did but I know that if every person had the benefit of hindsight then we would all have done things differently in our lives. But I'm just happy that I managed to have a semi-decent pro career. I'm over it now and happy with what I achieved but, when you're playing, that's when you get disillusioned because you see people who you've grown up with going on to bigger and better things. You see Peter Nicholas running out every other week at Highbury, Ian Walsh scoring goals for Swansea in the First Division, Kenny Sansom getting cap after cap for England and Terry Fenwick playing in the Cup Final and you can't help but look at yourself and wonder whether you stayed there too long.

By that stage of my career, I knew there was an expectation on me to produce at Palace. My brothers used to tell me that the crowd noise would increase when I got the ball, but that was partly to do with how bad the rest of the side was. Funnily enough, they actually recorded the crowd noise at one game on an old cassette and played it back to me but I wasn't thinking with my head when I played then. If your team is not doing well then that obviously means that the other side has more of the ball so, on the occasions that you do get the ball, you want to do something with it. That's not your mind thinking, that's your heart taking over, and you start to take too many players on. Football should be played more in the head than with the feet.

Personally, though, it was quite an enjoyable period for me because I did get on with Alan Mullery. Mullers was a man's man and managed like he played but it was always going to be difficult for him because he was Public Enemy Number 1 with the Palace fans, as he'd managed Brighton a few years before. He'd lost his head when Brighton played us and he'd run on the pitch and thrown some money down in front of the Palace support and gave them a two-finger salute, which went down well! So he was starting on the back foot. It's a bit like someone who has managed Southampton going to Portsmouth. It was hard enough for Alan Ball coming to Pompey having played for Southampton, and Palace fans, no matter their geography, will always consider Brighton to be their deadly rivals.

He could be an abrasive man, Alan Mullery, and, of all the managers that I played for, he was the only one that I thought, 'If I say something that you don't like then you're going to chin me.' He was good for me, though, because he treated me a bit like Terry Venables did, without the tactical nous, in the sense that he just let me play. In fact, out of all the managers that I had after Venables left, I played my best football for him. There were no frills and no complications with him and he actually said to me that he was going to bring an old favourite back to the club to try and help me out and that was Peter Nicholas, who had been at Arsenal for a few years. It helped me, but not necessarily the rest of the team.

However well I played, the club really did take a dive and we hit new depths in terms of both the players we had and our organisation. We were signing players – and we had some already – who just weren't up to the job and the Palace fans were frustrated. Honestly, Mullers made some extraordinary signings and did some strange things. I think that what best sums up the Alan Mullery era, and the fact that the organisation had completely gone at Palace, was that we signed quite a few veterans – players who were coming to the end of their careers. Gary Locke had once been a good right back for Chelsea, Les Strong had played hundreds of games for Fulham, Andy McCulloch only had half a leg and was on his way out, John Lacy had been a decent centre half at Tottenham and George Wood had been at Everton years before. They had been good players in their time but they were near the end.

At half-time one game, we were taking an all too familiar bollocking from Mullers, and George was looking at the ground. If you were an outsider looking in, you'd think that he'd let a couple of goals in and was disappointed. But instead of just looking down at the floor, he was looking from side to side too. Mullers asked him why he was shaking his head and told him to be man enough to look at him. But George told him that it wasn't that but he'd lost his contact lenses and was trying to find them. No one knew he wore them.

To be fair to him, George was still a good keeper, but all those other players came because of money. They weren't looking to progress. They'd been good pros and were decent enough still, but they weren't looking to get on any more. So we had them and players like myself and Billy Gilbert who were desperate to get out and it wasn't a good combination. These players travelled in from south-west London. Les had bought a pub near Hampton Court and Strongy had a great, old-fashioned Merc that the players used to call the Fun Bus because, no matter what the score was on a Saturday, the players used to arrive in it on a Monday, chuckling and laughing. Les would have had a good weekend at the pub because he was in a prime spot on the river by Hampton Court, so he loved his life. He'd do an hour and a bit training and then go back to the pub and have fun.

One day we got a couple of injuries. We had a player called David Boulter who had only just got into the first team and he didn't want to admit that he was injured too. He got through the fitness test on the Friday and the squad then went up on the board. We were playing Blackburn away and, by that time, the club had disintegrated to the point that we were going up to away games on the train on the morning of the game rather than by coach the day before. We'd had to have been playing in Scotland to have an overnight stay.

We had to be at Euston station at around 8 a.m. on the Saturday. We had thirteen players travelling and Mullers told us that the chairman had pushed the boat out and said that if anyone that wasn't in the squad wanted to come up and watch then they could too. Les Strong said that it would give him something to do as he'd brought in extra staff at the pub so he thought that he may as well watch a game of football and then get back for last orders.

The next day, we were all congregating at the station and Strongy was there. His eyes were blurry and he had this cashmere overcoat on and looked a little bit like a gangster. He kept telling us all about the night before and he was laughing and joking. Les was going on and on about this stripper who had come into the pub, and told us that he hadn't stopped drinking until 3 a.m. He was hoping for a good breakfast on the train as it was the best cure for a hangover. With that, Mullery turned up and handed the tickets out but the physio told him that David Boulter had phoned him and told him that he'd had a late reaction to his injury and he couldn't bend his knee, let alone walk.

We were all still laughing and joking with Strongy until Mullery walked up to him and told him that he was now playing. Strongy fell silent and I still wonder why Mullery didn't work out why all the players instantly burst out laughing. We went up there and Strongy, for a person who was normally quite bubbly, uttered about ten words all the way and didn't have his breakfast. He was trying to get his head together and spent the whole journey looking out of the window.

As we were getting changed, everyone was looking at Strongy because Blackburn's two most potent players were Simon Garner, who played up front, and Ian Miller who played on the right wing. In those days it was quite a well-known fact that Blackburn's biggest tactic was to get Ian Miller in behind the opposition's left back because he had pace to spare and get the ball into the box for Garner to finish. Their kick offs were always the same too. Kick off, get the ball down their right wing for Miller to chase, and cross to Garner. This was a lot of the reason why the players were laughing, because we knew their main threat and Strongy was up against it.

In his team talk, Mullery was going, 'Strongy, you've been here a thousand times before and played against players twenty times as good as this guy. You know he'll only want to go one way. He'll want to beat you for pace but you've got more than enough experience to handle that sort of player, haven't you?' We were all kicking ourselves. Luckily it wasn't me who was playing wide left that day as Les kept saying to the left midfielder, 'I need you to cover me. I need you to cover me.' He said to Jimmy Cannon, who was captain, 'For fuck's sake, don't lose the toss. Don't worry about what way to kick, just don't let them have the kick off. Let me get into the game.' Blackburn won the toss.

Well, they kicked off and Strongy was just frozen with fear. Miller cut inside, crossed and it went just over the bar by inches. For the rest of the half, Strongy proceeded to have the nightmare of all nightmares. He was being taken to the cleaners. His experience counted for nothing – it certainly wasn't worth anything when he was tanked up and had three hours' kip! In the changing room at half time, Mullers was trying to find out what was wrong with him, but he lost his rag and stormed out of the dressing room. Strongy said to us, 'Did you see that? He'd actually got his cross in before I'd even turned! They've kicked off, I looked up and he's already crossed the ball. How quick is this?' It was backs to the wall and we lost the game 2–1 and Strongy never played again. Mullery was like that.

In Mullery's second season, we beat Peterborough 3–0 in the League Cup but, between the first and second legs, we had a couple of league games and a spate of injuries. The manager said that all of our strikers were out injured so he told the chairman that we needed a centre forward. Mullers said that there was a young lad up at Norwich who could do a job for us who we might be able to get on loan. That was John Fashanu.

Fash was the archetypal 'I want to be a footballer' and, even though he might not have made it at Norwich, he came down and believed that he was going to make it in London. He turned up in a car called a Simca, which had three seats in the front, and he had furry dice as well – he couldn't get away with that at a club like ours. But, despite that, we played Fulham and he gave their centre half a torrid time; he was smashing him all over the place and we all thought that he'd be a really good signing. Even then – and he was only about twenty – he was a confident lad and he had quite a bit to say. I remember him turning to me and saying, 'I should think they'll be signing me here. Who have we got Tuesday?' and I told him that we had the second leg against Peterborough.

If you asked me what Palace went from after Venables left, this game sums it up. We went from being the third biggest club in London behind Arsenal and Tottenham and ahead of Chelsea and West Ham to a complete and utter Rag Tag Rovers. We were sitting in the dressing room and Mullery was telling us that this game shouldn't be too much of a problem being Peterborough and with us already 3–0 up.

Now, there was a lad that played up front for us called Paul Wilkins. He thought he was quite good but we all used to take the mickey out of him and his nickname was 'Wilf'. He was about 6ft 11in. Mullery turned to him and told him that we didn't need him as we had Fash, and Wilf looked gutted because he had thought that he was going to get his chance, so he went up to the Players' Lounge with the other young lads and started drinking himself into a stupor.

It was about half-six and we'd been there an hour and we were just starting to get changed. Mullery had told us the team and subs and then the door opened and the chairman, Ron Noades, came in. Whenever Ron was involved there was always something dodgy going on and he whispered something in Mullery's ear and Mullers turned to Fash and told him to take his shirt off because Norwich wouldn't let him play unless we guaranteed that we were going to buy him. Norwich didn't want him Cup-tied, but Noades wouldn't guarantee going through with the deal.

So Mullery turned round and said, 'Somebody go get Wilf', but word got back to the players that he was bladdered. After about ten minutes, Wilf came in and the worst thing was that he was trying to pretend that he was sober. His eyes were wide open but he was keeping his mouth down so Mullery couldn't smell the alcohol on his breath. Mullers told him that he was in the side and we were all thinking: 'He's bad enough when he's sober!' Wilf was reluctantly getting changed but he was saying, 'I can't play. I'm pissed. This is a professional level.'

Fash was sitting there, watching this. He knew Wilf was pissed, and he was shaking his head. Next thing, five to seven, there's a knock on the door and it's the chairman again: 'I've come to an agreement, Alan. He can play.' Fash's shirt is back on; Wilf was saved.

We'd been 3–0 up after the first leg so all we had to do was hold onto the lead, but we didn't and we came in at half time knowing full well that we were going to get the bollocking of all bollockings. Mullery was waiting at the other end of the dressing room and when the last player had come in, his team talk, as God is my witness, was 'Get out!' All the players looked at each other and he told us to get out again so we spent half time out on the pitch. We were just milling around, trying to keep warm because he just couldn't be bothered to talk to us. We'd thought that we were going to get a bollocking but he couldn't even bring himself to do that. His tactic worked, though – we got knocked out! We got beat 3–0 and lost on penalties and Noades was gutted because he wanted a few bob from a Cup run.

We were in the dressing room afterwards and I'd had a nightmare so I didn't want to get changed but, before long, I was sitting quietly in the corner of the bath and Fash was sitting there too: 'I can't believe this club.' He was very articulate, Fash; he was a bit like Garth Crooks. 'A complete and utter shambles, wasn't it? One minute I'm playing and the next minute I'm not. What sort of preparation is that for me and the team? It's a joke. The manager is a joke, the chairman is a joke – the whole thing is a joke.' All I said was, 'I've got to go along with that' and, with that, I got out of the bath. We were the last two in there and as I got my towel and walked back into the changing room, who was standing there but Alan Mullery. He heard everything, never spoke, he just turned around and walked out.

Next day, Fashanu was sent back to Norwich and Mullers said to me, 'You're not playing on Saturday.' I asked him how many more changes there'd be and he said, 'Just you.' I asked him why because, although I'd played badly, I was no worse than anyone else and he told me, 'Undermining me. It was like mutiny on a ship.' It was Newcastle away next so I thought that at least I didn't have to go all the way up there but then he turned to me and said, 'And you're travelling' so I went all the way up to Newcastle just to stand in the tunnel and watch the game. He was a hard man, Mullery. Basically, I was dropped because I agreed with someone but all I'd said was, 'Yeah, you're right' and Fash was banished completely! We could and should have ended up signing Fashanu. But the club then, and myself, were on the way down, and it wasn't pretty.

In fact, the only teams that we gave games to were the teams that came down from Division One or the ones that were at the top of the League. That was how apathetic we'd become. We beat Leicester and Newcastle, and Sheffield Wednesday won the League yet we beat them 1–0 and should have beaten them by more. To me, that sums up a team that is really in trouble: when the players can only lift themselves for games where they're not expected to win or do well. I put myself in that category too. We used to beat the top teams but we still ended up needing to win the last game of the season at home to Burnley to stay in Division Two. That's when I realised that it wasn't going to happen for us and that most of our players needed to get out.

It was the ultimate contrast. Although we won 1–0, there was me, Jim Cannon, Billy Gilbert and Jerry Murphy playing in that game and we all looked at each other. The four of us had gone so far backwards since the last time that we played Burnley to go up four years before. There were nearly 52,000 people in the ground in 1979 with another 10,000 that had got in unofficially and we were playing them that night to win the Championship and then, four years later, we were playing the same side to stay in Division Two.

Billy was one of the biggest to suffer when Venables left but he really was outstanding in Mullery's last season at Palace, which culminated in his move to Portsmouth. I remember in that game against Leicester, he was detailed to mark Gary Lineker and he played him very fairly and Lineker never got a kick. As I said, Palace were an enigma then and, in the same season, we played Newcastle and they had Keegan, Beardsley and Waddle up front and we beat them comfortably. Jim Cannon and Billy didn't give those players a kick that day.

It may well have been that final season at Palace when Billy had twice as many disciplinary points as we had as a team in the League and he was regularly making visits to the FA's headquarters at Lancaster Gate. He enjoyed tackling, did Billy, but he could play as well. Even now, when Billy loses his temper he's got the hardest frown that I've ever seen. He's got about fifteen frown lines and his eyebrows touch the crown of his head. I used to take the mickey out of him, but when I saw his face change that's when I used to stop because Billy couldn't let it go then. He was the type who, if he was having a fight and knew that he couldn't win fairly, would disappear and come back with something to help him. He had an armoury in his car.

He's a good lad, Billy, but there was a point where he'd snap. I've known him since we were fourteen and people say that Billy was hard when he played at Portsmouth but, by the time he'd signed for Pompey, all of his wild days off the field were behind him. He could still lapse, but it was a regular occurrence at Palace. The famous one was with the fella that nicked his parking space at Sainsbury's and Billy got charged with threatening behaviour as he'd pulled this huge knife on him.

Billy was angry at that time, like the rest of the players who had stayed at Palace. He knew that we hadn't fulfilled our potential, but he also knew that he was a good player. For me, the best centre backs were always the best pairings as they would always keep their eyes out for each other. I always felt that Billy Gilbert's best pairing was when he played with Jimmy Cannon at Palace. They both had good physiques but neither of them was built like a Noel Blake or a Darren Moore. They were athletic centre halves. If the ball came in the air we always felt comfortable that they'd either win it or make it difficult for their opponent to win the ball cleanly.

Jim Cannon was a great player; he was probably the most two-footed defender that I ever played with. He could play in any position too, in midfield or anywhere across the back. He was good in the air and strong in the tackle. But the great joke amongst the players was that Jimmy Cannon had the best memory at the club. It was photographic. Any goal that we conceded was analysed and that's common practice these days, but not so much then. Jimmy is the all-time appearance holder at the club but, if he played now, then I don't think that he'd have played as many games. Not because he couldn't defend, because he could, not because he wasn't good in the air, because he was, and not because he wasn't two-footed, as he was, and not because he couldn't tackle or wasn't quick, because he was both of those things too. His biggest problem would have been the TV cameras.

The reason is that, in every single meeting, when we discussed how we'd conceded a goal, the very first person that piped up was Jimmy and he always said the same thing: 'Well, I had my man.' Even if Jimmy was detailed to mark the centre forward at corners and then the centre forward scored a header at a corner, in the meetings Jimmy would say that he'd had to pass him on to Billy Gilbert or someone else and he'd taken their man. He played over 600 games for Palace and I played in a large majority of those matches and I don't think that he took responsibility for one goal in all that time. We'd laugh because he'd say that he knew exactly where everyone was and who was marking who, but his man never scored. He'd struggle now because the TV cameras would pick it up and he'd get dropped for not picking up his man, but none of us had the balls to say that he was lying.

He was an excellent player, though. He wouldn't have played the games that he did if he wasn't. But Jimmy could be difficult. He had a cutting tongue and could be unfeeling. When I was a youngster, you didn't want to hear him say, 'I've played 200 games and you're the worst crosser of a ball that I've ever seen', or 'If Venners weren't here, I'd smash you', because I had that a few times from him too. Maybe there was a tinge of jealousy from him about the way that us youngsters were treated, but what a player he was and his loyalty to the club was second to none.

Even though we stayed up, Mullery left and then Dave Bassett was manager for about a day and a half. Bassett called me and told me that he'd been at the club and would be taking over officially the following day. He outlined his plans to me and said how and where he wanted me to play. I thought it was promising as he was taking an interest and being positive despite the fact that he had a reputation for being a long ball merchant, so I thought that I'd give it a go but the next thing there was no sign of him. He must have had an about-turn that evening; I don't know if it was anything to do with speaking to the players, because I wasn't the only one that he spoke to. So he'd phoned me up and said that he rated me and wanted to play me in my best position, which was great, but then he resigned. That was me done at Palace. I was finished there.

BILLY GILBERT ON VINCE

As a kid, Vince always had a smile on his face. He was a bubbly character – full of laughs, making pranks. He was, genuinely, a really nice boy. Vince was a very, very good player as a youngster; a standout player in our Youth side, right from the earliest days. As far as I'm concerned, he was outstanding all the way through his career, to be perfectly honest, but, as a youngster, we always knew that he had something special there. Our Youth team had some excellent players in it. Kenny Sansom was a couple of years older than us and he was outstanding; we always knew that he was going to go on to great things but there were others too.

As a young player, I used to travel in with Vince and Jerry Murphy. Jerry and I were a little bit more worldly-wise than Vince though; he just loved watching television. We used to make a joke of it that he could tell you what time every programme was on during the day because he used to watch about three or four different tellies. We were leading a little bit more of a life, if you like, and we would never stay in whereas he would. He's changed quite drastically since but, back then, we always tried to get him to come out – but he was quite content to play his football, go home, and watch his telly when the rest of us felt that there was a big wide world ahead of us.

The documentary got him a lot of attention and possibly made the older players at Palace a little jealous but, for us youngsters, it got us into the spotlight too as we were involved in it a bit. I think the senior pros viewed him as a bit of an upstart and that was probably reflected in their attitude to all of us youngsters anyway. We were treated totally differently to the generation above us. Malcolm Allison changed everything in terms of the way we were dealt with as kids: we didn't clean boots, we never cleaned the stadium; we were probably the first young players not to have to do the things that the generation before had done. That put their noses out of joint. They saw how well we were treated and there was a bit of jealousy there.

Malcolm got us all in as kids at the same time and we won a lot of things early on in our careers. We had a winning mentality but I don't think that we ever really stopped to think about how good we were and what we could go on to achieve. As far as I was concerned, we knew that we had a good side with very good players in it but I don't think that we ever looked further ahead than the next challenge. We all hoped and thought that we would get into the first team – that was the goal as a youngster, to step up and get into that side – and then to continue to progress from there.

Because of the success that we had as kids, we were always in the limelight, so being tagged the Team of the '80s felt like a natural thing to happen to us. We were very young, though, with a very young manager and, in a way, we were set up to fail. This country enjoys setting people up and then watching them fall. That's the

THE EAGLES TROPHY

The Trophy being played for today has been donated by Mr. R.E. Bloye, chairman of Crystal Palace F.C. The competition has been organised by the Croydon Schools' Football Association. Seventeen districts in the London and South-East areas who were invited, took part. All players were under 15 years of age on the 1st September, 1974 when the Competition started.

The Croydon Schools' F.A. would like to thank Mr. Bloye for his interest and all the directors and staff of Crystal Palace F.C. for their support in allowing the final to be played at Selhurst Park.

Thanks are also due to Slazengers Limited who have donated a 'Player of the Match' award, to the Vice-Presidents club at Selhurst Park who have given today's match ball and to the referee and linesmen, who give up much of their spare time willingly and freely to officate at schoolboy matches.

Should a replay be necessary, it is provisionally arranged to take place on May 3rd at Selhurst Park, kick off 10.30 A.M.

THE EAGLES TROPHY FINAL

Under 15 - London and South East District Schools Association

East London Boys v Newham Boys

at **SELHURST PARK**
(By kind permission of the Directors)

on **Saturday, April 19th 1975.**
Kick Off 1.15 p.m.

TEAMS

EAST LONDON
(Green and Gold)

1. S. Dignum
2. D. O'Hara
3. D. Gregory
4. P. Miller
5. L. Dobran
6. D. Martin
7. G. Oliver
8. J. Murphy
9. S. Payne
10. S. Saunders
11. L. Hudson

SUBSTITUTES
Davies   P. Dixon
Greenstein   P. Mitchell

NEWHAM
(White shirts with red hoops and black shorts)

1. P. Hucker
2. P. Curbishley
3. K. Collins
4. V. Hillaire
5. T. Emanuel
6. H. Hughton
7. C. Henney
8. N. Morgan
9. J. Chiedozie
10. G. Moore
11. S. Faldo

SUBSTITUTES
W. Jacobs   J. Buttwell
K. Crowley   G. Gardner
R. Mcleod   D. Thompson

REFEREE   Mr. M. Bermingham   (Surrey)
LINESMEN   Mr. J. Handley   (Surrey)
          Mr. J. Moss   (Surrey)

DURATION OF MATCH : 35 MINUTES EACH WAY.
If, at the end of full time, the scores are level, there will be no extra time.

COMPLETE COMPETITION RESULTS

ROUND ONE

Ealing	1	Chelmsford	3
Islington	2	Aldershot	1
South London	4	Barking	1

ROUND TWO

Haringey	W/O	Bedford	
Islington	2	South London	4
Mid-Sussex	4	Merton	5
Blackheath	0	Newham	4
Croydon	3	Chelmsford	2 (a.e.t.)
West London	4	Hackney	0
Luton	0	East London	3
Havering	W/O	Hounslow	

ROUND THREE

Havering	1	Croydon	4
Haringey	10	Merton	0
East London	4	South London	1
Newham	2	West London	1

SEMI-FINALS

Croydon	1	East London	4
Newham	3	Haringey	0

My first game at Selhurst Park for Newham Boys Under-15s.
COURTESY OF IAN KING

FA Youth Cup winners. We expected to win whenever we played.
COURTESY OF NEIL EVERITT

A dream start. A goal on my full Palace debut at Millwall.
I thought I'd score thirty goals a season.
COURTESY OF NEIL EVERITT

A career highlight: playing for England Youth at Selhurst Park.
COURTESY OF NEIL EVERITT

The side of black footballers that I put together for Jim Cannon's testimonial.
COURTESY OF NEIL EVERITT

Losing 1–0 at Manchester United. Relegation felt inevitable that season.
COURTESY OF NEIL EVERITT

Four years earlier we'd beaten Burnley to go up as champions. Here, I'm celebrating Ian Edwards's goal against the same opposition that saved us from relegation into Division Three.
COURTESY OF NEIL EVERITT

A fresh start. Before my Portsmouth debut v Blackburn in 1984.
COURTESY OF COLIN FARMERY

Alan Ball insisted on hard work from his players. You couldn't coast through games.
COURTESY OF COLIN FARMERY

A day to forget. Sent off for Pompey in a defeat at Palace in 1987. A game I thought had cost us promotion.
COURTESY OF COLIN FARMERY

Other results went our way and our promotion celebrations could begin.
COURTESY OF COLIN FARMERY

ABOVE The Gremlins. I played alongside some unforgettable characters at Portsmouth.

COURTESY OF COLIN FARMERY

LEFT Alan Ball: one of the greatest people I've ever had the pleasure of meeting.

COURTESY OF COLIN FARMERY

Leeds is a massive club and I was proud to play for them.
COURTESY OF PRESS ASSOCIATION

Meeting up again with old teammates at Palace's centenary celebrations.
COURTESY OF NEIL EVERITT

With my grandson, Albie.

mentality of the British public. But, at the time, we didn't take too much notice of it. We knew we were a good side so we just tried to get on with it.

That side had grown up together – the players, the manager and coaching staff. Terry Venables was a character and was, by far, the best coach and man-manager that I ever played under. He used to join in with the players; he'd have a laugh with us and would sometimes come out and have a drink with us too. We went from the Youth team to the first team with him there and he was also the England Under-21 manager when Vince and I were in that side so we spent a hell of a lot of time with him growing up. He was like a father figure to us.

Venners' coaching was outstanding. He'd put individual sessions on for the attacking players, the midfielders and the defence. He made me a better player. In fact, everyone from that era became better players for having Terry and John Cartwright coaching us. When we first got to Palace, everything they did was like a Dutch set-up. The best way that I can sum it up was that I looked forward to going into training every day because there was always something different being done.

It was absolutely wonderful. To get to do different things every day was so enjoyable. It was genuinely a delight to go into training – we were learning so much – but, after Terry left, training became repetitive.

I was devastated when we lost Terry and that was reflected by everyone in the squad. To be honest, we never really recovered from it. It was like our father had left. Everyone was affected, even the senior players, but it was felt more by us youngsters because we'd grown up with him there. He'd left such an impression on us that it was a devastating blow.

Terry had played for QPR for a time before he became our manager and the chairman there, Jim Gregory, loved him. But, behind the scenes at Palace, there were a lot of rumours that the club were in talks with Howard Kendall about him coming in to replace Venners. I don't know whether that was just a smokescreen to cover up the reasons why Terry left, but there were was a lot of chat going round about it.

The next few years were particularly hard for the players who had been there with Terry – like me and Vince. We'd grown up as kids used to success and we'd been treated as if we were something special but the financial situation at the club wasn't great and there were sub-standard players there. That was down partly to finances but mainly to bad management. There were eighteen months or so at Palace when it was soul-destroying, to be perfectly honest.

But, as far as I was concerned, I'm one of those people that when the going gets tough, I get better and roll my sleeves up but some people haven't got that in their make-up. Possibly Vince could have stepped up to the plate more but it's easier for a defender, like me, because you tend to be tougher and you learn to look after yourself. What Vince probably needed was someone to put their arm round him and tell him that he was a hell of a player but that the team needed a little bit more from him. When Alan Mullery took over, he was a bit more like that. He'd put his arm round you and talk to you more than certain other managers would and Vince definitely needed that arm round him.

BILLY GILBERT ON VINCE

I didn't think that there was a chance of Vince joining Portsmouth. He'd left Palace at the same time as me and I didn't think that he'd leave Luton so quickly so it was a little bit out of the blue. One day, Alan Ball asked me what I thought of Vince so I told Bally that he was a hell of a player, would be good for the club, and that we should sign him. Within a week of that, he'd joined. It was great to see him because he is a great character and a very good player.

As a player, he was outstanding at Portsmouth but, from staying in all the time when he was at Palace, he was out every night at Pompey. Mind you, we had a hell of a lot of characters when we first went there. I've never experienced being around so many people who could drink as much as the other players could; it was fucking ridiculous. I thought that I could drink but I was a bit of a lightweight compared to some of the players there. It was a total eye-opener.

I think that Vince was probably happier in his personal life at Pompey but, football-wise, I think that we were both happier as professionals at Palace. I think we both would say that we had too much, too soon, as kids and that may not have done us too many favours. We never had to do anything for ourselves so we took everything for granted. We could have done with having to deal with a few knocks early on because, when the shit hit the fan, we just didn't know how to deal with it.

Having said that, if you look over our careers, we were still successful but we both could have done a lot more than we did. Hand on heart, if we'd knuckled down, we could have got the England caps that we should have had. That's the only thing I'd say looking back; we could have done better than we did.

VINCE

Vince is a great fella; he's my closest friend in football, but we don't see or talk to each other enough. We've known each other for years and years and, honestly, we should sit down once a month and have a couple of beers and a chat but we don't. Footballers are like passing ships. His persona is that he's a jolly chap who likes a laugh but he's very deep and takes a lot on board; he thinks a hell of a lot about things. Vince does have that persona where he says that everything is alright but he keeps a lot of things to himself.

CHAPTER 11

ENGLAND AND MOVING ON

I was gutted that I never got into the England Schoolboys side as a kid because I really wanted to. Local clubs used to run trips to go and watch the England Schoolboys internationals and I'd go along. I think I should have got in but I was unlucky in the trial. Billy Gilbert ended up captaining the side, Jerry Murphy was in it and Paul Waddington got in too. Palace ended up having about five players in that England team yet we were only in the Third Division.

I used to get envious of all of them going off to play for England Schoolboys. Peter Nicholas and Steve Lovell were with Wales as well so I felt a bit left out at Schoolboy level but, once I got to the pro ranks, I progressed a bit quicker than the others. When I got into the England Youth set-up, that was my first experience of playing with players who had been coached professionally by someone else and in a different way to me. They hadn't been taught by John Cartwright like I had. Some of the other players who were in that squad included Chris Turner, Chris Woods, Derek Statham, Terry Butcher, Russell Osman, Kenny Sansom and Gordon Cowans. I considered it to be an honour playing at that level. It was a great experience to play with good players who were in the first team at their clubs.

I ended up getting the honours at Youth level that I'd have liked to have got as a Schoolboy. We played in the Little World Cup in Belgium. I roomed with Russell Osman, who used to read the same book three times, something he put down to the fact that I made it impossible for him to concentrate. I always wanted everyone to like me so you can imagine what I was like with lads from all over the country representing England. It was one step up!

A really proud moment for me was when England Youth played against France at Selhurst Park. That was my first contact with Clive Allen and I scored in that game, and then we played France again and beat them in Paris, so we progressed to the main tournament in Poland. This was the only time, truth be told, that the squad of players tried their hardest to get knocked out at the first stage of the tournament, and we succeeded at this. Terry Fenwick was bad enough with homesickness when he was at Palace so you can imagine him in Poland! He was laughing and joking when we got knocked out as he wanted to go home from the first day. We just didn't want to be there.

Soon after, I got called up to the Under-21s. One of the reasons why Howard Wilkinson didn't gel with me when I went to Leeds stems back to those days. Dave Sexton was the head coach and Venners was assistant head coach and Howard Wilkinson was one of a few subsidiary coaches. Behind their backs, the players would call them 'Gofers' and I always remember Wilko saying how much he hated cockneys.

I always felt that I couldn't do any wrong with Venners at Palace and it was the same with the Under-21s. Dave Sexton was really close to Venners, because they'd spent time together at QPR and Chelsea, and he loved a joke but the only person that he used to tell them to was me. He'd put his arm around me and tell me a joke and, honestly, they were the worst ones you could ever hear but I just used to laugh and laugh. He was a lovely bloke, and a good tactician.

Because Venners was there and Dave Sexton liked us, me and Billy basically did what we liked when we were playing for the Under-21s. I can remember Billy telling me that he was going to have a shot in training but deliberately miss because then Venners would tell Wilko to go and fetch the ball. It happened and we couldn't stop laughing. He waited a long time but Howard Wilkinson got his revenge on me at Leeds. On my first day there, he said that he always thought that me and Billy Gilbert were flash cockneys with the Under-21s and he reckoned that his first impression was right. He ended up making my life a misery at Leeds.

It was an experience playing for the Under-21s, though, and I played with some great players. Bryan Robson was one of the best but he loved to party and have a drink. What a player, though. When I played with him, I could tell that he was going to be a legend.

We had a game against Scotland at Coventry when we were trying to qualify for the Little World Cup and they had a pretty useful team out and we'd suffered a few injuries. Garry Birtles pulled out so I played up front with Garth Crooks. We had

Gordon Cowans, Graham Rix and Bryan Robson in midfield, Gary Bailey in goal with Terry Butcher, Russell Osman, Kenny Sansom and Derek Statham in defence. It was still a decent team but we were drawing the game 1–1. Up to that point, I didn't know what the word 'inspirational' meant in football terms but, that day, Bryan Robson scored the winner. He'd already broken his leg twice in his career by then and he could easily have broken it again because he smashed this volley and, when he hit it, there were tackles flying in at him but he didn't give them a moment's thought. He didn't care. That's about as inspirational as it gets. All he wanted to do was to win the game and then, afterwards, it was like it had never happened to him. He was just sitting in the room playing cards with the rest of us.

Robson was a winner and you could just tell that he was going to be successful. People talked about Steve Williams and said that he was a winner too but he was a different type of player. We played in East Germany and I went through on goal but I pushed the ball too far and the keeper got there comfortably before me. I heard Steve Williams going absolutely mad because I didn't kick the goalkeeper in the neck. I told him to calm down but he shouted back, 'Calm down? Stud him in the neck!'

I ended up finishing my career at Exeter with Steve, and he could do some quality moaning. He was possessed by the devil on and off the field. Players like Steve and, later on, Mick Kennedy at Portsmouth, abused the opposition constantly and they were effective at it. The opposition would be so fed up with them that they'd lose focus and give us the advantage.

A couple of weeks after that game, we played Bulgaria, and Glenn Hoddle was supposed to play but he got called up to make his debut for the Senior side. Honestly, getting called up to play for the Under-21s was the greatest thing that ever happened to me as a footballer because I was only nineteen, and I was giving away a couple of years in age to all the other lads, and playing with unbelievable players like Hoddle, Robson, Sansom and Rix. People started to talk about me in the same breath as them and I did get a buzz out of it.

People would say that I was ahead of Mark Chamberlain, and John Barnes hadn't even been heard of then, so people often ask: 'What happened? Why didn't you get a full cap?' It was funny because Billy Gilbert had the same thing. If you speak to good judges and educated football people, they'd say that, at that time, Billy was in front of Terry Butcher, Russell Osman and Steve Foster and yet all of those players went on to get full caps and he didn't.

Billy has got a picture of us two with Terry Fenwick and Clive Allen in our England strips before a game at Southampton but, because of what happened to me at an early age, I got so blasé about it all. I can give all sorts of reasons. Maybe I shouldn't have stayed at the clubs that I did for so long? Maybe I didn't work hard enough? But I think it's that I got to a point in my career where I started to think that I didn't have to work as hard any more because I could do it and that's when you start to go downhill. Ultimately, you should always strive to be the best you can, and never become complacent.

VINCE

LUTON

My contract at Palace came to an end and I got a few phone calls from clubs. Gerry Francis, who I'd been quite close to at Palace, spoke to me about going to Coventry, as he'd gone there. They were the club that was most interested but then, out of the blue, David Pleat at Luton rang me. I really liked the way that he talked about the game. Every time I'd played against Luton they played good football and they had quality players there. He told me that he had a brilliant goalscoring winger called David Moss but that he was coming to the end of his career and he wasn't expecting to get much more out of him so he wanted me to come and play on the left wing and take over from him.

Pleaty told me that he'd watched me a lot and thought that I could do the job. He was aware that I knew Ricky Hill and Brian Stein and told me that he was going to sign a few other players too. But I would never have agreed to go to Luton if I'd known that David Pleat was going to take a backseat in terms of running the football side, which happened as soon as I got there. The manager didn't take any training. He left a fella called Trevor Hartley to do it all, and Hartley and I just took an instant dislike to each other. I immediately knew that I wouldn't be there very long.

Pleaty said to me after a week, 'Hilaire, I thought you had a better left foot than that. I wouldn't have signed you if I'd have known it was that bad.' All he kept going on about was my left foot and, for the next three years, after I left Luton, I kept getting Christmas cards from him with: 'Is that left foot any good yet?' written in it.

He was straight as a die, Pleaty, but he was a strange guy. He always spoke to you as if he was commentating; he never called you by your first name. His team talks were: 'When Hilaire gets the ball, I want Stein to make a run in behind the full-back and get the ball and face up. In the meantime, Donaghy will push up from left back.' It was just like he was commentating on a match. He was a funny man without meaning to be – very eccentric.

It was a shame it didn't work out, as I could see that there were good players at Luton – Ricky Hill was as good as any midfield player I'd ever played with and Brian Stein was excellent too. But some of the best players, like Garry Parker and Mark Stein, weren't even in the first team and they didn't get a look in at that time.

There was a bit of arrogance there that I didn't like, but it wasn't with the players – it was with the management. Pleaty resented Venables, which I found from a lot of managers during my career. He was a great football man himself and he talked a lot of sense, but the arrogance of him taking a back seat and putting his first team coach in charge of all footballing matters was wrong, because he hadn't won anything.

I liked Pleaty, though; it was an experience playing for him. He never raised his voice even when he was angry. I remember getting called into his office and he asked me how things were going. I told him that I thought it was OK, but that we needed someone in the middle of the park who could put his foot in. He told me that he didn't believe in playing football like that and that football was a purist's game. I said that we could get someone like Peter Nicholas from Palace for next to nothing as he could play but also mix it, but he told me that Nico wasn't his type of player.

Anyway, a couple of weeks after I got sold to Pompey, he went and bought Steve Foster, who didn't mess around, as well as Peter Nicholas and Mick Harford. They were three of the most uncompromising footballers you could ever come across and did not stand on ceremony. They took no prisoners. You need winners in a team yet, not long before, Pleaty had told me that he was a football purist.

The thing is, you don't need those players solely for their footballing ability. Personally, I needed them to keep me in the game, to keep talking to me and to keep getting me on the ball and to tell me that I needed to do something. That's what leaders do. People used to talk about the swashbuckling way that Manchester United played under Alex Ferguson but they wouldn't have been able to do that if they didn't have Roy Keane or Steve Bruce and Paul Ince and Fergie knew that. You can't just have people who can juggle the ball and catch it on the back of their necks because that's no good if you don't win the game.

Ultimately, I think that David Pleat gave up on me and I couldn't have stayed. I'm sure that if I had, he wouldn't have played me anyway, but his planning for that season was completely wrong in terms of the players that he signed – including me – because none of us were up to the mark. He then bought all of the players that he should have signed in the first place and took back control of the team himself.

I was a bit gutted, really, but, in the end, Pleaty told me that he'd had an offer for me from Portsmouth and was going to let me go. It was on Trevor Hartley's say-so. He was one of the few coaches that I came across who didn't like me on or off the field and the feeling was mutual. It was a shame because, as I say, there were some good players down there. To this day, I regret not staying after they signed those three combative players because that was basically what Luton needed. They then got to the semi-final of the FA Cup and, a couple of years later, won the League Cup too.

Portsmouth had previously come in for me when I was at Palace, when Bobby Campbell was manager. The rumours were that they really looked after their players with their wages, that it was a nice place to live and that they leased you a car, so I wanted to go there. But it turned out that the Palace player they were most impressed with at that time was Billy Gilbert, and he went there instead and I was very disappointed. So when I was told that Portsmouth were interested in me when I was at Luton, I knew that when I went down there I would sign for them.

JOINING POMPEY AND DEBUT

I joined Pompey in November 1984 but I didn't have a clue how to get there. I lived in Barnet, which was on the other side of London, and I knew Portsmouth was on the south coast so I followed the road to Brighton and then asked someone for directions. There was no M25 then and the M3 finished just after Basingstoke and then turned into narrow A-roads.

I used to meet Gerry Francis at his house or we'd meet at Fleet and then drive down together but, for the first three months, and this is no exaggeration, we were late to training every day. We missed the same turn-off every single day. When you drive down, there are two signs for Portsmouth and we always took the wrong one and seemed to drive round the houses to get there. We always had to ask directions; Portsmouth was like the Bermuda Triangle.

I thought I was a cheap signing for them considering that I was only twenty-four or twenty-five. I knew that I'd got into a bit of a rut with my career, but I found something at Pompey that I hadn't had since I was back in the Youth team at Palace. Bally didn't sign journeymen but he signed people who hadn't settled at other clubs and we all had great camaraderie.

At that time, Portsmouth didn't have a proper training ground. They alternated between a little gym at the football club and Eastleigh Barracks. My first day there was in the gym and we played five-a-side and my team had three England captains in it. There was Gerry Francis, who had just been signed. He'd played well on a short-term deal for Cardiff against Portsmouth and Bally thought that he could do a job until the end of the season. Bally was also in my team and so was Emlyn Hughes. He was down doing some training with Pompey. It was good for me to meet up with Nicky Morgan too because I hadn't played on the same team as him since I was fourteen and I was also back with Billy Gilbert. There were some good lads there and they made me feel welcome.

My first game was against Blackburn Rovers and I scored. I

usually did on my debuts: I scored on my full debut at Palace, for England Youth and the Under-21s but this was my best debut goal and I got carried away. After the game, TVS wanted to do an interview with me. I was euphoric but I wanted to get it done quickly because I was still travelling back to London. I didn't think anything more of it. The manager had given us the Monday off and I went back in on the Tuesday and, because I lived in London, I hadn't seen the interview on the local telly.

When I came in, Gerry Francis said to me, 'Cor! Your interview!' I admitted that I'd got a bit excited so I asked him to remind me what I'd said. Apparently, I'd said that Bally had signed me because I could dribble but, if there wasn't anything on, then I could pick a pass. I could get stuck in and could also get in the box and get my share of goals and that I could work as a team player but also as an individual too. Gerry looked at me and said, 'Bloody hell! Is there anything you can't do?' But I was just excited. I didn't usually get all 'me, me, me', but they were talking to me as if I was the best thing since sliced bread.

Luckily for me, the Pompey fans have always been brilliant with me from the moment that I signed but I would have been interested to see their reaction if I hadn't scored that goal on my debut, because I didn't play particularly well. I crossed one in and we got a penalty from that and I scored the diving header and that's all anyone seems to remember.

So I was lucky because I was made to feel welcome from the off, but I don't know whether my welcome would have been so good if I hadn't scored. Now that I've lived in Portsmouth for a long time, I've realised that people there don't follow the old adage of biding their time and establishing what someone is like – usually they either like you straight away or they don't. In my case, they liked me.

I could use Noel Blake as an example of someone who went the other way. Noel didn't start very well and wanted to leave the club early on. He had difficulty settling in having been in a big city previously and, after struggling initially, people got on his back. Once he found his feet, though, everyone began to like him.

I don't know whether I was well-liked because I started well or because of who I was, but I've always been well received in Portsmouth – even more so since I packed in playing. The majority of people here are quite humble and if you act in the same way then they tend to be alright with you whatever their circumstances. I've hardly met anyone down here that was born with a silver spoon in their mouth, which is unusual for a city with so many people in it. People from Portsmouth expect you to be humble.

Personally, I found a lot of the places around here are similar to the places that I grew up in in east London. I remember walking home through Summerstown one night and people couldn't believe it because they thought that Summerstown was 'Injun country', but, to me, I didn't think it was any different to where I grew up, so I didn't think anything of it.

I just feel comfortable and familiar here. If you walk through somewhere like Fratton then it's exactly the same as the East End in London. But I do tell people not to be fooled by *EastEnders* because east London isn't like that. Even in the '60s when

London was meant to be a lot safer, if you walked through someone's back door without telling them, you'd get a smack.

Portsmouth is a one-club city, so the players do attract attention. Even now, when I go out, all people want to talk to me about is Portsmouth Football Club. I go to London on a regular basis but the only time that I get recognised is when I'm in the Palace area. Anywhere else, there's no chance. At Portsmouth, you couldn't help but be out with the fans, and as long as you knew where to draw the line, then things were fine. If you played badly then you were an idiot to go out. I would never take the mickey and socialise when I'd played badly because supporters pay a lot of money to watch you play and you should respect that.

When I first came down, I still wasn't the Master Socialiser, though, and, a lot of the time, I was going straight back to London after training and games rather than going out. It was about a year and a half before Pompey changed me. For six or seven years at Palace, once the game was over, I would get my Kentucky and go home and watch the TV and that was my Saturday night. I always say that I grew up as a footballer at Palace but I grew up as a man at Portsmouth. At Palace it had only been about football, but out here I realised that there was more to life.

CHAPTER 12

THE GREMLINS

We'd had a bit of a camaraderie redevelop at the end of my time at Palace, which we'd lost when all the players went to QPR. We then had the likes of David Giles, Kevin Mabbutt and Billy who were good to be around, but Pompey was something else. People used to ask each other whether there was any reason why they had to go home.

At Portsmouth, it was very rare that any of the players went straight home after a game. I'd say that Kevin Dillon was about the only one who did, but he had a deep psychological problem called Kevin O'Callaghan and was a bit of a loner. Everyone else stayed around. I found it unique; I'd never been at a club like it. The drinking was quite excessive for me, though, because, no matter where we played, whether it was home or away, I wouldn't get home until Sunday morning.

Personally, I wasn't a big drinker; I never used to go out every night drinking – it was just when I felt like it. I'd usually be out after a game but, when I had bad games, and I'm talking about really bad games, they spoiled my weekend, no matter how drunk I used to get. That was the same throughout my career.

The drinking straight afterwards would help me forget for a little while but it would all come back to me on a Sunday.

I realised just how big the drinking culture was at the club at the first Christmas party. It was from that day onwards that I knew this was the place for me. If you read some of the other players' autobiographies, like Mick Channon's or Paul Mariner's, then you'll see them say that the Portsmouth side was the wildest bunch they've ever known and that they'd never been at a club like it. Yet neither of them had been around for that first Christmas party – that's how bad that party was. That's when I realised that I was in a team of mad men.

Billy organised that Christmas do as he had a few friends who had restaurants in Southsea. He told us that he had drinks and a meal sorted and then we'd have a show at the 400 Club, where there would be strippers. Billy had booked a restaurant and we had a big, long table and next to it were, what I considered, all the cowboys from Portsmouth – the builders and decorators. You know how blokes become boisterous when they've had a few drinks? Well, we just needed one match to light the touchpaper and that match was someone getting hit with a bread roll, which led to food being thrown and then to a massive free-for-all.

We all got kicked out, but we didn't mind because the 400 Club had opened by that time. In those days, not very far from the 400 Club was a joke shop and someone had the bright idea of getting some foam spray and, with that, every player bought at least a couple of cans.

Things started playfully, but then got totally out of control.

Punches were being thrown. Kevin O'Callaghan nearly lost an eye. He suspected that it was Kevin Dillon who did it, but that was never proved. The builders were getting involved; it was mayhem. In the end, the owner of the 400 Club got on the mic and told us that he'd call the police if we didn't stop. Everyone gradually quietened down, but he then told us that if we wanted the show to go on then A) the place had to be cleaned up and B) every can of foam had to be handed into a box that he had at the front. It was like a Western where all the guns get checked in. Billy took about five cans out of his pockets but the owner, Gordon, said to him, 'And that one in your trouser leg, Billy.'

I came out for some fresh air and someone had written in red ink on the wall of the club, 'Noel Blake has got the biggest cock you've ever seen'. It was mayhem. That was the birth of us as Gremlins. We were a bunch of players that had been plucked from all of over the country and, like the characters in the film, could cause chaos if we went out at night. After that, the Christmas party became legendary. We used to get tops printed to wear so that not only would we get in trouble but we made sure that we got recognised too. Each Christmas party got more out of control to the extent that, in the last two years, we just got given the whole pub to ourselves as the owners wouldn't have anyone else in there. We had to have them in private because we couldn't be trusted with the Portsmouth public.

Rumours spread and people thought that we did a lot of drinking on away trips, but we didn't. Contrary to popular belief, all of the drinking was done after games. We'd have fish and chips on the coach, an off-licence would never be far away for a few cans, and then we'd stop at the same pub, somewhere in Northampton, called the Crossroads for a few glasses of wine or some pints. Wherever we played north of Watford, we'd go back there and, then, when we got on the coach, we'd finish off the drink that we'd bought from the off-licence.

Things are so different now. The food is prepared for players to eat after games to aid recovery and players do warm-downs, but the thing we realised about warm-downs when we were playing was that if we did one then it would cut down on our drinking time.

Another difference between then and now is that it's very rare to see a Portsmouth player drinking at the club. When I played, it was the complete opposite and it was very rare that you didn't see a player drinking at the club and putting the world to rights. They'd be telling anyone that would listen why they had done well or badly. The players would then figure that it wasn't worth going home so we'd stay out. Back then, we could go out in Portsmouth in relative safety without fear of being abused or ridiculed. Obviously, you'd get the odd idiot but, by then, we'd be so far gone that we didn't care what people said to us. Now, though, that'd be unheard of.

As far as we were concerned, our drinking was even approved at board level. We had a director called Jim Sloan who we made an honorary director of the Gremlins. He used to be our eyes in the boardroom. Jim used to be a sight to behold on the coach coming back from games. Once he'd had a drink, we'd get all of our information from him because the Gaffer, even when he was drunk, was reticent with what he told us. Half the time, if you did get something out of Bally, then it would just be a criticism of you anyway.

Bally could be cutting when he'd had a drink, so you tended to stay away from him then, unless you felt especially brave. He criticised Micky Tait's footballing ability once so Micky threw a drink over him, but I don't think Bally remembered the next morning. In the end, the Gaffer learned to stay away from the players if he was drinking.

I remember we were due to play at West Brom but we turned round as we couldn't get to Birmingham, so Bally asked if any of us wanted to go and watch the Southampton game instead. There was a bit of muttering as some of us just wanted to get home, until Eamonn Collins told us that there was a free bar at Southampton and, suddenly, all our hands went up. Jim Sloan had gone up to the director's room as Bally was in there but someone turned him away and he ended up stumbling into the players' lounge where we were. Jim always used to say to us when we lost a game, 'Don't worry, lads. We might have lost the game but I beat them in the boardroom!' Well, he didn't that time.

When Jim came into the players' lounge that day, he was absolutely paralytic. I didn't know that it was possible for someone to be so drunk. Don't ask me how but, somehow, we got back to Portsmouth and found ourselves in the Pompey pub at the ground. We must have been like homing pigeons. It's a habit nowadays but I fell asleep in there as I'd been drinking for so long. The sight that I saw when I came to was a sight that I'll never forget: it was Jim Sloan asking for another whisky.

That guy cannot have been human. I physically could not have drunk one more drink – it was not possible. I'm a film buff and it reminded me of the John Wayne bit at the end of *The Greatest Story Ever Told* when they say, 'Truly this man is the Son of God,' and I thought, 'Truly this is the greatest drinker that ever lived.' He was a Gremlin ten, twenty or thirty times over.

Soon after I joined the club, we had a team meeting and Bally kept making references to a trip to Jersey that everyone had been on. It wasn't long after the team had got back but our results had started to turn and we were slipping out of the promotion race. He was having a go at us and I remember thinking that I would have taken offence at what he said if I hadn't been in the game for so long. He told us that we were all mongrels and that no one wanted us apart from him so we all owed him. I thought that he was going a bit power crazy.

The biggest mistake Bally ever made with us was to take us away and I found out the following year why he'd acted like that in that meeting because we went to Jersey again. You'd think that he'd have learned after the first year because the season went downhill after we came back but he didn't.

He always took us to Jersey. The drinking laws over there were different – the pubs were open all day. Now, going to Jersey for a Portsmouth player under Alan Ball was like a pilgrimage to Jerusalem or to Mecca. It was like the Holy Land to us players because those licensing laws suited us down to the ground. For a bunch of players who didn't like going home anyway, and only ever went home because the pubs shut, Jersey was heaven on earth.

My first Jersey trip was in the middle of the season. We

turned up at the hotel and were greeted by the manager, who told us that we'd worked hard so far that year so we were going to have a four-day break and there would be no training. We all looked at each other. Bally told us that he didn't want any of us going berserk; we were in a nice hotel and we needed the rest so he expected us to be responsible.

That night, funnily enough, I was responsible. I stayed in. It was only my second season at the club. The majority of the players had gone out but I watched the telly and had a few drinks and that was enough for me. It was quite late, about 1 a.m., when I was greeted by a sight that I'd go on to see many times while I was at Portsmouth.

I was rooming with Alan Knight and he'd had quite a bit to drink. Knighty was always very deadpan and he became even more deadpan when he'd had a drink. He started chatting away and said that a few of the lads had gone to the clubs and a couple had gone on to the casino. I could hear one of them coming in because he was singing 'The Greatest Love of All' at the top of his voice. I couldn't believe how much noise he was making; you could hear him banging into things and knocking on doors.

We'd left our door ajar and, all of a sudden, it was flung open and slammed against the cupboard and we were greeted by Alan Ball, wearing his flat cap. He sat on the edge of my bed and started talking in a language that, even to this day, I could not understand. Bally then started laughing to himself, fell off the bed, and he began pulling his trousers up, his legs sticking up in the air. After a minute, he got up and walked back out and started singing again.

Knighty and I didn't have a clue what he was going on about and we were chatting about it for about fifteen minutes until the other lads started coming in. Eamonn Collins asked if we'd seen the Gaffer. They'd all gone to a club and had to queue. Now the Gaffer hadn't wanted to bring too much attention to himself because he's quite distinctive. Apparently, he was pulling his cap down further and further over his face but some fella had come up to him and asked if he was Alan Ball. The fella then said the worst thing that you could ever say to Bally: he told him that he had put on some weight. That was a red rag to a bull, so Bally offered to race him over 100 yards for £50.

Anyway, the fella agreed to the race and, now, having previously not wanted to attract any attention to himself, there were about twenty blokes standing in a car park ready to watch a race between a guy no one knew and Alan Ball. Finally, we began to figure out what Bally had been saying because the Gaffer had been performing a running action when he came into our room. Bally had, by all accounts, pulled away from the fella and was looking back at him when, all of a sudden, he'd run into a bollard and hit the floor. He scraped his knees and that's what he'd been showing us when he was pulling up his trousers.

Eamonn finished telling us the story and then Bally came back to our room. By now, he'd had a shower and had a towel wrapped round him and he told us that we were all going to go down to the foyer to have a drink. We ordered some brandies, everyone was drunk, and the fella in the bar started complaining that we were all a bit noisy. It was about 2.30 a.m. and most of the other players were coming back now and Bally was telling them all to join us. The night porter told us that he wasn't serving any more drinks, but Bally told him that he didn't care because we had enough already, as someone had brought back a bottle.

By now, it was starting to get light and the staff wanted to get things ready for breakfast and they'd had enough of us. They didn't want any of the other guests to see us in our towels. The Porter was using one of those machines that they use to polish the floors and he was getting more and more irate and kept going round us. Bally was going up to all of us and hissing, 'Don't move! Don't move! Be a man. He wants us to move but we've got to be men!' By now, the fella started opening all the patio doors and we were in our towels and were freezing but Bally was shouting, 'Be men! He's not going to drive me out. You boys can go to bed if you want but I'm staying here!' Bally asked me quietly what the time was and I told him it was 4.45 a.m. and he said, 'We'll hold out until 5 a.m. We're not showing him that he's winning!'

It was déjà vu because when we came back we had another meeting. I'd put the 'mongrels' comment from the year before – when Bally had told us that no one else would want us – down to his passion but, this time, Bally came out with a statement that every player kept with them for the rest of their time at the club. He had a go at us about our behaviour on the trip, went quiet for about fifteen seconds, which is a long time in that kind of meeting, and then he looked up at the ceiling and shouted, 'You're a monster! I created you but I can destroy you!' It was a moment that none of us ever forgot.

Players like me, Blakey, Billy Gilbert and others were all known in football as people who were quite difficult to handle. I reckon he thought that it would give him a lot of credibility in the game as a manager if he could get us promoted and also show that he could handle this type of character. But, if anything, it was getting worse off the field.

Despite everything we'd go back to Jersey every year. Our trips were intended to be a mid-season break to instil team spirit but as soon as our plane landed our season would come to an end. It happened every year.

We used to look forward to it so much. It was only about a half-hour flight from Southampton and we had a habit that we wouldn't even unpack when we arrived; we'd just go out straight away. You didn't even look at your room, just shoved your bag in, and went out so you could make the most of your time. Quinny was a nervous flyer and when we landed he kissed the tarmac but we all started doing it because we were so happy to be back in Jersey. We thought it was the greatest island in the world. We all wanted to move the football club there.

The Gaffer used to tell us what hotel we were staying at but it was common practice that we all had to sort out our own taxis to get there. One trip, I told our group not to worry about going to the hotel and that we should go straight to the Tiger Bar instead. We turned up at this bar with our luggage with hardly anyone in there, and yet we were having the best time of our lives. Eamonn kept ordering us rounds but in bigger glasses each time. After two or three hours of drinking, we were rocking and reeling and no one more so than Paul Mariner. It was his first trip; he thought it was brilliant and he couldn't believe that we wouldn't even be training.

Eventually, someone suggested going back to the hotel and getting changed, before going out again. We came out of the Tiger Bar with our bags and jumped into a taxi outside. Marrers said to the driver, 'Pomme d'Or Hotel, my man!' and the driver said, 'But...' and Marrers told him, 'Don't ask questions! We ain't got time to waste. Pomme d'Or Hotel, my man. We've got money and you'll get paid!' The driver put his indicator on, did a U-turn, and said, 'You're here,' so Marrers said to him, 'What kept you?' The hotel was across the road from the Tiger Bar and we were so drunk that no one had noticed.

The following day a meeting was called in Bally's room and he told us that they wanted us out of the hotel. It was a higher-class establishment and the manager there had taken offence at our behaviour and he wanted us out before the end of breakfast. Bally became desperate and told us that there was nothing that he could say to him to change his mind and that, if we got sent home, it would get into all the papers and he'd be finished in the game! He said that he'd even bought him a big bunch of flowers but the manager wouldn't take them.

Bally had encouraged us to have a good time but we'd gone beyond where he wanted us to go. We were the monster that he'd created. Finally, we came to an agreement and Bally had to promise the hotel manager that, after we'd all had breakfast, none of us would come back to the hotel until after a certain time. We had to have breakfast and then vacate the premises straight away. We were like lepers. We had to go out all day so what else could we do? No exaggeration, we were drinking from 9 a.m.

Luckily we went up that season but I remember we played Middlesbrough on the Saturday after we came back from Jersey and we got a penalty. Kevin Dillon wasn't playing, so Quinny volunteered to take it. Now, I wasn't the best at watching penalties anyway and I remember standing by the dugout with my head in my hands because I couldn't bear to watch. Quinny was probably only second to Kevin Dillon in terms of his penalty-taking ability but, that day, I've never seen a penalty miss by such a distance. He nearly hit it out of the ground. All I heard was Bally shouting, 'You lot are never going to Jersey again!'

The next year, we were struggling to stay in the League but we'd drawn Luton in the FA Cup with a chance to get to the quarter final when the Gaffer had the great idea to take us back to Jersey knowing full well what we were like.

On the first night, me and Knighty were back in our room, talking about the evening when, all of a sudden, a meeting was called. We were told that we were going to train the following morning, which we thought was a bit odd – even though we were footballers. We had to meet on the sea front at 9.45 a.m. and we were all sitting on the sand waiting for the Gaffer. He had to cross the road to get to the beach in his studded boots and he was slipping and trying to keep his balance. We had a little chuckle but the first word out of his mouth was 'Gentlemen', so we knew that we were going to get a bollocking.

We thought it had been a fairly quiet night, but Bally went on: 'Lovely island, relax away from Portsmouth, a chance for us all to grab something to eat and give me and my assistant manager the chance to have a glass of wine and some food and discuss our plans. But you couldn't help abusing this great game of ours.' Bally was always very dramatic and graphic with his descriptions.

> I was halfway through my main course, which was steak and it was very nice, I was on my second glass of wine when a young man in a suit came up to me. I thought, 'OK, didn't take long but, you know, Alan Ball, World Cup winner. Someone's going to recognise me and ask me for my autograph.'
> I turned around with my hand ready to take his pen and he said, 'Excuse me, Alan Ball. We've had reports of a black man going berserk.' And, all of a sudden, that nice meal I had, that nice glass of wine, I didn't feel like eating or drinking it. You boys don't know how to behave. And because you want to act like kids, and because your centre-half spent a couple of hours in the nick while it was being straightened out, I will treat you like boys. Put your trainers on.

We thought that he was going to punish us by making us run, which he had done in the past, but he put us into two teams of nine and told us that we were going to play keep ball instead. I thought that would be much better than being run into the ground. We had the sea to one side, and the sand ran as far as the eye could see, so we asked Bally where the pitch started and ended because he always put some cones out but he told us just to play, so we played keep ball on the biggest pitch ever.

People were running with the ball for hundreds of yards. This game stretched for about half a mile. We started complaining but he told us to carry on. I've seen the pictures of how football was invented and that's how it was that day. We didn't have any bibs or different coloured shirts; we looked like a load of Sunday morning players just having a kick-about with each other and we did this for about an hour and a half. We were knackered. We lost about four balls on the tide, but Bally just pulled his cap down a little further, turned his back on us, and went back into the hotel. The next time we saw him was at dinner later that night. You'd have thought the conversation had never taken place because he went back to being Boss Gremlin so we all carried on on the piss.

Each time we went to Jersey, the season went downhill afterwards so Bally then told us that, seeing as we didn't know how to behave in Jersey, he was going to take us to Tenerife instead. That was even worse! By then, I think that the players were out of control. That trip was doomed from the start. For some reason, Noel Blake hadn't got his ticket sorted so Bally asked the whole squad whether anyone would do him a favour and give up theirs and come out a day later but he didn't get one taker. Not one. Not the married boys, not the youngsters, not one person would give up their ticket, even if it meant getting a whack from Blakey – big as he was – because we all knew what a laugh those trips were.

Blakey had the hump as he'd missed a day of the trip so, when he arrived, he wouldn't go out with the lads because he said that none of us were his mates. The Big Man was sulking and told us that he was going to go out on his own instead and that he was going to leave the club, all because he'd missed a day's partying.

Me and Knighty got back in the early hours and were lying in our beds. We fell silent for a few minutes and all we could hear was crickets as it was so hot that we'd left the balcony doors open. Then, out of this silence, we heard crashing, banging and dustbin lids falling. It must have been about 3.30 a.m. and then we could hear Blakey shouting, 'You Espanyoly Bastaaaaaaaards!' It sounded like a war cry and, deadpan as you like, without any emotion in his voice, Knighty said, 'I see Blakey's back from his night on the town, then?' It was the way he said it. He didn't speak to anyone for a couple of days, did Blakey. What made it worse was that he'd had his hair cut especially for the trip but he'd forgotten his gel for his new perm and his hair was getting more and more out of control.

That trip, Bally told us that we should go for a run, but we were all lying by the pool; it was about 11.30 a.m., and the drinks had already started to flow. Kenny Swain and Gary Stanley said that we'd all meet in the foyer in twenty minutes. They reminded us that we were professionals and we had to show some pride.

I was running with Billy and we all started off laughing and joking about Blakey. We'd run for about a mile and a half but we'd been drinking for a couple of days when, all of a sudden, 'Boom!' there was no talking, nothing. Both of us had hit the wall and what had replaced the talking was the heaviest breathing you've ever heard. We had our pride, though, and I remember thinking to myself that I got paid to keep fit and couldn't be seen to stop after a mile and a half.

VINCE

We were running this big loop of the town and Billy and I were quite near the back when we both saw our hotel up ahead. We ran into the foyer and through it, out to the back, and dived into the swimming pool and neither of us had said a word to each other. We'd only jumped into the pool to cool off but, when we resurfaced, Billy told me that he was struggling and I told him that I couldn't believe how bad it was. We weren't even running against a time, we just had to complete the course.

Needless to say, Kenny Swain was back about an hour before anyone else. It's funny really, because just doing that one run demonstrated how shallow we all were as footballers. Rather than show us that we should rein the drinking in, we were all back out on the piss that night.

CHAPTER 13

ALAN BALL

Alan Ball changed my outlook on life. Without a shadow of a doubt, he was one of the best people I've ever come across. Family was everything to him and football was too. He was so passionate and he had such humility. I'm proud to say that he called me a friend and he took me to so many clubs with him. I still miss the conversations that we had together. People always ask me what my favourite Alan Ball story was and there were so many, but the impact of them is lost on paper because you can't imitate his high voice.

Bally never tired of talking about football to anyone, even complete strangers, and I know how hard that can be. He'd never initiate a conversation but he'd always have an opinion and he wouldn't simply agree with someone just to get away from them, which I've seen a lot of players do. And the funniest thing about Bally was that he was never wrong.

I'd played against Bally before joining Portsmouth. When Palace went up to Division One, Southampton was the first team to beat us. They won 4–1 at The Dell and they had a good team then. I'd played against Bally before that game but, on this occasion, it was as though he wanted to show these young upstarts from London what it was like to compete. I remember someone got injured and he just ripped into the referee about the tackle and his face kept getting redder and redder. I was taken aback because he just didn't stop. They were 3–0 up at the time, but that didn't matter to him and it was a lasting memory for me. I knew then that he was a winner.

He used to refer to himself as Arthur Ball and I can remember him doing it in that game and he still did it when I went down to Pompey. I asked him who Arthur Ball was and he told me that the best way to play football and to stop the opposition from getting the ball was to play one-touch but that he was so good that he could have half a touch. He was actually calling himself 'Half a Ball'. Bally was the best one-touch footballer that I ever played against and he also gave 100 per cent effort all over the pitch. He was amazing.

When he had that spell at Southampton, you just couldn't get near him. He took a lot of that style to Portsmouth and I think that he saw a lot of those attributes in me. By that stage, I'd grown out of wanting the crowd to love me. I'd fathomed that the ball moves quicker than any footballer can and realised that you should only try to beat a player if you've got no one else to pass to. It took me a few years to find that out, mind.

Bally said to me that when he played for Lawrie McMenemy at Southampton he was told that if a player didn't have any passion or any devil inside them then they were no good to him. He thought that I had those strengths. Bally also didn't like cowards and that was one thing that you could say about me: I didn't pull out of tackles, because I'd learned from Venables how to look after myself and that's one of the reasons why I didn't get injured very often.

At Palace, the best thing about us in the early days was that the mixture was right between the competitive players and the ones with flair. Our spine was Billy Gilbert, Jim Cannon, Peter Nicholas and Steve Kember in midfield, and David Swindlehurst and Ian Walsh up front, and they all put themselves about, so we were always going to compete in a physical battle. Around that framework, the manager would then put the flair players who could win you the game. With Bally, though, everyone had to do their bit physically first and that meant that first and foremost we didn't lose the game. Some of the players were more effective at that side of things than others but the flair players also had to put a shift in too.

When we had that good three-year spell at Pompey, the nucleus of the players were all, in Bally's words, 'mongrels' and we all had strong opinions although the Gaffer's word was still law. He didn't like players just to lie down. He wanted us to have the same passion that he had – and we did. The best example of that was when we played Sheffield United and had three players sent off before half time. When we came in at the break, Bally didn't tell us how stupid we were, or complain about a travesty of justice – he just went about telling us how we were going to play with eight men. He didn't even give the sendings off a second thought because that's what he expected from his team. He expected commitment and hard tackles.

We had a terrible disciplinary record at the club and the reason why it was so bad could be summed up in two words:

Alan Ball. The team reflected his character. At Palace, although I knew how to look after myself on the field, we were taught to be technical, but, at Portsmouth, Bally instilled an attitude in us that winning was the only thing that mattered. He loved playing good football, but winning was what made it worthwhile, so we knew we had to win at all costs. Bally didn't want players to get sent off and he didn't encourage us to go and kick others, but he wanted us to win.

But when you lost games for Alan Ball, you knew that he might not speak to you for two or three days because he held you personally responsible for it. That didn't happen every time we lost; it was just when he wasn't happy with the way that we'd lost and he would go into a sulk. That was Alan Ball to a T. Some didn't like it but I loved playing for him, listening to his stories, taking part in his training sessions, and I loved the way that he looked at life.

There was no funnier man than Alan Ball when he was trying to put the world to rights. He sat me down once and told me a story and it's my favourite Alan Ball story. He had a glazed look and said:

Little Man, I'm going to tell you something about Bobby Charlton. If you see all those old clips of Bobby Charlton, all you ever see is him smashing shots in from forty yards or hitting sixty-yard cross-field passes. Let me tell you something about Bobby Charlton: for every shot he hit on target, and for every one of those passes, he had another ten that went miles over.

Bally's voice was getting higher. 'At the World Cup,' he said, 'Alf Ramsey used to say to him, "Alright, Bobby, when you get the ball, shoot or pass it sixty yards and don't worry if you give it away because Bally or Nobby will get it back for you to try again."'

He told me that Bobby Charlton gave the ball away more than any other player but the TV companies had the cheek just to show him smashing it into the net from forty yards all the time. His favourite line was that he was 6ft 1in. before he played in the 1966 World Cup and had to carry Bobby Charlton all the time. I asked him once whether I could detect a bit of animosity from him towards Bobby Charlton but he said, 'No, no, no. Great player, Bobby. Great player. Would have been nothing without me, though.'

It was very rare that anyone could say something to Bally that he didn't have a comeback to but, if he was stuck, then he would bring out his old favourite, 'Have you got a World Cup winner's medal?' or 'I was one of the best in the world in 1966. Fact!' so it was very difficult to argue with him. People used to say that in the 1966 World Cup, he covered every single blade of grass but that irritated him because he felt that it detracted from his footballing ability.

The profile of the national side has changed nowadays but I've never known anyone who was more patriotic. When Bally was at Exeter, he was on Graham Taylor's coaching staff for England and I don't think he took his England tracksuit off for three weeks. He wore it in to training every single day. He was devastated when he was told that he wasn't doing it any more.

To be honest, he would have been good at giving the team talks to England players these days, because he would have motivated them and got it through to them what it meant to represent their country.

We played a game at Sheffield United and, by that time, Bally's motivational team talks were a cross between Winston Churchill and a demented fan. He was good with the tactical side but then he'd always use this analogy to try and motivate us: 'We've got to be like outlaws today. We've got to ride in, take the money and get out of here because this is a pig of a place to come to so we need to rob them and get out.'

His favourite one – and he used to use it when we played at places like Grimsby and Shrewsbury – was, 'Right, you know they hate you. We've got the best houses, the best weather, the best women, we dress better...' I used to listen to this and think, 'But Gaffer, you're from Bolton!' Then he'd say, without fail, 'I tell you what, they'd even take the milk out of your tea here. That's how much they don't like you, so we're going to come here, make them jealous, and get out.'

He always talked from his heart. Everyone remembers Alan Ball for his high voice but, when he started speaking with emotion, you'd think that he was going to break down and cry: 'You know, boys. You go home and you just think, "It's OK, I'll try again next week," but it hurts. Don't worry about the manager. You've got your fat contracts,' and his voice would get so high it was ridiculous.

With some managers, their criticism wouldn't bother me but, with Bally, it did. He could take you to the heights with his praise but he could also bring you down again. He'd make you feel so good but he could really belittle you at other times. I suppose he thought that if he praised players all the time then he would make them lazy, but I much preferred receiving praise even when I didn't deserve it.

A lot of players would be affected because the Gaffer would go days without speaking to you if you were playing badly. The corridor by the dressing rooms was no more than six feet wide but, if you'd played badly on a Saturday, you'd be lucky to get a 'Hello' out of him if you passed him before the Wednesday or the Thursday when he knew that he'd have to start talking to you again. That was his make-up, though. He was genuinely upset because he thought that you'd let him down.

Bally would make it very clear if he thought that it was your fault the team had lost. He wouldn't actually say your name but he'd say your number or position so you were very clear who he was talking about. He did it to me when I went back to play at Crystal Palace with Portsmouth. I went through on goal, it was a very heavy pitch, but I should have done better with the chance, and George Wood, who had been a teammate of mine a year before, basically bent down and picked the ball off my feet. I fell down, George patted me on the head, and I picked up a load of mud and threw it into the ground, but I only did that to try and convince people that it was the muddy pitch that had made me miss the chance. It wasn't, though. We only had a couple of minutes to go and we ended up losing 2-1.

We'd played badly as a team and we'd deserved to lose but Bally came in and he left every single person in that dressing room in no doubt whose fault it was that we'd lost the game. He just said, 'If we don't go up then we know who to blame, don't we? Your right winger.' And all the others who had played badly, you could almost hear them sigh with relief, as they now figured it was my fault. For some players, that might make them want to prove him wrong but, for the majority, including me, it deflates you.

Probably the worst thing that I ever saw him do to a player – and it finished that player at Pompey – was what he did to Ian Baird. We've laughed about it since, but it was humiliating. I used to travel in with Bairdy because he didn't live far from me and we shared the driving. We'd played Charlton at Selhurst Park and we were awful; it was the year we went down from the old top division. We got beaten 2–1 and we were devastated because now we really were in relegation trouble. Bally told us after the match that we had to come in the next day for a meeting and to train on our day off.

Bairdy was trying not to let it get him down but he'd only scored one goal in about twenty games since signing for us. It didn't help him with the fans that he'd played for Southampton in the past too. He was sitting in the car quietly and told me that it was all starting to get to him. He asked me what Bally was like as a person as he was going to see him before training because he was really worried about his form. I was surprised because Bairdy normally had skin as tough as a rhino but I told him that it would show Bally that he cared.

Bairdy went off to see him and he came back down after about fifteen minutes and told me that he'd had a good meeting and felt better about it all. The Gaffer had said that it was between the two of them, they'd talk it through, and would do a bit of work on his finishing and on the rest of his game. But what Ian didn't realise was that he had been talking to someone who was under so much pressure that he was turning into a borderline schizophrenic because our form was upsetting him so much. Bally wasn't in the right frame of mind to be sympathetic, but we didn't realise that until afterwards.

All of a sudden, Graham Paddon announced that Bally wanted a players' meeting. He came in and ripped into me to start with because I'd had a personal Armageddon at Charlton. He then said to all of us, 'I had a player come to see me this morning.' Bairdy's eyes were like headlights.

> I was sitting at my desk thinking about what we could do because that performance was diabolical and then there was a knock on my door. It was my centre forward, gentlemen. My centre forward walked up to my desk and asked to speak with me and he said, 'Gaffer, I need help.' I sat there and I looked at him and I thought, 'You need help, son. You can't even fucking score in training.' How can I help someone like that?

He sold him two weeks later. He'd obviously sat there and thought about everything Bairdy had said and couldn't believe that he'd asked for help after twenty-odd games. He'd sat there fuming. We ripped into Bairdy: 'Between you and him, was it?'

Bairdy was funny; he was very dry. Earlier that season we'd played Charlton at home and I picked Bairdy up. I'd known Paul

Miller, who was Charlton's centre-half, as a kid. He was a hard man, gave a lot of verbals and he'd upset you with them and with his tackles too. Bairdy told me that when he'd been at Leeds, he'd had some battles with him but I told him that the key was to take no notice of Paul as he was alright really. He told me that he was a bit more mature now and keen to make a good impression so he wasn't going to get involved. I remember him saying, 'He can do anything to me.' Bally reminded him during the team talk not to get involved so Bairdy said that he knew better than that. Five minutes into the game, we were down to ten men. Bairdy's elbowed him.

The first time that I ever remember really losing my confidence was in a training session with Bally at Pompey. I promise you, the worst thing in football is not being embarrassed in front of 25,000 people but being embarrassed in front of ten or twelve of your team mates. That's what kills you, and Bally would do it on a regular basis. We had some players with good delivery in the team like Gerry Francis, Kevin Dillon and Ivan Golac but we'd had a couple of games when my own final ball had let me down a bit. When there's a part of your game that's going wrong, then you get self-conscious about it; my crossing plagued me throughout my career, but particularly at Pompey.

I was dreading the end of this training session because Bally had told us that we were going to finish with crossing. He ended the session and told us that he wanted three players out wide to cross the balls in and the rest of the players in the middle to try to score and I went to the group in the middle. Kevin Dillon was a bit like a shark because he could smell blood and he preyed on weaknesses and didn't let go. If you were under pressure then he'd know about it.

He smelt blood that day as he'd picked up that I'd had a couple of dodgy games with my crossing and that Bally had been having a go at me. He noticed that I'd gone into the middle so Dill shouted, at the top of his voice, 'What are you doing there, Vince? Shouldn't you be out wide practising your crossing?' Bally heard it and told me to go out wide with Ivan and Gerry and all I could hear was Dill chuckling to himself.

I let Ivan go first and, as usual, he hit a great cross in. Bally used to stand behind the goal and he was singing his praises. Gerry then did the same. I remember thinking that this must be worse than playing in front of 100,000 people, especially when Billy Gilbert asked who was knocking the next one in and groaned when he heard it was me. They drove the ball out to me, I controlled it, played it down the line and crossed it and it went bobble, bobble, bobble into the box. All I wanted was the Gaffer to encourage me but he screamed, 'Come on, Little Man. Get the thing up in the air!' When it was my turn again, I put it behind the goal. I couldn't keep the ball in play or get it in the air and then Bally's tongue started: 'Can't you do it? Can't you kick a ball thirty yards?'

Everyone was looking at me and I just wanted him to leave me alone. The last thing I needed was Ivan going, 'Wince, watch me. Keep your head down and wrap your foot around the ball.' I was hissing at him, 'Ivan, don't coach me in front of everyone. I'm twenty-five years of age. It's embarrassing enough.' Then Gerry Francis piped up. My head was spinning so I did the famous 'go over on my ankle' and told the Gaffer that I had to go in as I was injured. I could see Bally's cap going up and down in the background and he was muttering under his breath about my crossing. David Pleat's words about my left foot kept coming back to me too. Pleaty told me that he thought my left foot would have been better than it was and I bet Bally was thinking the same about my right.

I always thought that my game wasn't just about going down the line and crossing the ball, though, and Bally must have too as I was never dropped for it. I was dropped by loads of managers but the very best statement that I ever heard from a manager about being dropped was from Bally. In one of his many meetings, he told us that he'd had a player knocking on his door to tell him that he wasn't happy about being dropped and that he wanted an explanation. Bally told us all that his explanation to that player was the same as the one he was going to give us so that none of us ever came knocking on his door in the future:

> Until you knock on my door after I've put the team-sheet up and say, 'Thanks for picking me, boss' then don't ask me why I'm dropping you. I've never had a player yet thank me for picking them or ask why I've done it so I don't want any of you asking why I've dropped you.

I liked what Bally said and I agreed with him. Alan Mullery had left me out of the team for agreeing with two sentences that John Fashanu said after the Peterborough League Cup game but Howard Wilkinson at Leeds was from the same school as Alan

Ball and he didn't tell you why you weren't playing. At Palace, I never got told that I was being dropped, I'd just read it on the team-sheet. Venables just hoped that you were intelligent enough to work out that if you weren't in the side, and the team was getting results with the eleven players that were, then you weren't going to get back in.

Frustration stopped Bally from being a great manager. It was his frustration with players not being able to do what he'd asked them to do that could lead to him being destructive. He'd skirt round things sometimes but, if he ever came out and said that someone couldn't play, then you knew that he thought that person definitely couldn't play. You'd be surprised at some of the players that Bally didn't rate. I remember once, in one of his speeches, he said to Scott McGarvey, 'I've tried with you, Scott. I've tried and tried but you've just proved to me that you can't play and I've given you every opportunity.' That was in front of about five of us. By then, Scott's head was so low that it was between his ankles, not his knees.

Bally didn't suffer fools; he liked people who respected him and what he'd done in the game. Now, he had a lot of time for a lad we called 'Wurzel' – Darren Angell. He was about 6ft 5in. and played centre-half. He was a young lad who hadn't played in the first team but he still thought that he had a chance in the game. He got a bad injury but he worked ever so hard to get himself fit. Bally liked the attitude that Wurzel was showing but, bless him, most of the playing ability in that family went to his brother, Brett.

We had pre-season training and the whole club was training

together. Bally must have had a bad night as he stopped the whole session, sat us in front of him, and proceeded to talk about players and their poor attitudes. It was a hot summer's day and he was standing in a position where the sun was coming in over his shoulder. Now, Bally wasn't the most patient man; he'd been an intelligent footballer and he liked people to grasp what he was saying immediately. Where Wurzel was sitting, the sun was shining in his eyes. I could see this because I was sitting at Bally's feet and the sun was at my back.

But Wurzel didn't hold his hand up to shield his eyes. Instead, he started squinting and frowning so, therefore, he looked as if he didn't have a clue what Bally was talking about. Bally caught his eye and went for him:

And you, son. You look at me as if I'm talking fucking crap. What the fuck? You're the biggest example. You've got little or no ability and yet you're looking at me as if I'm talking shit. All I'm trying to do is help you! Get out of my sight. All of you.

We got back into the training session and Wurzel came over to me and asked me why Bally had had a go at him. He said that the sun was in his eyes. He was broken-hearted.

Kevin Russell, who went on to play 300–400 games for various clubs and became assistant manager at Wrexham, was the reason that Bally had stopped that session because he was having a bit of a nightmare. Before he had his go at Wurzel, he told us: 'I had a young lad come to see me earlier this week about a new contract. He wanted to know if he was going to get one from me and I've just been watching him in training.' He pointed at Kevin Russell, and forty-odd players turned to stare at him too. Bally went on:

> I'm going to do you the biggest favour I can, Rooster. You've got six months left on your contract and I don't want you to come into this club to train any more. All you've got to do is come in to collect your wages and, in that time, you look for a job outside football because you cannot play the game.

Rooster's head dropped; he was only eighteen years of age. By then, I was used to the things that came out of Bally's mouth, but Rooster's head was between his legs. But Bally meant it. Rooster went to see him afterwards and Bally told him that he'd never be a footballer while he had a hole in his backside. Kevin didn't have a bad career, in the end. When he walked out of that office, he realised that he had to pull his act together.

He was an interesting man to play for; the most interesting manager that I've had by far. Even just trying to read his moods when he came in was interesting. About 80 per cent of his moods were influenced by the result on the Saturday, which I didn't think was any way to go about it. One day, he even called a meeting to have a go at us because he'd had an accident in his car and he said that it was our fault. He told us that he was going to let the incident go but the fella that he'd had an accident with turned out to be Scottish, so he couldn't. I asked him why he had a problem with Scotland and he told me that when he played at Hampden

Park for England, every time he got the ball, all you could hear were 120,000 Scots impersonating his high voice.

Bally lived for the games and his whole philosophy was about the Matchday. As I've said, how we performed then determined how he was going to treat us for the next three or four days. We had a famous game against Fulham. They were a good team but we were 4–0 up by half time and it should have been ten, because we had the equivalent of a hurricane blowing behind us. Sometimes, if you're a footballing side, you prefer playing against the wind but this was probably the strongest wind I've known in a game and it was a huge advantage.

We were all pleased with ourselves, knowing the game was over, and Bally was delighted, as you can imagine, and was going round every player patting them on their heads. He gave a team talk and told us that the score could be anything by the end. He said that we could win it by six, seven or eight and we could really push their faces into the mud. He finished by telling us that we'd been outstanding and he wanted us to go on and show everyone in the stadium what a good team we were.

While he was saying this, the chief scout, Derek Healy, was going round to each player telling us that we'd played well but warning us to be careful as we'd be playing against the strong wind in the second half. He wasn't doing this loudly but Bally heard him and snapped, 'Derek, I'm doing the team talk. Leave the players alone. Their minds are set.' Derek apologised and walked out.

We then went out for the second half, with that strong wind against us, and we promptly drew the game 4–4 – and we could have lost 5–4 if Noel Blake had had his way. He could easily have got an own goal from somewhere because he'd given a penalty away and he'd had a couple of near misses from their corners. He was deadly with own goals that season to the extent that Bally used to whisper, 'Who's marking Blakey at their corners?' We never did tell Blakey that.

So we came in at the end of the game and I knew that Bally would have a go at us. He'd had a go at us when we'd drawn 0–0 away from home and got a good point at a difficult place, let alone when we were 4–0 up at home at half time and let it slip. We sat down. It was quiet at first when, all of a sudden, it started:

Gentlemen, you bunch of immature wankers. You had to go out there and try to win the game 6, 7 or 8–0. You're not happy with 4–0 at half time. You had to go gung-ho at them and they just picked you off and they could even have won the game. That just shows you how much you listen to me.

Our jaws dropped. We couldn't believe what we were hearing. We were shell-shocked enough at drawing the game, let alone hearing his words. He walked out and then all we heard was a dozen thumps coming from the treatment room. That then stopped, Bally emerged, gave us all the filthiest look you could imagine, pulled his cap down and walked out of the changing room. It turned out that the Gaffer had been in there headbutting the cabinet! Dill said, 'I told you, he's fucking mad!' I don't think that he spoke to any of the players until Thursday after that.

Despite all that, I loved playing for Bally because he wore his heart on his sleeve and, fortunately for me, he thought that I played more good games than bad ones. He often had a go at me, though, but I just didn't have it in me to tell him that I responded better to having an arm around my shoulder. He very rarely apologised for the way that he spoke to us although he had to once, six weeks after having a go at Paul Hardyman. We'd played Stoke City away and Hardy had a nightmare and it culminated in him being stretchered off. We had a meeting the next day and Hardy wasn't usually one to stand his corner but Bally ripped him to shreds. He told him that he'd been lethargic and that he couldn't catch his grandmother.

The next day, Hardy didn't come in and Dill reckoned that he hadn't recovered from Bally's bollocking and wasn't going to be a footballer any more. Later on, though, our physio came in and told us that Hardy could have died during the game because his appendix was on the way out. That explained his performance. Bally had slaughtered him, but it wasn't until he came out of hospital that he apologised to him in front of everyone. I think that's the only time I ever heard him apologise.

He actually resigned twice – most famously after a game at Wrexham. We were going through a sticky patch early in 1986 and we went down there and we scraped – and I mean scraped – a lucky win. I remember the game vividly. We were winning by the odd goal but I was having a nightmare and he took me off. I didn't even walk to the dugout. At Wrexham, in those days, we used to come out behind the goal, and I watched the rest of the game from there. With about eight minutes to go, I looked over to the dugout and the manager was starting to walk to the tunnel as he was so disgusted by our performance. We were winning at the time but we were so poor that he walked over and watched the rest of the game from behind the goal.

We won, so most of the players were happy because it was a hard place to go to, but Bally didn't speak to anyone. We got back to the hotel but, as I'd had a nightmare, I didn't want to go out. I went back to bed while all the other boys either stayed in the bar and had a drink or went into town. I woke up the next morning and had breakfast and spoke to Knighty and asked him what the Gaffer was like, but he told me that he hadn't seen him at all.

We got a message that we had to be on the coach to leave Wrexham at 10 a.m., so we all piled on and were ready to go. Everyone was there apart from the manager so they phoned his room, but there was no reply. Bally's room had been on the ground floor so we walked round. We looked through the window and there was bedding crumpled up in the corner and no sign of life apart from Bally's bags. We didn't know whether he hadn't come back to the room or had already gone home. All of a sudden, the bedding started moving and Bally was crumpled up in a little ginger ball and he jumped up and shouted, 'That's fucking offside!'

Jim Sloan went to get him and told us that Bally wasn't in a very good mood. We had some beers and whisky on the coach and were starting to have a good time, but the Gaffer just sat at the front and didn't speak to anyone. It was one of the louder trips that I can recall; we were laughing and joking and people were playing jokes and ripping seats.

As we were coming to the turn-off for the Southampton-based players, I started getting up along with Paul Mariner and Eamonn Collins but, instead of slowing down, the driver picked up speed. Marrers said that he was going to tell the driver that he'd missed the turning but the message came back that the manager wanted us all to go back to Portsmouth. We were bemused because it was 4.30 p.m. by then and we didn't know how we were going to get back to Southampton afterwards. We were all muttering, but Bally's face was as red as his hair and we could tell that he was angry.

We still thought that he was acting out of spite and that we'd get all the way to Portsmouth and then he'd tell us to make our own way back to Southampton, but Bally whispered something and got off. Word went round that there was going to be a meeting in the dressing room in ten minutes. You can imagine people like Kevin O'Callaghan and Kevin Dillon moaning. We'd been in the dressing room for about ten minutes waiting and we were getting bored. Micky Kennedy was arseholed drunk, so Billy Gilbert thought that he'd lighten the mood. He disappeared into the toilets and came out and said, 'Hey, can you do this?' and pulled his arse cheeks as wide apart as he could but, at that exact moment, Bally came into the dressing room. We were sitting there with big smiles on our faces and Bally said:

Right, gentlemen, I'll start. My captain, Micky Kennedy, he's an alcoholic. None of you care about the game. None of you care about your families. I listened to you for four and a half hours coming back on the coach and none of you care. You've got no pride; you're like a bunch of wild animals.

We were wondering where this had come from because we'd won the game. Bally went round the dressing room, dissecting everyone. But he didn't realise that he couldn't reason with people who'd had a drink and now all we wanted was to get home because we were tired. We'd heard it all before, so we weren't taking it in. Bally was in the middle of a complete and utter rant when Billy, who didn't tend to say a lot in meetings, cut him off in mid-flow and said, 'You know your problem, Bally? You're too soft.'

Everyone looked at Billy and no one spoke for what seemed like an eternity before Bally turned round and said, 'You know what? That's the most intelligent thing you've said in two years and, you're right. I resign.' He turned round and picked up his bag but, as he got to the dressing room door and opened it, we heard this cry: 'Oi! You've got my fucking bag!' He'd picked up Kevin O'Callaghan's bag by mistake! Rather than come back into the room, all we saw was his arm poking round the door and he dropped the bag and walked off. Kevin Dillon just said, 'Can we go home now?'

I was sitting next to Paul Mariner and he said to me, 'I've been in the game for eighteen years but I've never been at a club like it.' The boys broke out into an argument, which Graham Paddon couldn't control. After about six or seven minutes, Jim Sloan came in and asked what was going on as the manager had told him he was resigning, saying that the monster had turned on him and he couldn't control it any more.

We managed to get into a minibus to go back to Southampton, and we all thought that the manager was as good as his word and that he was resigning. But I'll remember this to my dying day. The next morning, we'd come in and gone to the dressing room and who walked in with his flat cap on but Bally saying, 'Morning boys, let's get down to the training ground and iron out a few of those faults.' Kevin Dillon shook his head and said: 'See, I told you, he needs help!'

CHAPTER 14

KEVIN DILLON AND KEVIN O'CALLAGHAN

The players we had at Pompey must have driven Bally crazy but, even though he signed characters that other managers wouldn't touch, we saved him time on the training ground because we knew what we were doing.

Having said that, Kevin Dillon was probably the most uncoachable player that I ever came across in my career. Bally would try to coach him, but they had so many arguments. Kevin didn't endear himself to Bally because he'd act as if he was taking no notice of the manager. Dill did very well for Pompey and scored some great goals, but he rubbed Bally up the wrong way. Bally would think that he wasn't listening to him despite him trying to give Dill the benefit of his knowledge.

Dill was totally devoid of emotion. If he played badly, it wasn't the end of the world, which is why I found it strange that he did well in coaching and as an assistant manager; he'd never dwell on it. Also, if he was having a bad time during a game, he'd never stop to think to himself that he better not try and hit a forty-yard ball, he'd still try and hit it. Dill was by far and away the best passer of the ball at the club and you'd have thought from the outside that Bally would love him but, when it came down to leaving someone out of the side, it would always be Dillon.

I remember that things were going quite well for the team and, although Dill wasn't playing particularly well, we were digging results out. That week we were due to play at Sunderland, which is where Kevin Dillon was from, and Bally decided, for a change, to pick the team early. He told us the team on the Wednesday and Dill, who had been in the side for most of the season and was going to his hometown club with all of his relatives going to the game, was left out. The Gaffer had only made the one change.

Now, on the rare occasion that Dill threw wobblers, he could really throw them. Bally took the team off for training and the ones who weren't in the side were allowed to do what they liked. We were training and, all of a sudden, Bally stopped and turned round and shouted out, 'What's Kevin Dillon doing?' There can't have been a soul near him for about 300 yards, and all Dill was doing was kicking the ball as far as he could, sauntering after it, and then kicking it back to where he'd come from. One of the coaches said that he'd tried to talk to him but Dill refused to speak to anyone.

We then had a meeting the next day about the Sunderland game. Bally was talking about their team and about a particular player on their side and he asked Dill whether this lad favoured his left side more than his right. Dill now hadn't spoken to anyone for two days and Bally was going: 'Would I be right, Dill? Would I be right? Would I? I'm talking to you, Dillon. Right, get yourself off and get out onto the training ground.' Dill got up and left and Bally said, 'You see that, lads? That's supposed to be a professional football player and he's sulking.' We won the game, but Dill didn't speak to anyone or utter a word from the moment he found out that he wasn't playing until the Monday after we came back from Sunderland. Bally put him back in the team the following week.

They'd wind each other up. We were playing Blackburn away in an FA Cup tie and Mick Quinn had scored early on but Blackburn had equalised and we came in at half time to one of Bally's legendary team talks where he 'lifted' the players: 'Well done, lads. You've done well to hang on in there considering you're playing with ten men. Kevin Dillon – did you come to the game today? All you other ten, you should be having a go at him. He's not even turned up for the match.' He then dedicated the next ten minutes to slaughtering Dill; I thought he was going to take him off, but he didn't.

We went back out and Dill was muttering under his breath about what he wanted to do to Bally. Five minutes into the second half, their keeper got the ball and cleared it. It wasn't a particularly good kick, although it still got to the D of the centre circle. It went straight to Kevin Dillon and he hit this volley from forty-five yards straight into the back of the net and we won the game. Afterwards, Bally could barely look at him and he muttered out of the side of his mouth, 'Good goal, Dill.'

Dill went off for his interviews and, when he got on the coach, we asked him what he'd said and apparently he'd told the press that the ball had come to him and he'd just hit it. He told us that what he'd really wanted to say was the truth that, as the ball was coming to him, all he could see was a little ginger face on it and he'd hit it as hard as he could. He said he didn't even know it was a shot. 'The ginger twat,' he was saying. He showed absolutely no emotions after the goal and barely spoke about it and I remember thinking then that he had some serious psychological problems.

I've already said that Kevin Dillon could smell blood like a shark. We played at Barnsley and the game was televised on *Match of the Day*, but I was having such a bad time and got substituted. I couldn't wait to get off; it was sub-zero temperatures and there was snow everywhere, and I sprinted off the pitch, straight down the tunnel. I got in the bath straight away, firstly because there was nothing else to do and secondly because, when you've had a bad game or been sent off, then you want to get in that bath, get changed as quickly as you can and get out before the manager can come in and have a go at you. As usual, I was gutted. I sat on the coach and didn't say a word to anyone. You get mixed feelings when the manager takes you off and the team scores a goal, and Dave Bamber had scored soon after I went off that day.

I was still living in Barnet in north London, as I hadn't been at Pompey for long, and I'd met the coach at Watford Gap, so I got off there on the way back and drove home. It had all been going very well for me up until then and it was probably my first really bad game. I'd not said a word from the moment I got taken off and I thought that Bally might have made a note of it and figured that it showed that I cared.

I came in on the Monday morning and, as I walked through the door, Kevin Dillon said:

Ah, there you are. You know, when I got home, I watched *Match of the Day* and I saw you run off and I haven't seen you since. Do you know, you ran off quicker than you'd run on that pitch in the whole of the game. Tell me, did you run off and go straight home?

He'd waited two whole days to have a go at me. I wanted to ask him whether he actually cared what he said to people, but I'd seen how he spoke to others and I realised that he didn't actually care about anyone's feelings, because he didn't have any himself. Luckily for me, Kevin O'Callaghan signed for us a little while later and Dillon switched his attention to him instead.

I knew Cally because he grew up in the same part of London as me. I'd known him since he was thirteen because he went to school with my brother but, between the ages of thirteen and sixteen, he became a huge moaner. I don't know what happened to him. Now, I thought that I could moan, but he was the biggest moaner ever. In fact, I have never met anyone who could moan with the same passion and intensity that he could and I initially thought it was because he was a winner, but it was actually just part of his character. I saw him moan about things that it was impossible to moan about. At his age, you shouldn't moan about bacon being too crispy or someone having more chips on their plate than you.

Cally fell out in a big way with Kevin Dillon – there was no love lost between those two. They could be so petty that they'd even refuse to call each other by their first names. They were both sponsored by Nike so they both kept ordering new boots from them just to see who Nike gave the best boots to, and then they'd boast about who Nike loved the most. They wanted to outdo each other all the time. It went from football boots to who had the best garden.

The two of them competed in everything. Absolutely everything. Who could take the best free kick. Whether it was a right-footed free kick or a left-footer. They were at it all the time. I can safely say that they're the only two players I came across in my career who were like that to this extent. They would genuinely argue about who had the better lawn at their house and they used to pass each other's houses and look at them just so they could say something about it.

It used to be funny because the arguments that they had were so ridiculous and they happened so much that the rest of us almost didn't hear them. It was so pointless. In fact, there wasn't a pointless subject that they didn't argue about, whether it was who was the fittest or who had lost the most weight. We could have lost 10–0 and, even then, they would argue about which one of them had played better. Cally was capable of doing some amazing things but, in hindsight, he might have done them just to show Dill that he was the better player.

When they'd had a drink, the abuse that they would throw at each other would become downright evil, but neither of them cared. They were just used to speaking to each other like that. It spilled onto the field and into half time too. Bally told Kevin O'Callaghan that he had to have more of an impact on the game and he said, 'I would if Dillon passed me the ball' but Dillon responded by saying, 'You know why I don't pass to you? Because you're crap!' This was going on at half time. I don't know if he did avoid passing to Cally, but most of the ball that I received during games was from Kevin Dillon.

In the end, Bally called a meeting to discuss the two of them. Bally told us that he didn't like what he was hearing from Dill and Cally and said he was going to nip the fighting in the bud because he'd had enough of it.

Whenever Bally spoke, he always used to set a scene and he'd be really dramatic. I remember once him saying to us, 'I just put my right foot into the bath and it was a bit hot and that's when it came to me...' It used to make me laugh. In this meeting, he said:

> I was walking down the corridor and I noticed that my lace was undone on my right foot so I bent down to tie it up and then I heard it: 'Hey, Callaghan? Callaghan?' 'My name's O'Callaghan.' 'Whatever it is, I bet you haven't got a pair of boots like these.'
>
> Gentlemen, I heard two grown footballers arguing over who's got the best pair of boots. It's got to stop. And, then, to top it all, they moved on from that to who has got the best garden. Who has got the best lawn? And you know what I did, gentlemen? I turned around, took a slow walk up that long corridor and shook my head.

It went quiet and then Kevin Dillon said, 'See, that's your fault, Callaghan.' That's what every day was like between them.

VINCE

Without doubt, Cally was the greatest moaner I ever played football with but, to go with his moaning, he also had the loudest tut that I'd ever heard, and it killed the other players, to the extent that they would want to fight him after games. Micky Kennedy threatened to hit him and Paul Tait did too, but it wasn't because of anything that Cally had said; it was all because of how loudly he'd tut if he didn't get the ball. I remember in one game even I told Cally that I'd see him at half time and, along with Mick Kennedy and Taity, Blakey, Billy Gilbert and Mick Quinn all did the same. His moaning and tutting got to us that much.

The last thing that you want to hear when you're having a bad game is a teammate moaning at you and Cally would always have a problem with someone. In the end, you'd just react. We played Shrewsbury, and Mick Kennedy won two crunching tackles – Cally called for it on the left, but Mick tried to knock a cross in and it went out for a goal kick. Cally tutted loudly and Mick turned round and screamed at him, 'If you tut at me one more time, I'm going to come over there and break your neck!'

I christened him Albert Tatlock, after the old *Coronation Street* character, because he moaned for fun. He even upset our kit manager before a game. No one else other than Cally moaned about the kit. He'd moan that his socks were too tight and that's why he had a calf muscle problem. Another time, we were geeing each other up just before a game when we desperately had to get a result, and, in the middle of it all, Cally turned around to the kit manager and asked him why we couldn't have shorts that had the dangly string at the front when you tied them. He told him that the shorts were a fucking joke – at ten to three when we had to get a result in the game. At five to three, when we were out on the pitch, he was coming up to the players and explaining that when he was at Ipswich they had shorts like that.

As a result he did have a few enemies at the club amongst the backroom staff. He knew more about injuries than the physio did and would tell him what treatment he should have. He knew what formation we should have and what team should be playing. I was a big moaner but I left it on the pitch; Cally, on the other hand, just couldn't leave it there.

Peter Osgood was brilliant with him. You couldn't have a go at Ossie because he'd just cut you to the quick. He was the Youth team coach at the time and was very protective of his kids, and they loved him for it. He wouldn't have anyone bullying them; he was like Bally in miniature. I remember Cally watching the Youth team train and, when Ossie came back in, shouting out to him, 'Oi, Ossie! What are you coaching them kids? A couple of them are fucking shit.'

Ossie turned round to Cally and said:

How many England caps have you got? Oh, that's right. None. You played for the Republic of Ireland even though you're from the East End of London. Is that because you couldn't get into the England team? I haven't told you that I've got a couple of England caps, have I?

Cally just sat there. It didn't matter how much money you'd made from the game – if someone had a better career than you then there was no argument.

Cally could back it up with his ability though. He was very confident and had a good left foot, but that could be overlooked because of his moaning. If he did knock a bad pass then it was never his fault. You'd either made a bad run or hadn't read what he was thinking or he hadn't been given the ball early enough. Paul Hardyman was the nicest guy in the world and once he got carried off at Stoke and was taken to hospital. As he was being put onto the stretcher, Cally was actually having a go at him and telling him that if he'd given him the ball earlier then he wouldn't have got whacked. He didn't even have any sensitivity when his teammate had just got injured.

CHAPTER 15

PROMOTION, RELEGATION AND SOME POMPEY LEGENDS

Despite everything that went on, we had a good side at Portsmouth. We missed out on promotion twice before we eventually went up and the reason for that is we had something missing during those seasons. We used to struggle at home and we needed players to want the ball and to stand up and be counted but we didn't always have that.

Bally changed, too, in the year that we ended up getting promotion, because he realised that you can't just 'out-football' people and you can't just out-muscle people either; sometimes you have to do a bit of both. In the two years when we just missed out, wherever we played, we played 4-4-2 with two wingers and two down the middle, but Bally finally figured that, perhaps, that wasn't the way to go about it.

We had to be more disciplined, so Bally had a meeting with us at the start of the promotion year and told us that we weren't going to be so cavalier any more. He said that he'd realised that playing two wingers every time was nonsense, so we'd only be doing that in home games from then on, and not when we played away. There were quite a few games when we went in with an extra defensive player instead. I was happy to say that he only left me out once and that, usually, it would be Kevin O'Callaghan who would miss out when Mick Tait would come in. Cally would, obviously, get the hump and moan about it. He used to ask Bally if he only had two numbers in his substitute's case – seven and eleven – as it was only ever me or him that got taken off. He even said once that he was going to throw the number seven away.

In those more physical games, we'd then have Tait and Mick Kennedy who were old-school footballers who loved a tackle and wouldn't have looked out of place in the '70s. The main creative element in the side would be Kevin Dillon, who could pick a pass out of anywhere and then, up front, we'd have a striker and a goalscorer in Paul Mariner and Mick Quinn. I knew my role; I was just another creative element in the team. I still had to compete, but I was expected to create too.

Anyone that came into our team, like Kevin Ball, who ended up being a legend at Sunderland, all had the same mentality. We knew what was expected of us when we were playing for Alan Ball: we were expected to die for the cause.

I even got sent off for Portsmouth at Palace when we needed to win to get promoted but we ended up losing 1–0. I pushed Andy Gray over. There were two reasons for that: the first was that I went back to my old club and we needed to win so my emotions were heightened. To be fair to them, Palace fans never gave me stick but, that day, they weren't shy in letting me know that they were winning 1–0 and we needed to win the game to go up. What compounded it, though, was Andy Gray was time-wasting and I'd known him since he was eleven years of age. He used to go and stay at John Burridge's house when he was a lad but now he'd turned into a giant and was taking the mickey out of me. I'd given him a couple of pairs of boots as a young kid, which didn't help my feelings about the situation so, out of frustration, I pushed him over the wall right in front of the linesman. Luckily, I didn't have a long walk to go off.

We ended up going up without playing. Our rivals for promotion, Oldham, lost 2–0 to Shrewsbury, which meant we were promoted. My sending-off and the defeat at Palace didn't matter. I remember that night really well. I phoned a couple of players and we met at a pub in the town centre and there are still a few pictures of me floating about with the notorious Pompey 657 crew celebrating promotion. We still had one game left and I could be a very rich man now, because there wasn't so much scrutiny on betting in those days. I'd have had any money you like on us getting beaten by Sheffield United on the last day of the season because some of the players weren't sighted again until the Saturday morning of the game.

At Portsmouth, I understood what going up meant to the Pompey fans so I had more empathy with them than I had with the supporters at Palace. I was nineteen when we went up with Palace in 1979 and we'd been used to winning all of the time. We'd played in front of 16- or 17,000 people when we won the FA Youth Cup in 1977, which we knew we were going to win – and we knew that we were going to win it the following year too. It wasn't as if we were playing mugs but we knew, at Palace, that we were better than anyone else so we didn't appreciate success as much. The more I think about it, winning all the time at Palace didn't teach us anything. Pompey had suffered lows, which made promotion so much more satisfying.

We went down straight away, though, and I hadn't expected that to happen. It wasn't a very good start to the season for me, personally. I was still serving a suspension for getting sent off at Palace at the end of the previous season, so I missed the first few games. To be honest, I only ever played one good game in every five that year and my form was sporadic, but I also think that Bally had lost it a little bit.

It was a difficult club to run but he played Paul Mariner at centre-half for the first few games because Blakey was injured, which was never going to help, so we didn't have the best of starts and then we couldn't turn it around. We didn't win our first game until the August Bank Holiday against West Ham and that was our fifth match of the season. I thought that we might be OK after that, but there was a game against Tottenham when I got brought down at 0–0 with about five minutes to go and Kevin Dillon missed a penalty, and then, against Arsenal, the same thing happened with about ten minutes to go. Winning those games could have given us impetus but we couldn't get any going and we ended up getting stupid results.

I do believe that if we'd started properly then we'd have stayed up. The big derby down here is against Southampton; they didn't sell any of our fans tickets for the away game there, but we went to the Dell and beat them 2–0, and we thought that would be the start of it. We also won at Tottenham, so the nucleus was there, but we couldn't get a consistent run together. Bally couldn't see it either. He thought the team was good enough, so he didn't change it – but we weren't. It was a real shame.

MICK CHANNON

Mick Channon was the driest footballer I've ever met. If you took swear words out of his vocabulary then he'd be a near mute but, in spite of that, I learned a lot from him. One of the main things that I learned was that people can't have a go at you if you're straight with them; they'll only have a go at you if you lie.

The only reason someone might not like Mick was because he was so black-and-white about things, but his attitude was that if you didn't like him, he didn't care. Noel Blake used to tell me that he didn't like Micky and he was going to knock him out. Now, usually, because of Blakey's size, people used to skirt round issues with him – I've seen players, coaches and managers all do it. They'd all pander to Blakey and tell him that he was great in the air and that he'd always win his tackles and if the ball came into the box then he should just get it away. But, really, what they were trying to say is that that was all he was good at.

Mick wasn't like that and Blakey didn't like it. We weren't playing particularly well in one game and Bally was talking to us, trying to put it right, but Micky Channon, in his West Country accent just said, 'Blakey. Big man. You can't play. All you've got to do is head it if it's in the air and kick it away if it comes to you on the ground. Don't worry about controlling it or anything like that because you can't do it.' With that, Blakey got up and he had to go into the toilets to cool down, and all you could hear was Micky shouting after him, 'Don't walk away when I'm talking to you, Big Man. I'm just trying to tell you the truth!' I thought Blakey was going to hit him.

This happened at Carlisle away, and one of the greatest things in my life happened on that journey home. Micky and Bally had to get back quickly and I asked if I could go back with them in the car, and I'd never heard anything like the conversation they had during that drive. They were so forthright and honest with each other. Micky just didn't care what he was saying. He was talking to the manager as if he was an ordinary Joe off the street: 'I can't believe you played him, Bally… that decision you made was a joke… if you're not careful, Bally, then you're going to get the sack.'

To be honest, the one thing that got in Mick's way at Pompey was the actual football and he complained about it often enough. On a matchday, we used to have to report between 1.30 p.m. and 1.45 p.m., but he used to come in at 2.15 p.m., put his kit on, and then disappear. We didn't see him again until ten to three because he'd put all his bets on and he wanted to watch the races.

We played Fulham in my second season at Pompey and this illustrates just how much notice Mick took of the team, the game and everything else. We'd been holding on by the skin of our teeth to the top three places and Bally told us that he was going to throw some kids in. Now Kevin Ball is a major winner, and ended up having a really good career, especially at

Sunderland. He played in a similar style to Micky Kennedy. He was a young player then but, despite that, everything he used to do was aggressive; there was absolutely no fear in him.

Now, bear in mind, this was a very important game. We drew 1–1 and it was a disappointing result, but we'd had a chance when the ball came in from the right and Kevin Ball could have knocked it in with his tongue but he threw himself full length at the ball and tried to head it with all of his power. He was horizontal to the ground and he put it wide and we all stood there in disbelief, staring at him.

At the end of games, I was always one of the last out of the bath, and after that game Micky was still in there too because he used to like soaking his old bones. He was lying there swearing as usual about us throwing a win away. With that, Kevin Ball got into the bath. He'd been delayed getting changed as he'd been having some treatment. Now, Kevin Ball didn't like Micky Channon at all and when he got into that bath, he started having a pop at him.

Micky was sat in the corner and didn't say anything and Kevin said, 'There's not enough of us taking responsibility. It's do or die here. We've got to get results.' He was still only about eighteen but he was going on about our attitude and saying that we didn't want to win enough tackles and that it made him sick. With that, he got out of the bath and Micky Channon had still not said anything for five minutes. As God is my witness, he then turned to me and said, 'What's that lad's name again? Did you hear him going on? He was the fucking worst one out of the lot of us! What about that chance he missed? What was his name again?' He'd played a vital League match with someone and he did not know who they were.

He didn't care. When we used to have team talks on a Thursday, he'd be trying to get away as he had to be at Newmarket for the racing. On a Friday, we used to train for an hour, tops, and yet Mick would only come in for ten or fifteen minutes. But, to be fair to him, his career was winding down by then. Bally actually reckoned that Mick got better as he got older and he was probably the best one-touch player that I played with after the Gaffer himself. It was an experience playing with him.

Micky told me his philosophy one day when he was sitting in the dressing room. He said:

> Do you know what makes a football club? It's that team that runs out on a Saturday because, without that team that runs out on a Saturday, there wouldn't be a football club. Without those eleven players, the rest of this club wouldn't be here. And, do you know what? Those reserves are parasites. I hate reserves.
>
> Every morning, when I come in, I'm going to open that door to their dressing room and say, 'Morning, Reserves' because they'll hate that.

…and he used to do it without fail. He'd come in to our changing room every morning giggling to himself going, 'They hate me but I don't give a fuck.' He used to emphasise the word 'reserves' and he used to make it last about ten seconds: 'Morning, Reseeeeeeeeeeeeeeeeeeeeeeeeerves!'

NOEL BLAKE

The first time I met Noel Blake was when Palace beat Birmingham City at Selhurst Park. I came out of the dressing room and I don't know if it was because I was black or not but he pulled me over to him and said, 'I want you to find me the steward that hit me and I'll be waiting here for him.' I didn't know what he was talking about, but he said that one of the stewards had hit him when the crowd had run on the pitch at the end of the game and he wanted to find him. I told him that I'd be back in a minute and that was the last time I spoke to him until I went to Portsmouth. Two and a half years later, I asked him if he ever got hold of the steward…

As far as playing ability was concerned, he was a good centre-half. He was a great header of the ball and him and Billy Gilbert got voted into the League Team of the Year in the second year that Billy was there. Blakey was considered to be a hard man but he didn't actually get a lot of bookings or sending offs; Billy was the one who picked up all the points. They had it off pat: when the ball was in the air, Billy would drop off and, eight times out of ten, Blakey would win it cleanly and, if the ball was knocked up to the striker's feet, then Billy was very good at reading that and would either win the ball in front or go through the back of the player.

Billy would get booked more often because you got penalised more for challenges on the deck than in the air, but Blakey was always a very clean jumper as well; he didn't throw elbows and he had a very good spring. Quite rightly, he's a legend at Pompey and he won the crowd over even though he didn't have the best of starts at the club. He's a legend to all the players as well but that's because of what went on in the dressing room and the extraordinary things that he would come out with.

As an example, we'd just been on a pre-season tour and, when we came back, Bally called a meeting. He told us that he'd just been to see Luton Town play and they had given him an idea that we were going to use. In football, if you don't call out a name when the ball is coming to you then you give away an indirect free-kick for ungentlemanly conduct but, if you shout, say, 'Leave it, Tim,' then the other team know exactly what you're going to do, which is fine.

Bally told us that Luton shouted, 'Sid' and 'Fred': 'Sid' meant to flick it and 'Fred' meant to dummy it. Bally thought that this code was brilliant. He asked us if anyone had any ideas as to what we could use as names. We were all standing there thinking about it when Blakey piped up: 'How about Swede? We've all come back from Sweden so how about Swedey Swede?' As hard as we normally tried not to laugh directly in front of Blakey, on this occasion, we all just rolled around and were laughing in his face. For the rest of the session, we were all shouting, 'Swede!' whenever he had the ball.

For a man who worked so hard in the gym and, apparently, had great stomach muscles, he had no stamina. That was possibly his only weakness as a centre-half. A lot of teams realised that you couldn't beat Blakey in the air so you had to make him work very hard and run into corners and channels and tire him out because his recovery wasn't the best in the world. Blakey would rather play against someone who was eight feet tall and have a battle with them.

I always used to laugh as Blakey's playing boots actually curled up at the end; his toes pointed up at 90 degrees. He did think that he could play, though, which may actually have been his other weakness. Bally used to encourage me to give the team as much width as possible whether I was on the right or left. During one game, I'd barely touched the ball, so I went over to the other flank to see if it would be any different.

The opposition went on the attack, but it broke down and Blakey had the ball at his feet. He hit this pass to the left wing and it was still rising as it flew out of the ground. If you were twelve feet tall, you wouldn't have got a head on it. It was on the north stand side, and that was some feat to get it out of the ground. As it went out of play, Blakey put his hands on his hips and shouted, 'Where the fuck is he? Why don't he just stay on one wing?' Honestly, the ball still hasn't come down.

Blakey scored five or six own goals in his first season at Pompey. At first it was a serious issue but, in the end, it just became a joke and we used to laugh about it. We played one game where the opposition had a centre-forward playing up front called Mick Ferguson, who used to play at Coventry. Neil Webb had scored to put us one up, but then they fired a cross in and Ferguson went to the near post, Blakey was a bit late to track him, and it rocketed into the roof of the net. Ferguson took all of the applause.

When we came in at half time, Bally was moaning that the marking was a bit off, but the big man said that he'd slipped and that's why Ferguson had got there before him and got his volley in and he couldn't do anything about it. What we didn't know at the time was that was a blatant lie. The game was shown on the telly that night and, when we watched it, Blakey didn't slip, he beat Ferguson to the ball and he smashed it into the roof of his own net. He told me later that he thought that as they'd both got to the ball at the same time, he might be able to get away with it. We walked in on the Monday morning and we were looking at each other going, 'Blakey's goal, wasn't it? He bulleted it into the net!' It showed us that all the own goals were actually getting to him to the extent that he was trying to deny them.

He must have broken the record for scoring own goals. He got another one when we were playing at home in the promotion run-in, and things were getting a bit tense. There was a scramble in our box and Micky Kennedy tried to clear the ball and shouted, 'Away!' but it hit Blakey on the stomach and flew into the net. That one couldn't be helped and we drew 1–1. We were all sitting there after the game but no one was saying anything because it had now gone beyond a joke. All of a sudden, Blakey broke the silence and said, 'Do you know what? I'm going to have to stop doing my stomach exercises. That would have hit any other person and hurt them but because of my abs it's flown in.' We all just stared at him.

IVAN GOLAC

Bally had signed Mick Channon from Southampton and he thought that he'd had another masterstroke when he signed

Ivan Golac from them too. Now Ivan was a quality player but all of those players who played at Southampton at that time, like Keegan, Ball, Channon and Chris Nicholl, were outspoken and straight-talking. They were such good players and so experienced that they didn't feel the need to be sensitive; they were blunt with each other and they didn't take what was said to heart. Ivan Golac was actually less sensitive than Mick Channon but, because of his accent, what he said sounded endearing and you didn't realise that he was actually having a go at you.

Ivan had a good career but he was tight; he loved his money. In those days, we used to meet at the club and then go to the training ground and all the players used to take it in turns to share the driving. He had a 2.8i Granada but, for about two weeks, Ivan didn't offer to drive once so we asked him one day for a lift and he said, 'My car stays here. You don't pay me to drive my car to training ground. You pay me to drive to club. Someone else take me to training ground.' He was the first person to have a one-seater Granada!

He was only with us on loan for six weeks, but I loved the time that I spent with him. He used to change next to me and I remember him coming in and he took his shirt off and he had a vest on. Micky Kennedy was a tough northerner and he just started laughing at him. Ivan was a real footballing centre-half and he ended up taking Micky under his wing but, to this day, Micky doesn't realise that it was because Ivan thought that Micky couldn't play football. Ivan told me he was going to try and improve him as a footballer so, every day, after training finished, Ivan used to tell him to practise some skills with him.

Anyone else would wonder why he was only working with them but Micky thought it was great and he loved Ivan for it. Ivan even tried it with me one day. He said to me, 'How have you managed to play football so long when you can't cross a ball?' I laughed and told him that I wasn't Micky Kennedy so he should leave me alone!

He used to call me 'Wince' because he couldn't pronounce the 'V'. I sat next to him on the coach going up to Barnsley once and he said to me, 'Oh, Wince, Wince, Wince. Look at this team. Only you, me and Webby can play. We just play triangles all the time – me, you and Webby.' I had a nightmare that day and got taken off and the final straw was when Barnsley had a throw-in and Ivan told me to mark in front of the player that he was marking. They took the throw-in and he said, 'Winny' and I thought that meant that he had the ball so I ducked, the Barnsley player got it, went through and nearly scored. I asked him what he was doing as I was having a bad enough game as it was and he goes, 'I said "Win it"!'

I looked up and I could see Bally taking his cap off and shaking his head. It happened a few times after that but it was my first taste of the Gaffer saying to me, 'Come off, son. You're embarrassing yourself, your family, me and those people that have come to watch you. I'm doing you a favour.' I ran in and I had a big dollop of snow on my head and I sat in the changing room gutted.

CHAPTER 16

THE CAST OF GREMLINS

MICK QUINN

Our training at Pompey was based on possession football because it was Bally's pet hate if you gave the ball away, so we'd do hours of small-sided games every week where we could be awarded goals for making a certain number of passes. What Bally was trying to do was to encourage us not to give the ball away, but he also wanted to encourage the other team to press quickly to win the ball back.

On Quinny's first day, we had a similar session and Bally told us that eight consecutive passes would get a goal. Even though we had a lot of players that liked to get stuck in; most of them were reasonably comfortable on the ball too and we were passing and moving, knocking it around, and Bally was counting the passes loudly until one team lost the ball and we had to start again.

But Quinny wasn't getting involved in any of the passing; he was just standing by the goal that he was attacking. Kevin Ball was marking him and he loved it because Quinny was just standing still. We'd got up to seven passes and eventually got the ball to Quinny's feet and two people, including me, were up supporting him. All he had to do was give it to one of us and we'd score a goal, but he tried to turn and shake Kevin Ball off and he shot from an impossible position and it flew over the bar.

Bally shouted at him to knock off a simple ball as he'd have got a goal for another pass, and a couple of us said the same thing to him, but Quinny turned round and, in his big, broad, Scouse accent, shouted, 'Correct me if I'm wrong but you win games by scoring actual goals. There's the onion bag so get it in there! Fucking eight passes … just get it in the goal. If you pass me the ball, you ain't going to get a pass back!'

That summed up Quinny to a T. He was a natural goalscorer. Nothing else existed to him apart from scoring. That type of player is single-minded and they're not happy if the team wins but they don't score. Something I've noticed is that a team with an out-and-out goalscorer very rarely win prizes on a consistent basis. Those players can be selfish and that affects the team.

Quinny could shield the ball well but it was all to his own ends. We used to ask him why he couldn't hold the ball up if it was for the team's benefit and to get players in around him and he didn't have an answer. You could forget about playing a one-two with him. You'd knock the ball up to him and it would bounce off him but if you knocked it to him around the box, it was like going into a spider's web; a defender could not get that ball off him. Quinny's touch only ever let him down if it was in the build-up; it was perfect if there was a shooting opportunity, and that is a fact. He was happy as long as it ended up in the onion bag.

Billy Gilbert wasn't a great one for tolerating people who were out-and-out goalscorers, but he put up with Quinny, because Quinny punched his weight. He was aggressive. Quinny scored goals wherever he went but you could never play a young kid next to him because that young kid would not make the room to let Quinny be a predator. They'd make their own runs and expect Quinny to make room for them but he wouldn't do it.

Bally had Mick Channon up front with him at the start and Quinny did well with him while he was still at the club and then, after Mick Channon left, he played up front with Nicky Morgan. They were similar players although Nicky was a better footballer than Quinny but there was only ever going to be one player that Bally was going to keep, and that was Quinny.

When we went up, Bally signed Paul Mariner and, that season, Paul only got about five goals, which isn't a lot for a centre-forward. Quinny got about twenty-eight. Marrers was experienced enough to let Quinny have the limelight. Me and Kevin O'Callaghan chipped in with eight and ten goals respectively, which helped the side.

There were a lot of rumours surrounding players that Bally supposedly didn't get on with, but it nearly always boiled down to the fact that he didn't think they were doing enough on the field. Alan Biley was an example of that. Quinny was an out-and-out goalscorer, like Biles was, but his sole aim in the game was to score goals and he'd get hurt scoring goals or trying to do so.

Quinny didn't worry about getting hurt. You knew what you were going to get from him, whatever the conditions were. He was so single-minded and he'd have definitely passed the Frank Lord Test, because he certainly would have kicked his gran to score a goal. And all Bally wanted to know was that if there was a chance, even if the player didn't have the best ability or was having a nightmare in a game, that player would be prepared to do anything to try and score a goal. I'm really not having a go at Alan Biley here, because he scored a lot of goals for Pompey, but Quinny would do whatever it took.

I lost count of the number of times that people came up to me and spread terrible rumours about Bally and Alan Biley's relationship, but it was all rubbish. People just couldn't understand why someone who scored two goals one week might not get selected for the following game, but if they were to look at the facts and break them down, they'd see why. Alan Biley had a decent career – he scored goals for loads of clubs like Portsmouth, Everton, Brighton and Derby – but, to me, he was too much of a nomad and couldn't settle. Biles had to play alongside someone up front and he kept searching for that perfect partner and club.

The best English goalscorer that I can remember was Gary Lineker, although Shearer got close to him as he got older. Before Euro '96, when Shearer didn't score for twelve games, there was a load of talk that he should be dropped but Venables showed what a great manager he was by sticking with him. Shearer went on to score a load of goals for England after they played Sheringham alongside him and found a system that suited him.

I'd be very interested to compare the percentage of goals the top strikers from my day like Gary Lineker, Clive Allen, Micky

Quinn and even Alan Biley scored away from home, compared to in home games. I would say that the great goalscorers probably got as many as 40 per cent of their goals away from home, and that makes a huge difference to a team. Arguably, Lineker's greatest goalscoring feat was when he scored all four for England away from home in Spain. I never rated him as a footballer, and I played against him a few times but, as a goalscorer, his record speaks for itself. No matter where he played, Lineker was a threat and you could say that about Mick Quinn too.

Quinny was a great finisher but the best goalscorer I played with was Clive Allen. He just had a bit more variation. He could score from any distance whereas you wouldn't expect Quinny to get on a free kick from thirty yards out. Clive could just as easily score with a dead ball from thirty yards or tap one in from a yard or do a piece of individual skill and score. Quinny was stronger, more physical, and a better header of the ball and was more aggressive, while Clive was more subtle. Both of them lived for goals.

If you look at Quinny's record, a lot of players suffered in terms of their goal return to get the chances for him – like Paul Mariner – but it's a gift to stick the ball into the net and you can't coach it. You have to be single-minded. When Quinny came out with that comment in training, it summed up why Bally had signed him.

It was completely different to what I'd experienced at Palace because I'd been raised on the idea of teamwork under Venables and, in the system that we played, the hardest-working players on our side were the forwards. Dave Swindlehurst and Ian

Walsh only scored eleven or twelve goals apiece when we got promoted to the top flight, which wasn't great for your main strikers, but because of the system we played, every time they lost the ball, they defended from the front, which Venables liked. So we had the best defensive record when we went up. To the layman, it would have looked like we had a great back four but any manager will tell you that you can't just defend with your defenders. The whole team has to do their bit.

Quinny has got a massive reputation. He was very quiet when he first joined, but he ended up being one of the leaders of the Gremlins. He got in with the heavy drinkers like Tait, Blake, Kennedy and O'Callaghan, and he went over the hill and came back a Gremlin. I remember the manager was having a pop at him about his weight, as he'd put a few pounds on. Bally told him to start thinking about his diet.

On one of the many afternoons that we all met up at the pub, we asked Quinny what he was going to do about his weight, and he told us that he was going to take on board what the Gaffer had said and cut down on his drinking. I then announced that I was going to get the next round in and all the boys shouted out the drinks that they wanted. I asked Quinny what he was going to have and he said 'Vodka and tonic', so I reminded him that, five minutes ago, he'd said he was going to start a diet. In response to this, he said, 'Oh, yeah. I better start as I mean to go on. Make that vodka and slimline tonic.' For the next two years, it was vodka and slimline, as he was watching his weight, but I guess when you were drinking twenty of them, it didn't matter so much.

He was probably the biggest joker in the team and I remember him getting himself in a spot of bother and ending up in Winchester Prison for a couple of weeks and we missed him for a few matches. The manager called a meeting on the Friday before one of those games and told us that he had a letter from Micky Quinn from inside Winchester Prison. Quinny had asked the Gaffer to read it to the boys as he wanted to inspire us for Saturday's game. Bally read this letter out and it started with Quinny saying that he missed us and, as this letter went on, you'd have thought that it was *Papillon* and that he had been inside for about ten years.

He described the conditions he was living in and said that he had someone looking after him and he hoped that he'd see us soon. We were all laughing and it put us in such good spirits that we lost the game the next day. Quinny was back in the team the week after he got out of prison, when we played at Ipswich and we won 1–0, and all was fine for about three weeks until the police came down to the training ground to arrest him again, but it was a case of mistaken identity. Typical day at Portsmouth, really.

POMPEY CHARACTERS

The characters were so diverse at Pompey. It was like Bally was putting a jigsaw together. Every player that Bally got rid of, he replaced with a real character. They were amazing people and they all had their own stories to tell. I came across more characters playing for Portsmouth than anywhere else in my career. There were a lot of them who I'd played against before when I was at Palace, but I'd had no concept of what they were really like as people. I'd known some of them, like Cally and Kevin Dillon, as youngsters and, at times, I couldn't help wondering whether I'd changed to them as much as they'd changed to me.

Scott McGarvey was there when I first joined and I felt very sorry for him. He was a lovely bloke, but he was a leper in Portsmouth. You didn't even want to be seen to be talking to him on the pitch because he'd taken over from Mark Hateley and that was sacrilege to the supporters. To his credit, Scott never let it get him down, but he always said that he wished Bally hadn't told the local papers that he'd make the fans forget about Hateley. He reckoned they might as well put it on his gravestone. Every morning Bally came in, he looked at Scott, and you could see him thinking, 'You are the biggest mistake I've ever made.' It was a shame for Scott because he was such a nice guy.

Scott was really good friends with Nicky Morgan, and they were always together. Nicky scored eight goals in his first eight games one season and Bally said that he was the best hold-up man in the business, but Bally and Nicky fell out and Nicky ended up being sold to Stoke. To be fair, Nicky did sample the south coast nightlife well before the Gremlins came into being. Scott and Nicky weren't shy about letting people know that they'd been out either. That didn't help because Nicky wasn't the fittest at that time. Later on in my career when I was at Leeds, I saw that Bally had got the Stoke job and the first person he sold was Nicky Morgan. I spoke to Nicky a few years later and he reckoned that he'd been a legend at Stoke until Bally turned up.

The thing about Pompey was that Bally signed players who you'd think were decent pros but they'd all turn out to be rebels. They had some psychological problems. I mean, I got fucked up at Crystal Palace and Billy Gilbert was the same. Dill had a bad time at Birmingham and I'd played against Micky Kennedy loads of times and he'd had a similar background. He always wound opposition players up; it was part of his make-up.

The thing about Micky was that he was the nicest guy in the world off the pitch but then he would have a complete change of character for ninety minutes; he would become a different person. I never even saw him shake hands with the opposition after a game. The only time he'd shake hands was when he was captain at the toss. He just didn't care, but if you ask anyone who knew him, they'll say he was great company, and he still is. But some of the trouble that he started!

Bally didn't encourage the bad behaviour but he did encourage the camaraderie. It sometimes did get heated, though. I've lost count of how many fights there were at the training ground. There have always been fights in training at every club but we used to have one a week because we had people who didn't hold back, like Micky Kennedy, Paul Tait, Billy and Blakey. Bally loved it. We'd just let people get on with the fights; even Bally would stand to one side, watching. There'd be no one pulling people apart, but it would be over as quickly as it started.

We were a physically strong unit. Paul Wood and Kevin Dillon had the best stamina along with Mick Kennedy, especially as he pushed his body to the limit off the field. Kenny Swain was an excellent pro, as was Paul Hardyman and Kevin Ball, although Kevin couldn't do anything without being aggressive. He was probably one of the most physically strong people that I came across. He was always one of the first picks in the five-a-sides because he didn't think it was fun to play in a different position; he just wanted to play at the back and hurt people.

We used to have some battles on the pitch too. We had a problem with Blackburn and we also had a flare up in the tunnel after a game with Wimbledon. They were the main games for us in terms of a physical rivalry and we always knew that it would go off when we played them. Dennis Wise bit my finger once and it was at that point that I realised Wisey was the spawn of Satan. He wouldn't let go of it, and he thought it was hilarious when I confronted him about it in the Players' Lounge after the game.

The biggest flare-up I was involved in during my career was during a night game against Millwall. There were still a few players around at that time who you just knew you shouldn't fuck with. There was a lad who used to play at my Sunday club and he was well known even then. He looked twenty-five even when he was fifteen and he went on to be a cult hero at Millwall. His name was Terry Hurlock.

In this particular game, Hurlock and Kennedy were going at it. Bally had set us up for this match and dropped Cally, so we had a midfield of Kennedy and Tait and it was one of the few times that we didn't go in with two wingers. Bally stocked the team up with heavy artillery and Millwall had Hurlock, Les

Briley and Fashanu up front so it was always going to be a real war. Early on, there was a brawl involving about sixteen players and even the referee stood to one side and I stood with him because it wasn't my scene either.

On a football field, players are usually the biggest cowards in the world because they fight knowing that nine times out of ten it's going to get stopped quickly. It's not like a Sunday morning game where people threaten to see you after the match, although that did happen at Pompey sometimes. Billy Gilbert waited in the tunnel a few times. I suppose we were the nearest you could get to a pub team. But, in that match at Millwall, the players were actually trying to hurt each other.

Near the end of the game, I remember thinking to myself that Fashanu was a real handful and I was really glad that we didn't have to face him again for the rest of the season. Afterwards, Bally was going on about Fash because he'd caused us all sorts of problems. We were due to play Wimbledon on the Saturday and who did they sign a couple of days before the game? Fash. And not only did he play in exactly the same way and terrorise our entire team, but he smashed Kevin Dillon's cheekbone to boot. We missed Dill after that because he was our one real creative talent that season.

Justin and John Fashanu were the only two centre forwards that I've seen bully Noel Blake although, I suppose, Billy Whitehurst did too, to be fair. Billy and Blakey had a bust up in the tunnel at Hull, but they were like spinning tops because it was a hard surface and they were both wearing metal studs. They were sliding around and, needless to say, no one else got involved in it. Blakey might also add Mick Harford to that short list, but I think that Mick had the Indian sign over Blakey from their days at Birmingham.

Because of the way that so many of our players acted, other people's characters were brought out. People like Kevin Ball and Paul Wood were quiet lads when I first got to the club and they just got on with their jobs, maybe just wanting to scrape a living out of the game, but they went on to play hundreds of games at various clubs; playing for Portsmouth toughened them up. Liam Daish was another. I think that the stick that they took from the other lads made them a bit harder.

When you get stick, you go one of two ways: you either crumble or it makes you harder. You either take it and you give it back – or you don't and then you suffer. Liam Daish, when he was only sixteen and a half, had a fight with Blakey. Blakey pushed him, but Liam pushed him back harder. Blakey is not a small geezer but Liam stood there toe to toe with him. That was the sort of character we had at the club. It was a good place to be.

I remember Andy Ritchie coming down just before Quinny joined. Bally told us that he'd signed Andy, he'd taken his medical, and he was going to do well for Pompey and Andy even joined in with us at training. Andy might not thank me for telling people this, but the next day, Bally called one of his meetings that he became famous for and told us that we weren't signing Andy any more as he'd failed the medical. With that, the door opened and Andy walked in crying his eyes out and told us that he was just getting his stuff.

When Andy walked out, Bally said, 'You see that lads. There's someone there who was desperate to play for this club. Do it for him.' Bally could be quite emotional but, as soon as he finished that sentence, you couldn't hear what he was saying next for the laughter, led by Kevin Dillon. Dill was his usual compassionate self. He was going, 'What sort of man is that? Crying over a move! Pathetic!' You'd think that there would have been a respectful silence after he left and, at any other club, that would have been quite a sad moment because he had been desperate to join Pompey.

I was a little bit sad because I knew Andy from my England Youth days and he was a nice lad. We all called him Desperate Dan, as he looked like the character from *The Dandy* and we were all picturing Desperate Dan crying because he hadn't got his move. In hindsight, though, if Andy hadn't failed his medical then we wouldn't have had Quinny.

Quinny came along and he just fit into this jigsaw puzzle. Each player had their own unique character; there wasn't one player at Pompey who behaved in the same way as someone else. New signings were the same. By then, I was experienced enough that I tried to make new players feel more comfortable, and part of that was by taking the mickey out of them. That's what I always tried to do and I was the one who gave out the nicknames.

Bally signed Kenny Swain, who had won the European Cup at Aston Villa, and Kenny, for a minute, thought that he would bring a bit of professionalism to the club but, from the very first meeting he had, he got it ripped out of him. He'd won the League, the European Cup, played at Villa and Chelsea and he made the mistake of thinking that Portsmouth was like a normal club.

Bally used to ask players in meetings if they had an opinion, but we all knew that there was no point in giving yours because it wasn't going to be right. But Kenny took it upon himself to pipe up: 'Yeah, Gaffer, you're spot on with what you've said and you're spot on with everything you're doing.' With that we got changed and all you could hear was Kevin Dillon and Billy Gilbert going, 'Spot on?' From that moment, Kenny Swain's nickname was 'Spot'. We got him drinking in the end, but he was one of the better pros.

I'd played against Paul Mariner a lot of times, but I'd never have thought that he'd be the way he was off the field. He was a real fun guy and he completely lost it when he came to Pompey. After that famous meeting following the Wrexham game when Bally resigned, Paul said that he'd been a pro for sixteen years but he'd never been at a club like Pompey. He said that he couldn't believe what he was seeing and hearing, and we all told him that he'd get used to it.

Bally used to tell us that no one else wanted us and that's why we were mongrels, but the biggest mongrel we had was someone who played the least, and that was Eamonn Collins. He was about two feet tall. On a pre-season tour of Sweden, we were playing a game and Eamonn asked to come off as he said he had stomach pains. He got back to the dugout, put some trainers and a tracksuit top on and went to the burger bar behind the stand, bought a burger and started watching the game!

More often than not, Eamonn used to get on the mic on

the coach back from matches and be the main man for getting the songs going. Like I say, he didn't play many games but Bally used to take him along anyway for the social. He was uncontrollable. Eamonn didn't drive and I used to pick him up on the way in to the ground sometimes and, on a couple of occasions, on the way home, I dropped him off on the motorway. It wasn't at a turn-off, it would be in the middle of a motorway, but he used to tell me that he'd cut across the fields. I had good eyesight, but even I couldn't see a single building. Regardless, he'd say that he knew where he was going.

I roomed with Alan Knight for three years. He was a very deadpan and unruffled character; nothing fazed him. One day, a meeting was called, and it was a reasonably familiar theme: someone had got into trouble for something that wasn't football-related. The meeting was in the middle of the week, very early in the morning and we'd won on the Saturday so we all knew that it must have been about something one of the players had done. The meeting was called, but there was no Alan Knight at the club. Apparently, he'd been involved in an accident and they'd had to cut Knighty out of his car. Andy Gosling, who was the reserve goalkeeper, was shitting himself because he realised that he might now be playing. Bally had to learn his name because, up to that point, he didn't have a clue who Gos was.

Bally asked us to take turns to go and see Knighty as he was in such a bad way. I used to travel in with Andy Gosling. I told him that Knighty had come through for him in a big way, so we should go and see him. We went to his house and rang the bell and Knighty answered. He looked as if he'd been hit by about

50,000 darts. He gestured with his fingers, pointing at his face, and he invited us in but we didn't know what to say, so we told him to stick the telly on and it came on the *BBC South News* that Knighty had been involved in a huge accident – so he turned it back off.

I figured that I might as well ask him what happened. He told us that he remembered going to the Rifle Club, but he couldn't recall anything after that until they pulled him out of the car. I asked him whether he remembered anything else and he said, 'Yeah. As I left the club someone told me to drive safely and I told them that I would.' Maybe you had to be there but he said it in such a deadpan way.

He was out for a number of weeks after that and, whenever Gos was in the team, it was because something bad had happened to Knighty. Gos was a remarkable person himself because he smoked forty cigarettes a day and he drove everywhere as if there was a nuclear bomb going off. He'd only drive you to the end of the road but he'd have to hit 80mph before he got there. Gos was about 6ft 5in. and he was a heavy whisky drinker. He was a funny guy and wouldn't take anything seriously; he would admit, without shame, that he was only in football to pick up his wages. He used to admit that Bally didn't even know who he was. He was just one of many characters at that club.

ALAN KNIGHT ON VINCE

I was excited when we signed Vince. It felt like a major coup for Portsmouth to be able to attract someone who had played in the Team of the '80s under Venables. I'd played against him and I knew that he was a very exciting, pacy winger who would fit in well. The club had always had that type of player so he ticked all of the boxes. The expectation levels were super-high because of what he'd done at Palace but he didn't disappoint at all. He was better than I'd hoped.

We were very lucky to have him and Kevin O'Callaghan on the wings as they were by far the best wingers in the League at that time. Vince terrorised defences. Kevin Dillon was a big part of that side because he was our creativity but so were Vince and Cally. They were so important to the balance of the side. Wingers can go missing sometimes but, eight times out of ten, they'll win you games. If one of them had a bad match then the other would step up and, if both Vince and Cally were firing, then we knew we'd win the game.

He was really quiet when he first turned up at the club. He'd never go out and would just go home and watch the telly all night until the dot came up. I shared a room with him for three or four years and we'd sit and watch telly together on a Friday night *before games. We'd sit and drink tea and coffee and I'd be smoking too. But then he found whisky and coke and it created a monster.*

Once Vince got into that culture, he embraced it big time. In fact, it was him who came up with the nickname 'The Gremlins' for the boys but, if we were the Gremlins then he was 'Gizmo'. He was the lead Gremlin and he'd cause havoc. Vince knew how to have a good time and I've actually woken up on pub floors with him. He'd have a drink and get merry but he was always good value; he wasn't a beer monster or a drunk. He loved to have a chat and tell a story and he still does now – he hasn't changed.

That was one of the reasons why Bally liked him so much. Whenever we went away, Bally would always come and grab me and Vince. I think his reasoning was that I was a bit of a beer monster and could drink and Vince was good quality and liked a laugh. Vince would tell a good story but also laugh at Bally's jokes even if he'd heard them a thousand times before. Bally loved players who had flair and ability: players who would go out and express themselves and show their God-given talent and that's why he had a special soft spot for Vince.

One of my favourite memories of Vince was in Jersey and actually involves Bally too. We'd been down in the foyer drinking but we eventually came up to our room at about 3 a.m. and put the radio on. 'The Greatest Love of All' by George Benson was playing. Alan Ball burst through the door and started singing it at the top of his voice as it was his favourite song. The night porter came in and dragged him out and had a go at him about the noise. Me and Vince were sitting on the bed laughing so hard. We almost got chucked out of that hotel.

Bally used to take us to Jersey all the time but I think that was because he had a lot of friends out there and he just enjoyed the island. He liked to get the players away to relax. We'd have an iffy time whenever we got back but we'd always pull it round eventually.

We just had a group of players that fitted together. We had our lunatics that were a bit scatty like Kevin Dillon and Cally but we'd all eat, drink, fight and battle on the pitch for each other, and the socialising that we did was a key aspect of our success. That group has gone down in Portsmouth folklore and there are all sorts of stories that fly around about us but Bally allowed us to socialise as long as we worked hard and played hard in the matches. Then he'd back us all the way.

He treated us as men and, in return for that, we did everything within the rules. We wouldn't drink two days before a game; we'd work hard when we had to. We had a quality group of players and we enjoyed our football. It was all about team culture and team bonding. A lot of clubs were doing it; it was part of football at the time. Wimbledon were one of those that socialised a lot too when they weren't kicking us up and down the pitch.

The year we were in Division One there was a lot of stuff going on behind the scenes at Pompey that led to the team breaking up. It was so sad, after all the hard work by that group of players that got us promoted. The chairman was looking to sell and had stopped investing in the football side, which was a big, big mistake, and the team started to split up.

It started when Micky Kennedy left in the middle of the season and then Blakey and Vince left too and they both ended up at

Leeds. It just started to fall to bits. I suppose, after missing out on promotion a couple of times, we'd been lucky to stay together as long as we did but it was a real shame. Vince had to do what was right for him. On a personal level, I was gutted. I would have loved for that team to stay together for ever.

Vince is incredibly well-thought of and well-liked in Portsmouth now. People down here nickname me 'The Legend' but he's as much a legend as I am because he stayed in the area after he retired and his daughters and grandchild are from Portsmouth. That's why he's held in such high esteem by everyone around the place. I was the same. I'm originally from Balham in south London but I came here when I was sixteen and stayed.

Everyone down here sees the bubbly, effervescent character but, on the other side of that, he is like a lot of sportsmen in the sense that he is deep, and he used to get really upset about some of the criticism that he'd get and he used to take it personally. It would hurt him when people got a little personal. To his credit, he had the strength of mind and character to overcome it. I'd always give him stick too that his crossing was crap. In return, he'd say that my kicking was rubbish and would put him under pressure as they'd curl out towards him so he'd have to go up for headers to win the ball and Vince wasn't the tallest so he hated that.

I could tell a million Vince stories but most of them couldn't get published, and shouldn't, especially now he's got a grandchild. As I say, I've woken up with him on pub floors and there were all sorts of shenanigans that went on but it's probably best just to say that he's a great guy and friend.

CHAPTER 17

THE GAFFERS

BILLY BREMNER

My contract ran out at the end of the season and Portsmouth didn't come back to me with an offer until I'd agreed to go to Leeds. Bally came round to my house and said that they'd give me what I wanted but it was a bit late by then. I told him that I wanted to try and play up north. Leeds was a big club and they'd offered me a two-year contract.

Billy Bremner originally signed me for Leeds but he was only there for a few more months after that. I loved him. All our training consisted of was five-a-sides. He used to join in and he was still the best player; he was fifty-five or fifty-six but he had a better touch than the rest of us. He used to go round playing that reverse ball that he played for the whole of his career and made everyone look stupid.

When I was at Palace, Venables didn't take part in sessions. I remember Venners from his QPR days: he was a thinking footballer, and you tend to find that managers who are thinkers as players are also thinking managers, and they take a backseat.

Managers who, as players, were full of energy, tended to take part in sessions: Alan Mullery, Billy Bremner and Alan Ball were like that. It was easy for me to see why they got so many International caps.

Billy Bremner was great. He was emotional, but if you lost a game, he forgave you a lot more quickly than Alan Ball did. I wish that I could have played under him for a bit longer, because the boys loved him. Every day, he couldn't wait to finish the training session with five-a-side so he and his assistant, could join in. It's a regular thing at a football club that players get given the yellow jersey for being the worst trainer and he used to come in and take the votes every day without fail. He'd try and influence the players over who to give it to.

Norman Hunter was Billy's Assistant. If you imagine a play-fight at school, kids always try to get the last punch in and, gradually, as it goes back and forth, the punches get harder and harder. Norman was like that. He joined in on five-a-sides and you realised why he had the reputation he did, because he clearly didn't know where to draw the line. Ian Baird didn't take any prisoners when he played – he was a hard player – and he caught Norman in one of the five-a-sides accidentally and, the next time that Ian got the ball, Norman went over the top on him. He could have broken Bairdy's leg but he didn't even apologise; he just got up and walked away. I remember looking at him and thinking that he hadn't even hurt Bairdy because he wanted to – he just did it out of habit. He didn't stop to think that he was assistant manager and he needed Bairdy to play on the Saturday. It was in his blood.

I remember a training session with Billy Bremner that sticks out in my memory. Billy wasn't a great one for tactics; he just wanted his teams to go out and perform – a bit like Alan Ball. He signed Noel Blake, but we then had about five centre halves at the club so we couldn't figure out why the Gaffer had signed him unless he wanted to play with three at the back. Lo and behold, we came in on a Thursday and had a rare meeting and Billy told us that we were going to play with three centre-backs in a game against the reserves. None of us had played like that under him before and Blakey was going to be the one in the middle.

Now, everyone knows that if you play with a back three, the one in the middle is going to be the one with the ball all the time and have to bring it out from defence. I looked at John Sheridan and he looked at me and then I looked at Blakey, because he used to wear these boots that curled up at the end like Ali Baba, and I thought: 'This is going to be good.' The shout from Billy Bremner was: 'You've got great feet for a big man, Blakey.' That was the worst thing that you could say to him because his chest puffed out even more – it was about fifty-six inches. Mick Channon used to say at Portsmouth that the big man couldn't play, and that reputation should have stuck.

So we were playing the reserves and Blakey was having a nightmare. He was going back to the goalkeeper and getting the ball from him in the six-yard box and trying to dribble out the back and then knock eighty-yard passes like Ronald Koeman. He was getting robbed when he was dribbling and he was slicing the ball out of play. After about ten minutes of this torture,

Billy shouted, 'Hold it! Hold it! Big Man, your body position is all wrong when you're getting the ball and bringing it out. Go and stand at the side and watch me and I'll take your place.'

As I say, the Gaffer had this reverse pass that he used to use where he'd look one way and then play it the other but it had been raining so it was a greasy surface; he was wearing trainers and slipping everywhere. He was trying all these drag backs and flicks and I was laughing because I was thinking, 'He can't want Blakey to play like this?' Then, the next day, Billy called us in again and told us that we were going to play with a flat back four on the Saturday after all as it would make us a bit stronger at the back.

We went down to Portsmouth for the game, which I was really up for as it was my first visit back there, and we got beat 4–0 so we weren't that much stronger at the back. Quinny played up front and gave us a torrid time. My last memory of that day was that I went back down the corridor where the dressing rooms were and there were only two people left in our dressing room: Blakey and Billy Bremner. The gaffer was trying to explain to the Big Man how to bring the ball out at the back. I just carried on walking, laughing.

I hasten to add that when Pompey came up to Leeds for the return game we beat them 1–0 and the worst person in the world scored the winner: Ian Baird. I laughed because he took so much stick at Portsmouth and, when we mobbed him after scoring, he just kept saying, 'I wish Bally was still their manager… I wish Bally was still their manager', but they'd sacked him by then.

HOWARD WILKINSON

Things changed after the first couple of months because Billy – who was a Scottish version of Alan Ball – got sacked, and my arch-enemy, Howard Wilkinson, turned up. I'm not sure that I gave up on Leeds but I did give up with Howard Wilkinson. I loved Leeds United, it's just a fantastic football club, and I have to say that the fans, despite all of the stick that I took whenever I'd been up there with Palace or Portsmouth, were brilliant with me. Pompey fans think, quite rightly, that they're passionate, but Leeds take it to another level. It's another one-club city and it's an amazing club, but I gave up because of the manager.

Wilkinson had loads of qualities. The first thing I have to say is that he won the League, so he deserves massive credit. He was organised and professional but his persona was so dour. If you've never lived in Yorkshire but are aware of the stereotypes of Yorkshiremen, then he fitted every single one. He came across as rude and you couldn't joke with him. He had no warmth at all but, to his credit, Wilko was the first manager I played for who gave us individual dossiers on a Friday night about the opposition. He also gave us a list of foods that we could choose from to eat and he brought psychologists to the club. Nevertheless, the players eventually stopped playing for him.

Wilkinson said that we were going to play percentage, high-energy, high-tempo football, which no footballer wants to hear. I'd been around by then and all that means to a footballer is that we have to run more. I remember one of our first practice games when we were training with the reserves. Mervyn Day got the ball and we'd all pushed up. We had Ian Baird and John Pearson in the side and Gary Speed, who had the best spring for his size of any footballer I've seen. Now Mervyn Day was a phenomenal kicker and he caught one and it went to Gary Speed and he jumped up and powered a header.

Wilko stopped the game and told us that if ever we couldn't win a header ourselves then we had to be prepared to get kicked or headbutted to prevent our opponent from getting a clean header on the ball. He said that we should charge at them if we had to. I turned round and looked at Ian Baird and John Pearson because I thought that was their game but Wilko shouted and I turned back and he said, 'I'm talking to you!' and he was pointing at me! He said that Mervyn would be aiming the majority of his kicks at me and I realised that my games would consist of trying to win flick-ons and then chasing after them and chasing back.

Wilko told us that when we were defending, he wanted all of us to defend, every single player, and, when we attacked, he wanted most of us to go forward. It was perpetual motion but we had good footballers there like John Sheridan and David Batty whose games weren't based on high-tempo running, they were based on possession. He told us that we'd start a training session and that when he blew his whistle, he'd shout something and we all had to sprint to that position. We didn't know what he was talking about so he told us to play and after about ten to fifteen seconds, he blew the whistle and shouted, 'Corner for.' It didn't matter where we were on the pitch, we had to sprint and get into our positions for a corner in our favour. Then we'd play again and he'd shout, 'Corner against' and we'd all have to sprint again. This was how it went on. The training was atrocious. It went on for about three hours in the morning and two hours in the afternoon and it was all geared towards playing at a high-tempo. We even had to sprint to a throw-in; we weren't allowed to walk.

In our first game, we played against Swindon Town and we drew 0–0. I had a friend from Portsmouth who came up to watch and, at the end of the game, he said to me, 'Do you know what? After a little while, when you hadn't touched the ball for about fifteen minutes, I thought that I'd count how often you ran the length of the field and you did it thirty-eight times and touched the ball five times.' I told him that not only did I know that but that Wilkinson had told me that I'd played well. I thought I'd be dead in about three weeks.

To us it was a joke what he was asking us to do. We had to run onto the field and, at half time, we had to run off just to show how fit we were. We were awful in one particular home game, and Mark Aizlewood, who was our captain, came over to me and said, 'That was a nightmare. Look how long I'm going to spend in the toilet at half time...' and he stayed in there for the whole break just so he could avoid Wilko. After that, we used to have two or three players go to the toilets at half time until Wilko got wind of it and he used to go in there to see if anyone was hiding from him. The younger lads were afraid of him but it did the older players' brains in – it was like playing football for a dictator.

At all the best teams I've played in, we never wanted to leave the training ground, but Wilko used to take training and he'd just talk for ages. He had nearly as many meetings as Alan Ball did and he went on and on and was so wrapped up in what he wanted to say. Coaches often used to ask the players if they had anything they wanted to add, but Wilko wouldn't even give you that opportunity. He didn't want any feedback. He was always open, but only if you made an appointment. The other managers' doors were always open, full stop.

Wilko had managed Sheffield Wednesday before he came to Leeds and, when I first played against them, it was the season they got promoted. As was Palace's habit at that point, we tended to raise our games against the good sides and beat them as we still had some good players at the club. That particular time we were struggling near the bottom of the Second Division but we rarely got beaten by the teams at the top of the table. The big factor was that we had some players who had seen good times but were unlikely to see them again unless we were playing against a top side. It was a good chance for me, Billy Gilbert, Jim Cannon and Jerry Murphy to remind people that we were still good players.

I'd never played against Sheffield Wednesday under Wilkinson before they came to Selhurst that day, but we'd heard all about the cross-country running they used to do and how powerful they were; they'd barely been beaten since the start of the season. We'd had a couple of injuries and I had to play up front and, at that point, I'd never played against a team with so much energy. I'm not talking about being closed down quickly, because you expect that to happen, but they did things I've never seen happen on a football field.

We kicked off, and I was playing up front with a guy called Andy McCulloch, who had played for Wednesday himself. Andy wasn't very mobile so he was going to try and win the flick-ons and I was going to try and get on the end of them. We started off and the ball went back to our centre half who knocked it forward, but Andy was offside and the ref blew up for a free kick. That is the point in a game when you relax and, normally, wait for a side to get the ball and let their teammates get into position but not this time. I'd never seen anything like it.

It's common practice nowadays for a goalkeeper to take free kicks outside the area but Wilko was the first to do it. They got the ball back as quickly as possible and, from nowhere, Mick Lyons, who used to play centre half, sprinted upfield, their keeper came and booted the ball up the pitch and, suddenly, me and Andy McCulloch were fifteen yards offside. I looked at Andy as if to say, 'What's going on?' The two of us must have been caught offside twenty times in the first half because we couldn't physically keep up with them. There wasn't a point when we could rest against Sheffield Wednesday. You never got a moment's break. They always got the ball in play quickly and they were always on top of you. The ball would be out of play and they'd still be running here, there and everywhere.

We beat them at Selhurst but then they beat us 1–0 at Hillsborough and went up. The thing that I admired the most about that Sheffield Wednesday team was how fit they were but, if you play like that, then you have an early sell-by date. Looking back on my career, I console myself with the fact that things at Leeds may have been very difficult for me under Howard Wilkinson but, with the exception of Gary McAllister, others who might have been considered to be flair players all came to a standstill under Wilko. It's like they physically had to do things that they'd never been asked to do before and they couldn't handle it.

I was talking to Mark Chamberlain about it and he said that he'd played his best football at Stoke and had won England caps while he was at that club. He then got a big move to Sheffield Wednesday but lost about two yards of pace when he was there. He told me that when you play for Howard Wilkinson, you are constantly trying to keep up, and you sacrifice speed of thought and guile for being super-fit. You rely on being fitter than the opponent that you're up against rather than relying on your wit being sharper than theirs. Wit wasn't good enough for Wilko; he wanted you to run hard from the first minute to the last minute.

I only missed one game in my first season under Wilko but it was hard and I can honestly say, looking back, that I didn't enjoy one match under him. You have to work hard; people pay money and they're entitled to think that you should give 100 per cent, but they should also look at a professional footballer and think, 'I couldn't do this or that and that's why he's a pro and I'm not.' They shouldn't think, 'They're a fit side. If I was fit, I could play for this team.' That shouldn't be the case for people watching games. If that was the case then someone like Mo Farah would be playing for Manchester United. Talent should be what separates professional footballers from the public. The game is quicker these days and it has moved on, but there are still players at a lower level who are as fit as the players at Chelsea,

Manchester United and Arsenal; it's what those top players can do on top of their fitness that sets them apart.

If you play a team that's hard-working and your team is hard-working too, then it's a toss-up as to which team is going to win. But if you are both hard-working and one team has got more match-winners than the other, then it's the one with better players on the ball that's going to win. It's been said in dressing rooms in football for years and years. If you match the opponent's appetite for hard work, then your skill is what will make the difference.

Wilko's school of thought was that you should run until you can't run any more but, if you run until you can't run any more, then what happens when the ball comes to you? You're fucked. That's why you have to have a bit of thought: you choose when to work hard rather than doing it all of the time so that when a chance comes along, you can take it.

Gary Lineker used to say the same. He didn't care if he saw players running here, there and everywhere – he wasn't going to do it because he wanted to conserve his energy for when the chances came along. The first thing that goes when you get tired is your mind; you've got to stay alert and sharp. You couldn't criticise Lineker because he'd get you goals. He wouldn't bother chasing a full-back if he knew there was no chance of catching him. There was no point.

I know Wilko ended up winning the League at Leeds, but it's the same secret as for every other manager. No manager has ever won the League on their own; believe it or not, you do need some good players and the more good players that you acquire, or have to start with, then the easier your job becomes. I believe Wilko assembled those players by accident rather than by design. That midfield he had at Leeds was the best in the country, bar none – it possibly would be now too – and it was the midfield that basically won them the League: Speed, Batty, McAllister and Strachan.

But when Wilko came to Leeds, I know for a fact, because I was there, that David Batty and Gary Speed weren't going to be in his plans. Batts didn't like the training under Wilkinson or the way that the manager spoke to him, and Gary Speed might as well have not been there. It was only Leeds getting a few injuries that forced Wilko to have a look at Gary Speed because I don't think he could see past Speedo's good looks. He thought that he was just another poser. It was only when he had to play him that he realised his assets. Speedo could jump as well as someone who was six or seven inches taller than him; he had a good left foot and was a good athlete, and Wilko came across it by accident.

Leeds' midfield that won the League had everything a team could ask for. You had three people who could guarantee you eight to ten goals, which got you thirty goals from midfield; then you had a wide-sided left footer in Gary Speed and then Gordon Strachan on the right; there was a ball-winner in David Batty and a playmaker in Gary McAllister. All four were internationals.

It was then a case of getting someone in who knew Wilko's methods, and who could finish off the good work that his midfield put in. That person was Lee Chapman, who'd played for

Wilko at Sheffield Wednesday. Chapman was ideal for the way Howard Wilkinson wanted to play his football in those days. But, as much as he's a great organiser, Wilkinson has never found that formula again.

I remember George Best saying something once about David Pleat that summed Wilko up too: 'Why use one word when 100 will do?' But Pleaty's philosophy on football was a lot more attractive than Wilkinson's. Wilko's philosophy was based on hard work and a lot of thought, but Pleat's idea was to have a lot of gifted footballers playing with a lot of thought and there's a big difference.

The contrast between Wilko and Alan Ball was also interesting. Bally tended to lose his rag on the line during games or in meetings but he didn't lose his rag at half time; he'd systematically slaughter you, but he wouldn't lose his temper then. In the Leeds dressing room, you never wanted to catch Wilko's eye, so we used to jostle for position to make sure that we weren't directly in front of him. He was having another go at us one day and there was a tray of teas on the treatment table in the dressing room and he said, 'How many more times do I have to tell you about going offside when there's no pressure on the ball?' He whacked these teas and one of them went all over David Rennie's shoulder but he was so scared that he didn't move even though the tea was so hot, you could see steam coming from his shirt.

In my first season there, we were due to play Watford away and, on the Thursday before the game, Wilko called me, John Sheridan, David Batty and Gary Speed together and told us that he had a free kick he wanted us to try in training, because he might want us to use it against Watford. He couldn't have picked four worse people as we were the ones that liked a laugh the most. Wilko got the ball twenty-five yards from goal and said that he wanted us four to make another wall a yard between the ball and the opposition's wall, facing the ball with the goal behind us. Then he said, depending on what side of the penalty area the ball was, he wanted me to run over the ball to my right, Shez to run over the ball to his left, David Batty just to run straight over it and Gary Speed to run over it to his left and then turn and curl the ball into the goal with his left foot. He said that if the free kick was on the other side, we'd do exactly the same thing, except John Sheridan was meant to run over it and curl it in.

We ended up walking through it about a dozen times and, by sheer fluke more than anything, it worked in training. So he was pleased and said that if we got a free kick on the Saturday then we'd try it in the game. The four of us were all muttering to ourselves so he couldn't hear, but we were saying that there was no way that we'd try it in the game as we wouldn't have a clue what we were doing.

Come the game at Watford on the Saturday, we were having a nightmare and, surprise surprise, we got a free kick twenty-five yards from goal. We wanted to take it quickly to get out of doing Wilko's plan, but we heard a shout from the dug-out from Wilko going, 'Try it! Try it!' We were all saying, 'Oh my, God!' as we put the ball down. Bobby Davidson, who played for us, was standing on the end of the Watford wall and he was chuckling away as he knew that we didn't have a clue what was going on.

The four of us were standing there and we turned our back to the goal and we were starting to panic because the ref was telling us to speed it up. With that, David Batty said to me, 'What's this one again?' and I replied, 'I don't know, I'm just going to run', so he said that he was just going to run too. The four of us all ran over the ball and no one kicked it and the Watford players were shouting, 'Waaaaaaayyyyyy!' The ref shouted and told us not to mess around, so I told Shez just to hit it anyway and it went straight into the crowd.

Half time came and I thought we were going to get it because the manager liked a rant at the best of times. We sat down and the door opened. Wilko had a habit of pacing up and down before he spoke while he was collecting his thoughts. His first words were, 'Right,' and he took a couple of deep breaths, 'the free kick was an abortion. I don't know what you were doing.' We could see that he was trying to hold in his anger: 'What happened?'

We all said that we thought that the other was going to hit it and then he started going on about how bad we'd been in the first half. There was a treatment table in the middle of the room and he tried to kick it away with the sole of his foot to show how angry he was, but the table was screwed to the floor. So he said, 'I want you to give me 50 per cent more effort than you did in the first half and then Alan Sutton can treat my fucking foot because I think I've broken it.' Needless to say, we never tried the free kick again.

What made it worse was that Stefan Edberg, the tennis player, who was a massive Leeds fan, had come to the game and had been introduced to the team beforehand. There was this huge contrast between this massive star who had won six Grand Slam titles and was the model professional and us messing up that free kick. Honestly, it was embarrassing.

Once Gordon Strachan had been signed, I realised that I wasn't going to play on the right side so I played on the left instead, but then Gary Speed got into the team in that position the following year. I only missed one game in my first season at Leeds, but I knew I had absolutely no chance in the long term with Wilkinson. The only thing that kept me going and stopped me knocking it on the head completely was the quality of the other players that he also dumped into the reserves, who were in exactly the same boat as me.

Even someone like Vinnie Jones, who is right up there with Kenny Sansom in terms of confidence, was dumped for a short while. There was almost nothing you could say to Vinnie that would shake his own belief that he was a top, top, top player; the only time I ever saw weakness with him was with Howard Wilkinson. I was privy to the incident when he told Vinnie that he was in the reserves because he was rubbish and Vinnie actually came and sat down next to me and asked me if he'd really been that bad on the Saturday.

So, with Vinnie on board, we then went to Leicester City and played their reserves. We had the usual banter because there must have been about 10,000 games worth of experience in that reserve side. Just name the player and he was in that team: John Sheridan, Batty, Speed, Beglin, Aizlewood, Chris Kamara and now Vinnie Jones too. It was just one big joke to us playing for Leeds United reserves.

Our coach was a real school-teacher type and he did the team talk, which we never took any notice of, but he said at the end of it that he was going to make Vinnie the captain. We were all chuffed for him. Vinnie led us out at Filbert Street, and the stand opposite the tunnel was really low, and he had a ball in his hand and he half volleyed it, trying to put a bit of backspin on the ball so it came back towards him but he kicked it over that stand and out of the ground. My accomplices at the club were David Batty, Gary Speed and Glynn Snodin and we all looked at each other and just started laughing.

I hated my time under Wilkinson. In the evenings, I would go out and then come back to the club, be let into the manager's office, have a few drinks from his drinking cabinet and then go back out on the town. One story that sums up Howard Wilkinson is that even if Leeds were playing your local team and that's where all your family lived and you wanted to meet them after the game, you had to first ask him forty-eight hours before the match if it would be OK to stay at home afterwards. His reply was always the same: 'We'll see how we get on.'

Being my first season at Leeds, I still had all my friends, my family and my house down south. It hadn't been a problem for Billy Bremner, because anyone with a modicum of sense would realise that you were staying in a hotel in Leeds during the week, away from your family, and you just wanted a night with them before reporting back at the correct time on the Monday. I wasn't asking to travel to the game on my own. I understood that the team should be together before a match, but I used to ask the club secretary to arrange for my car to be taken down south so that I could have it after the game.

Wilko wasn't being awkward because he thought there was a chance he might call us in for Sunday training; he never ever did that. He did it to show you who was the boss. If we did lose the game then you still had to go up to him again and ask if you could stay down. Six times out of ten, he'd say yes, which, really, isn't a very high percentage, all things considered.

We were due to play Oxford United away and I'd arranged with my mate, Sam, to come up and stay with me in Leeds for a couple of days before the game. Oxford was only an hour and a quarter away from where I lived, so Sam drove my car down to their ground, which meant I would be able to get to Portsmouth by 7 p.m. That would have been really good for me as it would enable me to see my family and friends. I stress that this wasn't a problem with Billy Bremner and, sometimes, he'd even tell me to come back on a Tuesday as he was sensitive to the footballer as a human being.

We lost the game 3–2 and didn't play very well. We took decent support down there; Oxford weren't doing very well so it was a bad defeat. Wilko wasn't very happy with our performance and was having a go at us in the dressing room and I vividly remember him having a go at John Sheridan as he didn't think that he was taking the game seriously enough. He got the hump even more as he thought that Shez was laughing, so he told him to stop smiling. He obviously had never looked at Shez closely enough because Shez always had a smile on his face; he couldn't wipe it off. He was like the Joker.

Wilko ended up keeping us back for half an hour to have a go at us and then he told us he wanted us all back on the coach. I reminded him that he'd said that it would be OK for me to stay down if I asked his permission, but he just repeated, 'Back on the coach!' Now, I'd already told loads of people that I was going for it that night in Portsmouth and made arrangements; I had all my nightclub circuit sorted out and I was also going to see my daughter which was the main reason why I wanted to stay down.

While I was in the bath, I concocted a plan that I would go for a drink in the Players' Lounge while the coach was coming round to pick everyone up and then I would hide behind the bar so that the secretary wouldn't find me when they realised that they were one short. The time came for everyone to get on the coach and I said that I wasn't going. I told the other players that I'd handle whatever Wilko had to throw at me on Monday. The players all reckoned that Wilkinson wouldn't leave without me, but I refused to go. I hid behind the bar at the allotted time and I told the bar staff so they'd cover for me. The secretary came in and asked for me but a couple of the Oxford players told him that I wasn't in there. It felt like about twenty minutes, but it must have been about five, before my mate, Sam, came in and told me that the coach had gone.

The whole of my drive back to Leeds on the Monday morning was spent thinking about how much I was going to get fined and how much Wilko was going to have a go at me, so I was trying to think of an excuse. I thought that I'd get in first, so I asked Mick Hennigan if I could see the manager and he told me that he was coming out for training anyway. I ran up to Wilko and said, 'Cheers, Gaffer. Thanks for leaving me in the middle of

Oxford.' His reply to me was: 'Were you inconvenienced?' I told him that I was and that, because he'd left without me, I'd had to get a train to London, then to Portsmouth, and had spent the whole of my Saturday night travelling. He asked me again if I was inconvenienced and I replied, 'I've just told you that I was!' and he said, 'Well, that's good then', and he turned his back and walked away from me. I knew that he'd think that if I'd had to run around and had a hassle then it was OK. Little did he know that I'd had a great night and a magnificent Sunday.

CHAPTER 18

STAYING SANE

Howard Wilkinson had this habit of picking his team through training and you knew that if you weren't involved in the set pieces then you wouldn't be playing in the game come Saturday. One day, he told Peter Haddock, who was one of the other centre-halves, to mark someone, so Ian Baird turned round to Noel Blake and told him that it looked like he'd been bombed. We finished training and Blakey was in a foul mood. Our assistant manager was a guy called Micky Hennigan, who tried to be the link between the players and the manager. What he knew but dared not tell the manager, because he'd lose the players' trust, was that our nickname for Howard Wilkinson was 'God' because he thought he was never wrong, but we only called him that behind his back.

We used to have to make an appointment to see Wilko – he was that arrogant. Blakey walked over to Micky Hennigan and said, 'Micky, I want to see God and I want to see him now.' Micky told him to go and have a bath and he'd try to sort it out. There was me, Bairdy and Blakey wallowing in the bath, and Blakey was seething. Me and Bairdy were chuckling away discreetly and having a few glances at Blakey. If you've ever seen a hippo in the water, you can just see its nostrils and that's what Blakey looked like. With that, Micky Hennigan walked into the room and put his head around the door and told the Big Man that he had an audience with God. Blakey responded, 'I'm sick and tired of that coward. I don't want a fucking audience. Just me and him, face to face.' Me and Bairdy sunk down into the water.

For the two years at Leeds, one of my best mates there was John Sheridan. He was a very funny man. Whenever Blakey used to come in through the door, Shez used to sing an old Junior Walker song which I knew because I was a big Motown fan. 'I said "Shotgun. Shoot 'em 'fore they run now. Shotgun!"' One day, Blakey asked me why Shez always sang that song whenever he walked into a room. I told him that I didn't have a clue, but the truth is that I did, because one of the first things that Shez said to me was, 'What about Blakey's nostrils? That's a double-barrelled shotgun if ever I've seen one!' But no one ever had a go to Blakey's face. In fact, the only person I've ever seen do that was Micky Channon – 'I'm just telling you how it is, Big Man. You cannot play!' – and Blakey wanted to kill Channon.

After I'd completely gone over the edge at Leeds, I used to come in at all sorts of times. One day, I bowled in a little bit late and Ian Baird was sitting in the dressing room and he looked at me and said, 'You don't give a fuck, do you?' I said, 'No. Not any more. I'm not playing for him. He's completely fucked me off.' All I wanted to do was a bit of training and then get out of there and go to the town centre for a drink. That was all I wanted to do.

I told Bairdy that I'd always fancied being a rep for a sports company. Although it was only me and Bairdy who were having the conversation, there was a roomful of people in the dressing room and they were all listening in. Bairdy asked me what kind of money I'd get for that and I told him that I'd probably be on a basic salary with some kind of commission. With that, Blakey got up, adjusted his boot and kicked the toe into the ground. He didn't say anything until he got to the door. Then he turned around and raised his eyebrow and said, 'I'd imagine when you work for that kind of company that you'd be on a basic salary with commission,' and, with that, he walked out. He'd just repeated everything I'd said and yet done it in a way that implied that he was being really astute. As he shut the door, Gordon Strachan jumped up, put his ear to the door, listened to make sure that he was walking off down the corridor and he said, 'Right, boys, you can laugh now.'

There was another thing that happened with Blakey at Leeds that opened him up to ridicule, and people actually laughed in his face this time because they couldn't keep it in any more. We had the most powerful reserve side in history because loads of big players had been pushed out by Wilkinson. We had a game one day and a few of us got there early – one of the few times that I did – and we were sitting in the foyer. Jim Beglin was there and he was another of the Blakey Baiters, behind his back. Blakey sat down and was reading a paper. All of a sudden, Jim's gone: 'Can you smell that, Vince? Someone smells nice.' I didn't have any aftershave on so Blakey said that it was him. Jim asked him what the smell was and he said, 'I've got that Polio on' – instead of 'Polo'. I picked up the paper and put it over my face so

Blakey didn't see me laughing, but when he left the room I said, 'Is that the aftershave that makes you walk funny?'

Vinnie Jones, who ended up at Leeds, had a huge reputation from his time at Wimbledon. I actually didn't realise what a good striker of the ball he was until I played with him. He was a good passer of the ball too. The good thing about Vinnie, and most other hard men, was that they never tried to do things they couldn't do. Some people used to say that they were poor players, but they always played to their strengths. That's down to strength of character; it takes someone with a special type of character to limit themselves to what they're good at.

Vinnie had a special confidence about him. To give you an example, we had a table tennis table outside the dressing room at Leeds, and I was one of the better players. Gordon Strachan used to give a running commentary standing at the side, and I can clearly recall him saying, 'Wee man, you're different class at this game.' One day, Vinnie Jones came in from training and I was playing table tennis. Strach asked Vinnie if he'd seen me play, as I was top-quality and I used all the spins and slices. Vinnie just said, 'He ain't that good' but Strach told Vinnie that he was crap, so Vinnie told me that he'd play me for £100.

All the young players were watching and it was like one of those old Wild West films where someone comes into the bar and challenges you to a duel. Everything stopped and word got round and, suddenly, everyone was crowded around the table watching. Strach was making it worse because he kept saying, 'This is the easiest £100 you'll ever make, Wee Man!' I don't know what it was but I felt more nervous than at any time in my career.

My hand shook as it held the bat, and Vinnie was winding the situation up, but he was crap at table tennis – honest to God, he was crap. But, instead of slicing my serve, or putting loads of spin on the ball like I normally did, I was hitting my serve into the table so that it bounced up really high over the net, and he was just smashing the ball back. I got beat – simply because he was so confident that he could beat me.

But Vinnie was always going to make it in life. I said that he would play within his limits on the pitch. On the training field, he did like trying to show people that he could play, but none of us would have it, particularly Strach. One day, we went out to train and we were milling around waiting for the coach to come out and there were some footballs on the ground. You can see any kid in the park do this, and I happened to look at Vinnie out of the corner of my eye as he tried to roll the ball backwards and then flick it up into his hands. As he flicked it, he kicked the ball over the fence, and then turned around to see if anyone had seen him. I burst out laughing and he just said, 'Of all the people!' I shouted out to Strach, my partner in crime, and told him what I'd seen. The fence was about eight feet high and the ball was on the other side of it. Vinnie was desperately trying to make out that he had been trying to flick it over the fence deliberately.

Vinnie had a reputation as a hard man, but David Batty was even harder. I played with Batts when he was eighteen or nineteen and, even then, he used to kick people in training. Of all the hard men that I played with, only Batts and Mick Kennedy wouldn't draw the line at kicking their own players. Batts perfected a technique where he would hit players in their follow through. He was more of a niggly fouler whereas Mick Kennedy was more flamboyant. Mick perfected a tackle where the first thing that he would do was hit the ball and then, as he hit it, he would roll his body so that his momentum would carry him over the ball so that he could hit the player too. It would wind opponents up because players knew he was trying to catch them but, most of the time, refs wouldn't give a foul because he'd played the ball first.

Batts had a great career, but he didn't really like football. I met him at eighteen and he was a typical example of what people from the south think Yorkshiremen are like. He had no fear of anything; nothing fazed him at all. I knew when England had their penalty shoot-out against Argentina in the 1998 World Cup that if Batts missed he wouldn't break down in tears because it wouldn't matter to him. All that mattered to David Batty was his family and he realised that it was only a game of football – if he had to take a penalty again the next day, then he would gladly do it, because it was his job.

He used to make me laugh. He would come out for training and, however cold it was, he wouldn't do a warm up. Discipline, team shape, organisation and team talks all bored him to tears. All he wanted to do was kick the football about, and he used to run out, walk up to the nearest football, lash it as hard as he could, and then run after it. I remember when Howard Wilkinson first joined the club, he thought that Batts was really dedicated to the game because he'd be out there kicking a ball about but he wasn't – he simply liked kicking a football. He had no interest in studying the game at all, or even watching it. He had no interest in tactics; he just wanted to get out and play and compete.

I remember we were playing a nothing game – we couldn't go up or down and neither could the opposition – and Batts said to me, 'Eh, Vinny. You see that girl over there by the corner flag? I'm sure I've seen her down the town. Do you recognise her? When we get a corner, go over there and have a look.' That's how much notice he was taking of the game and then, thirty seconds later, he kicked someone up in the air and promptly got booked. It was like being in the playground and that's why he infuriated Wilkinson.

I have to commend the lad, though, because, although he went around kicking people all the time that I was at Leeds, whenever he got kicked himself, he would get straight back up and he wouldn't moan at the ref or the player who had hurt him. He knew that if the same opportunity arose, he would hurt that player too; it didn't matter who they were. His thinking was so black-and-white. Batts was the most laid-back hard man I'd ever come across. He had a bad disciplinary record, but he was a good player; he was comfortable on the ball and I liked him.

Gary Speed was also a close mate when I was at Leeds. He used to have a smile on his face all the time and would laugh at anything I did. It was so upsetting when he died. He was so happy-go-lucky. Just after I'd stopped playing, I started working in hospitality at Portsmouth, and Newcastle came down when he was playing for them. I hadn't seen Speedo since I'd left Leeds, but I bumped into him and asked him if he could do a big favour for a mate of mine who had helped me out when I'd finished playing, and get him a Newcastle shirt. He told me that he'd see what he could do and, after the game, he came out of the dressing room with his own shirt and all of the squad had signed it and Shearer and his names were in pride of place. That summed him up really. He was a great guy. I loved being in his company and he was a good player too.

DRINKING AT LEEDS

We had a lad called Brendan Ormsby who we'd signed from Aston Villa, but he'd suffered a lot of injuries since he joined. Brendan was the type who didn't get out a lot and, if he did get out, had to make every single excuse in the world to his wife but some of those excuses were brilliant. Brendan was probably the most custard-pied person at the club, but he was one of my favourite characters. To sum him up, one day at training, someone said that they'd seen Brendan's car parked at Roundhay Park, which was a big park in Leeds, sometime between 12.30 a.m. and 12.45 a.m. the previous night. But when he looked again, it had gone. We asked him why it had been there and he said, 'I wanted to go out with a few pals for some drinks so I told the Missus that I had a golf-do to go to but she's like a detective. I'd had a few drinks and then, as I was driving back, I knew that she'd check everything so I had to stop, put my golf slacks back on because I'd gone out in them to fool her, put my golf shoes on and get my clubs out and I was just whacking the turf in the park to get some mud on everything because I knew that she'd check!'

One day we were sitting in the Peacock, which was the pub opposite the club, and we were having a good session and we asked who was going to stay out. John Sheridan said that he would, and Gary Williams, who was Brendan's closest mate, said that he was going to stay out for a little while too. Brendan said he wanted to stay out, but his wife was expecting him back, and he'd try to get back a bit later.

He went off and Gary Williams told us that in about fifteen minutes, we'd get a call on the mobile. We didn't know what he was talking about but he just said, 'You watch.' Fifteen to twenty minutes later, his mobile was ringing, so Gary told me to answer it but not to say anything. I answered it and I just heard Brendan say quickly, 'Ring me back!' I called him and said, 'Brendan, it's Vince' and he replied:

> What do you mean there's a presentation? It's a bit short notice ... this isn't on, you know ... I do a lot for that club already... what do you mean the manager is going to be there as well? What time does it start? 7 p.m.? I'll get there as soon as I can but I hope it ain't going to go on too late.

And that was it. He did everything to try and get out.

In the days when you were only allowed to have two subs, Wilko would still take eighteen players to away games with him. Even if he knew that you weren't going to play, he'd take you with him and then, as a squad, you'd train together. He had a lot of experienced players at the club with their faces pushed out of joint and, one day, he said he wanted to have a meeting, but only with the eleven players who were going to be playing. He read eleven names out and told the rest of us that we were going to train with the reserve team manager, but he wouldn't be in until 2 p.m. We were told that we could come back then for an hour's stretching and then go home.

By now, Brendan had been fit for two and a half months and he wanted a chance, but Wilko didn't even acknowledge his presence at the club. We had been told to be back at the club at 2 p.m. but we knew that we weren't going to be doing any training, as the Gaffer had said that we were just going to be stretching, so someone asked if the rest of us fancied going to the Peacock for a few drinks. Now, one thing about Brendan was that he couldn't drink. Honestly, his maximum was two pints and he would be rocking and reeling.

Most of the reserves decided to go to the pub because we lived too far away to go home and get back. We weren't going mad, though, because we knew we still had to return to the club. I had three or four whiskies, but Brendan had a pint and was getting loud, and then he had another pint and started becoming the life and soul, telling a few stories. We were all laughing and joking when, all of a sudden, one of the apprentices ran over from the club and told us that the Gaffer knew we were there having our lunch – which we weren't because none of us had eaten – but he wanted us to come back now. It was 1 p.m. We thought that we were going to be doing a few stretches at 2, but the apprentice said that Wilko now wanted a practice match at 1.15 p.m. and then added that Chris Fairclough had got a strain, so Brendan was going to play in the first team in this game.

Now, we were all wetting ourselves and it got back to all the other lads that Brendan was pissed. Brendan was playing centre-half and everyone knew he was drunk: Vinnie Jones, Strach, McAllister, everyone. But Brendan was trying so hard to appear sober because it was the first time that he'd been acknowledged by the manager and he really wanted a chance. Wilko was speaking to him and Brendan was trying to keep a straight face and act normally.

Mervyn Day was playing in goal and he told us that the first time he got a chance, he was going to launch one straight down the middle for Brendan to deal with. Lo and behold, a couple of minutes into the game, the ball has gone back to Mervyn and Wilko's shouted out, 'Right, Mervyn, launch one down the middle. Back four: I want you to drop off, win the header and then push up from there.'

Mervyn was the best kicker I've ever seen for a goalkeeper: wherever he wanted to put it, the ball would go. He launched one and Brendan shouted out: 'Brendan's ball!' He went to give it this big header but completely misjudged it and, as the ball dropped, he watched it hit the ground, bounce back up and hit him in the face. You've got to imagine the players. We were cracking up. The thing that made everyone laugh the most was that, after someone cleared it, Brendan checked his studs as if he'd slipped and that was why he missed the ball. Everyone was pissing themselves and Wilko got the hump and moaned that none of us could take anything seriously. Brendan had a nightmare, mistiming tackles, and I don't think he kept one ball in play. That was it for him.

There wasn't the same drinking culture at Leeds as there had been at Portsmouth but anytime myself, John Sheridan, David Batty and Gary Speed went out, we'd invite one of the younger players to come with us and we'd put them in charge of our welfare. We'd tell them where we lived and that if anything happened, it was their responsibility to make sure that we got home. We'd give them our taxi money at the start of the night with our address. They wouldn't have to buy anything all night – their only job was to make sure that we got home safely so that we didn't wake up in a gutter or in a cell. I'd tell them that, at the point they thought I'd changed character, that was when they had to get me home. I'd say that no matter if I screamed or shouted, they had to get me home.

On a list of the nicest players you could meet in football, John McClelland would be right up there. He didn't drink and didn't have many close friends at Leeds, so I befriended him and he used to make sure that I got home OK. He was a bit older than me and he used to treat me as if I was a young pro. Many's the time that he would drop me home, which was about fifteen miles outside of Leeds, and I'd wake up in the morning wondering how I'd got there. Then he would greet me at training the next day with his dulcet Irish tones and ask if I'd slept OK, and I'd tell him that he was the nicest man that I'd ever known.

PRACTICAL JOKES

I was always a practical joker but every joke I played seemed to backfire on me and Wilko would always catch me out. One day, I was down the town centre and I saw a joke shop that had a row of these dancing daffodils that moved when it was noisy. It just came to me that I'd stick them on the ledge in the dressing room. We had experienced players who were disgruntled at not being in the team, like Mark Aizlewood, John Sheridan, David Batty, Gary Speed and me, and our assistant manager at Leeds, Mick Hennigan, used to have a go at us for the sake of it, and we'd all had enough of it.

So I came in with the flowers one day and stuck them above the door and told the boys to look at them move when Hennigan went into one. Lo and behold we played the game, at half time the manager came in, and, right on cue, Micky ripped into us about us not earning our money. But all us players were concerned about was watching this 'pop group' above the door. He didn't understand why we had smiles on our faces while he was shouting.

Wilkinson brought in afternoon sessions when he arrived so we'd finish training in the morning and then we'd all have lunch in the canteen at the training ground. *Neighbours* was really popular at the time and Noel Blake was avidly into it. We'd eat lunch and watch the first part of *Neighbours* before we had to go back out for the afternoon session. They used to show the same episode every day at lunch time and then repeat it in the late afternoon, and John Stiles reckoned that Blakey used to watch it twice so that he could figure out the plot.

We had a first team squad of about eighteen to twenty players and, when we had to report back for the first afternoon session, there were only about six players there. Micky Hennigan asked me where the rest of the lads were, so I told him I didn't know, but I'd secretly told all of the lads that we had to report back at 2 p.m. when it was actually 1.45 p.m. Wilko hadn't got out there yet so I said to Mick, 'I don't know how to break this to you, but a few of the boys said that they'd be out as soon as *Neighbours* has finished.' The six of us went on our warm-up and the other boys must have looked out of the window and seen us running so they all came rushing out and the six of us started singing the *Neighbours* theme tune. It got back to Wilko that it was down to me, and he fined me £100.

That wasn't my only fine. The dressing room had these bulbous handles on the doors and, because I had dry skin, I used to put Vaseline on my hands after I showered or bathed. One day, I was leaving to go home and I tried to turn the handle but, because I had so much Vaseline on my hands, I couldn't turn it. That gave me an idea. I figured that if I smeared the handle on the other side of the door with loads of Vaseline, people were going to try to come into the room as normal, assume the door would open, and walk straight into the door.

The next day after training, I got a tub of Vaseline and smeared the door knob. The door had a frosted window so you couldn't see exactly who was on the other side, you could just see shapes. We were waiting in the dressing room and I asked three or four of the apprentices to hang around on the other side and let me know what was happening. About three or four people walked straight into the door and we were laughing. The players who were getting done were calling me a 'bastard', but they thought it was funny. Next thing, there was another 'Boom!' and we laughed again. I got up and opened the door and the apprentices outside weren't laughing any more. One of them hissed at me, 'The Gaffer!' and I ended up getting fined £500.

Another time, we played at West Bromwich Albion and we stayed at a really nice hotel. I was rooming with Ian Baird and the towels and the robes were really nice so I told Bairdy that I was going to take some. He said they'd notice that they were missing and they'd charge us. So I told him that after we'd gone down to breakfast, as the maids were making up the rooms, I'd take a few off their trolley. I got up for breakfast and I told him to leave the door ajar, as I could see the maid was at the bottom of the corridor and I didn't want to be waiting around for him to unlock it as I'd have to run back after I took them.

I could hear the maid singing in one of the rooms as she was tidying up, so I took about four towels and I ran down the corridor. I got to our door but it was shut so I started kicking it. I was hissing, 'Bairdy, Bairdy, open the door, open the door!' and I must have kicked it about half a dozen times and, finally, it opened really slowly. The reason that it wasn't left ajar was that I'd got the wrong room and I was standing in front of Wilko. He had shaving foam on his face and a towel wrapped round him and I just said, 'Alright, Gaffer. I've got the wrong room.' He shut the door in my face without saying a word and I had all of these towels in my hands. I hadn't even realised that he was next door. I went back to my room and Bairdy was pissing himself. We then had to go down for the team meeting and Wilko, thinking he was very dry and funny, said to me, 'You had rather a big bath, didn't you?' I was always getting caught... without fail.

FINISHING AT LEEDS

I pretty much identified that I didn't have a future at Leeds halfway through my first season there as Wilko signed Gordon Strachan. He played in my position so I played the rest of that season on the left. I knew that you didn't sign someone like Gordon Strachan from your bitterest rivals and then not play him. I was playing alright; I'd played a lot of my career on the left, so I didn't mind. It didn't bother me and it was an experience playing with Strachan for those games but I felt this wouldn't be a long-term solution for Wilkinson. Strach was a great player with a great attitude, and always looked as though he enjoyed playing the game. His experience taught him not to take too much notice of Howard Wilkinson and so he just got on with doing his job.

Wilkinson didn't make Strach the player that he was at Leeds; Strach had learned that himself through his career. He had learned to live the right way, to eat the right food and to look after himself physically; he worked hard and trained like he played. He ate pasta, had no butter or margarine on his bread, ate loads of bananas and he only drank half a lager a week. I don't know whether that was out of choice because, to be honest, he couldn't handle his drink anyway. If he had a glass of wine then he'd be all over the place.

He was a great pro and a very funny man and it was extremely rare to see him get angry off the field. I've seen him since and he nearly crushed me when he hugged me. Strach brought something to Leeds that then rubbed off on Speed and Batty. It didn't so much on McAllister – I'd previously played against him when he was at Leicester, and he was a good player anyway; that's why I say that the Leeds midfield came about by accident.

I expected not to be in the team after that season finished. Gary Speed was beginning to establish himself. Wilko had played Speeds at left back for a couple of games but he was really a midfield player. Footballers know when they're not going to be involved because they don't get chosen for practice games. Wilko was very careful not to have any practice games where the first team were playing against the players who were left out, because it wasn't kids who were being left out – there were lots of experienced pros who weren't in the side, and our noses were out of joint. These were players with 200 to 300 games behind them; it was a lot easier for me to bear as I wasn't on my own.

There were players like Jim Beglin, who had played in the European Cup Final, Gary Williams, who had won the European Cup at Villa, Glynn Snodin, Mark Aizlewood, who was captaining Wales up until a year before, Brendan Ormsby, Imre Varadi, Mervyn Day, John Sheridan and John Pearson, who had been with Wilko at Sheffield Wednesday, and Chris Kamara who was probably the fittest footballer that I played with. Even Vinnie Jones had a spell in the reserves after the first game.

Other than Howard Wilkinson, I thoroughly enjoyed my time at Leeds. The people at the club were great and so were the people in the town but, in the end, I was bored. I had three or four meetings with the manager as he wanted me to leave the club and he kept asking me what I was doing with my life and told me that I couldn't just stay there. I told him that I wanted to go but there was no point going if no one wanted me.

People say to me that I'm harsh towards Wilko because of the way that he treated me but my answer is that they should ask anyone that played there at the time what they thought of him and they'd all say the same thing. He even managed to have a barbed go at me when I left Leeds on a free; he couldn't even be nice to me then. He said that I could go to Stoke and he asked me what Leeds had paid for me. I told him that it had been decided by a tribunal and they'd paid £200,000. I didn't think that was a lot to a club like Leeds but he replied, 'It just shows how far you've come. This club wasted good money and, in just two and half years, you've devalued yourself by £200,000.' That was how he spoke. I did what I'd done for the whole time that he'd been at the club and I let it go in one ear and out the other.

IAN BAIRD ON VINCE

When Vince signed for Leeds, it was a surprise to me. I never thought that he'd leave Portsmouth as he seemed to have such a good relationship with everybody there – especially the fans and all the staff.

He was the court jester at Portsmouth and he was also a very good player for them. Portsmouth had been really successful while he was there; they'd hit the post and the crossbar with regards to getting promoted but then they'd finally crossed the line and that added to my surprise that Vince left. He certainly didn't take a long time to settle, though. He came up to Leeds in his own inimitable way and livened up the place. He was his usual shy self. He was Vince.

He hadn't changed at all. In those days, most sides invariably played a 4–4–2 and Vince would be the wide right player. He still had that unbelievable natural talent. When he first arrived, Billy Bremner was manager and he wanted the side to play passing football on the deck which helped Vince as that suited his game. When Billy was there, he was flying and there was a period when we were doing well.

Even though Leeds were in the Second Division then – or the

Championship, as it's now known – it's still Leeds United and people don't realise how big they are until they get there. Vince was a football man and knew all about Leeds' history but I don't think that even he realised, until he got there, what the club was really like. Honestly, we were probably a mediocre side when he first joined. Billy was trying to make signings off the back of two years of disappointments where we'd been five minutes from reaching the 1987 FA Cup Final and we were also within five minutes of reaching Division One, but we were still getting gates of 25–26,000. It's a big club, that's for sure.

Billy Bremner leaving hurt Vince but I think he was hurt more by the fact that it was Howard Wilkinson that came in after him. Vince had played under Howard when he was in charge of the England Under-21s so he knew all about him. Howard was dour and he was the polar opposite of what Billy Bremner was like. Billy had been a world-class player and a Leeds United legend and was voted the best player in their history. His training was based on the way that the old, successful Leeds United sides had trained. It always involved a ball and five-a-sides, which suited Vince's play. We'd work very hard for one day a week but the other days consisted of playing football.

Howard Wilkinson was brought in to get success and he totally changed the mentality and the ethos of the football club. He came in and took down all of the pictures of the old, great Leeds players in the reception area and he stamped his own mark on the place. If you look at the previous sides that Howard had managed – Notts County and Sheffield Wednesday – they didn't play in a style that fitted in with a player of Vince's ability. To get the best out of Vince, you needed to get the ball to him and, ideally, to his feet so that he could do his little tricks in the final third. That's how we'd played when Billy was manager; we were very much a pass and move side. When Howard arrived it was turned into a long-ball game and there was a totally different mentality.

But everybody tried when Howard first joined because everybody wanted a place in the side and to be part of Leeds' future. I wouldn't say that Vince ever worked too hard on his fitness because he was naturally fit. In the Billy Bremner days, if we did a running session, he'd do enough to get through but there was a period under Wilko when Vince worked really, really hard because he wanted to play for Leeds. Everyone did because of the size of the club.

In that initial period, Vince was still doing really well but he began to struggle under Wilko and it was soon made obvious that Vince wasn't part of his future plans. Howard had arrived in the October and we had some limited, initial success under him but we didn't get into the play-offs that year. His remit was to get the club into the old First Division and Vince and a lot of other players' days were numbered. Howard was given money and he brought in the likes of Vinnie Jones, Mel Sterland and Gordon Strachan. When Strach was brought in, he was in direct opposition to Vince as they played in the same position but there were a lot of other players who knew that the writing was on the wall too.

If you're an experienced player, like Vince, who has been very successful and played first-team football all his life and been there, seen it and done it, to suddenly be put in the freezer was not very nice. It wasn't just Vince either; the reserves had loads of good players in their side. The reserve league up there was called the Central League and had Man United, Man City, Liverpool and Everton in it and it was a really good standard and there were a lot of players in that team that were made to feel rejected, but Wilkinson didn't give a flying fuck as long as he got what he wanted.

From then on, Vince, being the way he is, did the best he could to get away. I'm not pigeon-holing him because a lot of players would do the same if they knew that the writing was on the wall for them. Those players at Leeds knew who they were and the biggest example of how Howard singled them out was that Vince and a couple of others weren't allowed to be in the team photo for the coming season.

At the time, Elland Road was getting painted. One of the funniest things I've ever seen in football was Vince putting on a painter's outfit and standing in the team photo with a pot of paint and a painting brush. Howard saw it and told him in no uncertain terms to fuck off out of the photo. But Vince knew that his days were numbered and that there was a clear divide between the squad players that were going to be involved and the ones that weren't. The ones that weren't were basically stuck in the freezer, so Vince turned into the painter.

He was the court jester, Vince. One of the funniest stories I can remember about him goes back to our Portsmouth days when we had a pre-season trip to Sweden and Bally put us in a hotel that was above a nightclub. You just didn't do that with that squad of players that were there. It was like an 18–30 holiday. Even Bally was in the nightclub every night and he admitted that it was the biggest mistake he'd ever made bringing that squad there. Vince was in charge of all of the videos and entertainment and they were piped through the main reception and we'd have porn videos coming on.

Vince was lucky because the camaraderie that they had at Portsmouth was a special one. Let's face it: they were on the piss most of the time. You had Kennedy, Quinny, Billy Gilbert, Vince, Kevin Dillon and Taity who would be down the Social Club most afternoons. But they seemed to have that bond that enabled them to be successful.

I always thought that Vince wore a bit of a mask because one of the biggest things that we'd laugh about with him was the Team of the '80s tag from Palace. Those players – the likes of Gilbert, Murphy, Sansom and Vince – were all expected to become superstars but only one of them, Kenny Sansom, did. I remember Billy Gilbert telling me that he'd had a kick in the bollocks when Terry Venables left Palace and went to QPR and he didn't take him with him and signed Terry Fenwick instead. I imagine that Vince felt the same.

Let's not forget, Vince Hilaire was a superstar. People forget that. He was on A Question of Sport and, because it's my era, I remember how good a player he was. He got to his spiritual home, which was Portsmouth, and he had his spiritual manager in Alan Ball because he knew that Bally believed in him. Alan Ball used to just tell Vince to go out and play and Vince probably thought that Billy Bremner could give him the same. He would have done and he would probably have extended Vince's career if he had been manager at Leeds for longer. But, as soon as Howard came in,

VINCE

who was the polar opposite to Billy, that was it. Howard was a 'beat you with a stick' manager and, to me, Vinny was on a downward spiral then. It was goodnight, God bless for him. He probably started drinking more and lost his focus.

Vince was always made out to be the joker, and he was, but he was also a very serious footballer. He thought deeply about the game and I thought that he was really intelligent about football. When it came to training and playing, there was nobody more professional than him.

Make no mistake, Vince was a real football person. He is the funniest lad that I've met in football but he's very deep. I spent a lot of time with him at Portsmouth. I was a young lad and I was struggling badly there. I'd signed and it didn't go right and all of the fans were on me but Vince was very good to me and always supportive. He was a good lad and he could light up a place, but only if he felt that he had the support behind him and, as soon as Billy went, he didn't have that support any more.

CHAPTER 19

THE END

I can honestly say that Stoke City was the only club I played at where I've been barracked by my own supporters. I had a problem with the fans; they couldn't warm to me and the feeling was mutual. But I didn't want to be at Stoke in the first place and I lost the plot there, even more so than at Leeds. I didn't like the place, I didn't live there, and I couldn't wait to get back in my car every day to get back to my apartment in Leeds.

I only signed for Stoke because of Alan Ball. I did well there on loan, initially, and quite liked it but, when I signed permanently, I obviously spent more time there and didn't like the place. I'd played much better in my loan spell than I did after I signed permanently, which is often the way, but going there was all about Alan Ball for me. Unfortunately, Bally wasn't very popular with the Stoke fans so, consequently, anyone with links to him was unpopular too and didn't get a chance.

Being with Bally for so long, I tended to know when he was feeling a bit cantankerous or whether he'd had a drink the night before and had a hangover so I knew when you had to make sure that your training was spot on, or you were going to pay for it. At one point we were training and, for the umpteenth time, the forwards had made the wrong run so Bally stopped the session.

We trained next to the ground and it used to be heavy and boggy. Bally told the forwards that he was sick and tired of them not being able to make the right runs and he marched onto the pitch with his flat cap and his tracksuit on. Bally told everyone to stand still and gave the ball to the right back and, as he was talking, he started making this arced run that he wanted the forwards to make to stay onside. He was wearing moulded boots, though, and he started to slip as he was running and was trying to keep his feet but he landed flat on his face and his flat cap went down over his eyes. All the players were looking at each other, trying not to laugh. He was in a right mood and he jumped up and looked at all of us and he just shouted: 'You stupid fuckers!' and walked off. It was the talk of the training session and all of us were mimicking it.

At that point, it was like the last days of Pompeii and we knew that something was afoot. Results were bad and we had injuries and he didn't have the players he needed. I wasn't there for very long after Bally left and I couldn't wait to get away. It's the only club that I've ever walked out of but I don't think that anyone noticed, as I was that bad.

I thought that Graham Paddon let Bally down after Bally got sacked, as Paddo thought he could do the job better and he took over for a while. I got ill at that time, which was a rarity in my life; I had a really bad case of sinusitis and was in a bad way for a couple of weeks. I was stuck in Leeds on my own but, in the end, I had to go in so the doctor at Stoke could see me and he agreed that I was struggling; I couldn't even open my eyes.

THE END

I hadn't trained for two weeks but Graham Paddon told me that I had to play on the Saturday. I explained that I hadn't trained and he knew that I wasn't the fittest anyway but he said that I'd be alright. I didn't want to play for Stoke full stop by that time as everyone had turned on all of the old Pompey boys – Mick Kennedy, Blakey, Lee Sandford and me – because of Bally, but Paddo insisted that I played.

We kicked off and the ball was passed out to the right to me; I went to trap it and it went under my foot. The ball was going at snail's pace, which was a good start, and then, the next time I got it, I tried to take on the full-back and he picked his nose, ate it and then took the ball off me. The first fifteen minutes of the game carried on in that vein. I was just having an Armageddon. I glanced at the dugout and I saw the sub warming up and I thought, 'Surely, he's not going to humiliate me after fifteen minutes?' but then I saw my number come out and I realised that he was taking me off.

It was embarrassing. I was right over on the other side of the field but the game was immaterial to me by then and I was just thinking on my feet about what I was going to do when I got subbed. There was a break in play and my number was put up and the crowd cheered as they wanted me off so I decided to limp off the field for the whole width of the pitch to make people think that I was injured and that's why I'd played so badly.

As I got to the edge of the pitch, I looked into the dugout at Graham Paddon and said, 'Cheers, Paddo,' had a shower, found my girlfriend and my little 'un and we got in the car. I also spoke with a lad from Portsmouth, who was still on trial from Alan Ball's days, and told them all that we were driving back to Portsmouth and I was never seen at Stoke again. They fined me three weeks' wages and I didn't speak to Paddo again. My contract was terminated.

Ultimately, I didn't have a problem with Paddo but I did have a problem with Stoke City and the place. I just didn't like it and I've got nothing good to say about the place. My theory is that it's a jealousy thing. I'm not just talking about Stoke as a football club, I'm talking about the area, and I make no apologies for it because of the way that I was treated. I've racked my brains about how a place can be so bad and I just hope that the people of Stoke can realise that if you're in the middle of a triangle that consists of Liverpool, Manchester and Birmingham, then no one is going to go to Stoke, and they need to get over it.

There were a couple of highlights at Stoke, but they happened off the pitch. You come across loads of different characters in your career and Tony Gallimore was right up there with people like Peter Nicholas and Noel Blake for doing the daftest things that you're ever likely to see. He was a good player and had a decent left foot. One day, we put him to the test, though I didn't think for one minute that it would work.

He'd been complaining about his boots being on their last legs, so I told him he should go to the kit manager and the secretary and get a chitty signed so that he could get some new ones. He asked what a chitty was and we told him that the secretary would ask what boots he wanted and then he'd put down the amount on a piece of paper and then he'd sign it. He asked what he should do then, and we told him that he should take the chitty to the bank.

THE END

We didn't think any more of it but then, the next day, we came in for training and Gally said that he'd got into trouble with the manager because the police had got involved. He told us that he'd done everything we told him to and had got the chitty, taken it to the bank, and had got into the queue as it was busy. He'd finally got to the cashier's desk and Gally told us that he'd slid the piece of paper under the counter but the cashier had asked him what he wanted her to do with it. Gally told her that he wanted some money and so she'd slowly reached under the counter and pressed the security button. He said a huge noise had gone off and, the next thing, three coppers had run into the bank and the cashier pointed at him. She thought that he was holding the bank up as he'd asked for money!

Billy Whitehurst was someone I'd played against throughout my career, and then I ended up in the same side as him at Stoke City. He never backed away from anyone and I saw him have some fisticuffs in the tunnel at Hull with Noel Blake. Billy wasn't frightened of anything, but he was a nice guy and we used to travel in to Stoke together with Wayne Biggins. I was used to people who looked big but didn't necessarily act hard, but Billy refused to shed his hard-man image at any time. He couldn't help it.

We used to drive across Yorkshire, through the back roads, and it was quite a drive. One day, we stopped in this small village outside Stoke at a pelican crossing and we were a bit late. This old dear started crossing the road and Billy just bellowed at the top of his voice: 'Did you press that fucking button? Did you? Some of us have got work to get to!' I thought the woman would have a heart attack. She must have been in her eighties.

I wanted us to stop the car and check that she was OK, but he was fuming just because she'd pressed the button on the lights.

I followed Bally around and, whenever he saw me struggling, he'd take me to a club with him and he did so again after I left Stoke. Because of all the years I spent with him, I developed quite a good impersonation of him. Whenever the phone rang and I heard, 'Alright, Little Man. How are you doing?' I knew that he was coming to get me again. Bally was now at Exeter and he called me up after I walked out on Stoke. I walked into his office and he was sitting at his desk with his little legs swinging. That was probably the funniest talk he gave, particularly bearing in mind what a competitor he was and the fact that he wanted to win at absolutely everything.

He told me that I'd love it at Exeter, that Devon was a great place to live, the people were great, and that he'd changed as a human being and he'd realised that football wasn't the be all and end all. Bally told me that there was going to be no pressure and that we just had to try and get enough points to stay in the division. I thought that he seemed really chilled and that maybe he had actually changed.

When I signed, we went on a run of about six or seven games unbeaten. He then called a meeting and told us all that we could be anything we wanted to be and that we could go up and go places and I remember thinking, 'He's started again…' From that moment on, when he changed his priorities from simply enjoying it to wanting us to get promoted, I think we only won another couple of games up to the end of the season. We could have gone out of the League if other results hadn't gone for us.

I was a bit older when I went to Exeter. At Portsmouth, Alan Ball wouldn't have it if you didn't do your fair share of work and track back and defend. He hated cowards. But, by the time I got to Exeter, I realised that I was only interested in going one way on the football pitch and that was forward. So, along with not running for a football, I realised that I was too long in the tooth to run back as well but, luckily, I played in front of Scott Hiley, who not only had good footballing ability but had good lungs too, which was handy.

It's no coincidence that Scott Hiley did such a good job that Bally then went and bought him when he managed Manchester City. He was a very good player, an excellent right-back, and he did all of my running for me. I told him, very early on, that I could either make him look good or bad and, if he passed it to my feet, then I would make him look good. I said that it didn't matter where I was on the pitch, even if he thought that I was going to get kicked, as long as he passed it to my feet, then I didn't have a problem. But I also told him that if he knocked the ball over the top or knocked it inside the full-back for me then, not only was I not going to chase it, I'd also make sure that the crowd thought that he'd knocked a bad ball.

So Scott understood that the golden rule of any player who played immediately next to me, or behind me, was that you should only ever pass it to my feet. I was capable of making the best passers look bad – if I had to over-exert myself to stretch or run for any pass, then I didn't want to know. Before Scott, Barry Horne used to repeatedly play balls inside full-backs and expect a flying winger to get on the end of them, but I used to just stand next to him, pointing at my feet. Barry used to end up apologising to me in so many games but he'd then say that he'd forgotten that he wasn't passing to a normal footballer! I'm glad Horney ended up having a good career; he realised that his main attributes were his excellent work rate, tackling and simple passing.

While I was at Exeter, a friend of mine was going through a bad patch with his clothing business. He had a lovely shop in Portsmouth and clothes were a great passion of mine and, every time I came back to Portsmouth, I used to go into his shop and look at his gear. He used to tell me to take clothes; he always did me a really good deal and no money used to change hands over the counter. He did that for me for about two years.

A few years later the inevitable happened and he told me that he was going to lose the shop. He asked me to lump as much of his stock into my car as possible; he'd close the shop for the day, and we'd go to Exeter and try to sell the stuff to the players down there. We left early and the car was packed and I told him that I'd squared it with Bally that we could use the away team dressing room as a shop and he could hang all the clothes up around it.

We'd got beaten on the previous Saturday and Bally didn't take us for training; he wasn't talking to us because we'd lost. My mate did a bit of business with some of the lads, but he was a bit quiet afterwards. I'd seen him talking with Bally while we were training so I asked him what they'd been talking about. My mate told me that after he'd laid all the stuff out, he thought that he'd watch us train for a little while. Bally had pulled up in his car with his tracksuit on and his dog with him and my mate introduced himself to him. He'd said to Bally, to make conversation, that Exeter obviously hadn't had a good result on the Saturday but he thought they'd stay up. It went quiet. Bally was still standing with my mate who got a bit intimidated and he thought that he would have to make some more conversation with him about football so he asked what everyone was doing in training.

Bally pointed over to the first team squad and explained that we were playing keep ball because we didn't have a clue how to keep possession. Then he pointed at the Youth teamers and he told my mate that Exeter had some good kids down there that may eventually come through. Now, at Exeter, we had a lot of older players who, if they'd been cattle, Bally would have refused to take them to market, and they were training on their own. With that, my mate asked what the group of older players were doing and asked whether they were injured.

Bally didn't even turn around but he pointed behind him and said:

That's the shit of the world. Don't even look over there. They come here and just pick up their wages and go home again. They don't care about themselves, their game, they're nothing. Their families and their families' friends should all be ashamed of them so don't even look at them.

Apparently, it went silent. Bally adjusted his cap, got back into his car and drove off. Those players were just banished.

Exeter was my last League club. I was only thirty-one or

thirty-two, but the way that I lived my life at Portsmouth had caught up with me. I had been released by Exeter at a relatively young age but I couldn't see that I had any more years left in me playing the game and I thought it was the end of my career. Unfortunately, I still had another three years until I could get my pension so I didn't know what I was going to do and then, one day, the phone rang at home and I heard, 'Alright, Little Man? How are you doing?' It was Bally. I thought he was going to give me one last hoorah, as he'd gone to Manchester City, and that maybe he needed a little bit of experience there.

As he was talking, I told myself that I was going to accept anything that he offered. He asked what I was doing with myself and I told him that I was struggling a little bit as I had no club or other job. I was just waiting for him to ask me to come up and join him at City but he said, 'What do you think about a summer season at Butlins?' I thought that I must have been hearing funny so I asked him to repeat it and he said, 'A summer season at Butlins. I can't do it now because I'm Manchester City manager but I thought of you straight away.' I thought it was sweet that he'd thought of me but I figured it was beneath me until he added that it was £100 an hour, so I asked him where I could pick up my red coat! That was the last job Bally ever got me.

CHAPTER 20

JUST VINCE

I didn't feel bitter when I packed up. Alan Ball said it was one of the hardest things he'd ever had to do when he told me that he couldn't offer me another contract at Exeter. I believed him. Bally was always genuine with me. In fact, it was easier for me to take coming from him because it wasn't someone that I hated ending it; the only person I could blame when I looked in the mirror was me.

In hindsight, and I'm not trying to be facetious, I wish I had collected those footballs when I was playing for England Under-21s instead of getting Howard Wilkinson to get them. Maybe my life would have turned out differently. It's funny how things work out. I was nineteen or twenty but laughing at Howard Wilkinson may well have been the thing that affected my career at Leeds. It's a fact that for every action you take – no matter how small it is – there's always a consequence. Taking the mickey out of Howard seemed so small and irrelevant at the time, but it came back to haunt me.

I love Crystal Palace and Portsmouth dearly. As I've said, without Palace I would never have been a footballer and without Portsmouth I would never have enjoyed life as much as I did; I wouldn't have two lovely kids and a grandchild without Portsmouth but – and I have no hesitation in saying this – the biggest football club that I played for was Leeds. I would love to have had a bigger impact there.

When Bally let me go, I had no idea what I was going to do next with my life. You'd think that I'd have learned my lesson when John Cartwright told me all those years before that you never think that you'll get old. When I was released by Exeter, I was a little bit older than he was when he said it.

I thought of John when I spent a night in prison for unpaid parking fines. I got picked up in Portsmouth and bundled into a police van and even some of the coppers thought it was embarrassing how much of a fuss was made. But that night in prison didn't make me truly reflective. I was still happy-go-lucky then. I was thirty-three and had been finished playing for about six months, but I still had the same mentality that I'd had at twenty-four or twenty-five. It's strange because even though I was in a prison cell, I felt safe because it was in Portsmouth.

Being in Portsmouth enabled me to cope with retirement. I don't think that I'd have managed if I'd been anywhere else. You've got to remember that it's a city with a village mentality so everyone knows everyone else. I'll be forever grateful to everyone here that helped me out. Things were a lot easier for me than they should have been but, in hindsight, it might have made me grow up a bit quicker if people hadn't been so quick to help me.

So I was around people who knew me. I had a very good friend, Peter Lee, who had a Chinese restaurant, and he looked after me, and another guy called Peter Yung, who I'd also got to know when I played for Portsmouth, did the same. They both owned restaurants so I never struggled for something to eat. They really helped me – particularly, Peter Lee.

The fact is that I, like so many players from my era, lived for the moment. Look at photos of us signing for clubs and you won't see any agents or lawyers alongside us in the picture. It's the player and the manager and that's it. Modern-day players have people around them guiding them and telling them what to do with their money and they're well looked after. It wasn't like that for us.

Financially, things were difficult. I remember going on one of my walks around Portsmouth one day wondering what I was going to do with myself and I saw a guy called Ian Forbes – known around the town as 'Froggy' – who had a reputation as a member of the Portsmouth 657 crew. They were notorious around Britain. He was one of their main men, but he was trying to make his way in the building business.

Froggy liked his football and he pulled over and asked how I was. I told him that I was struggling a bit. He asked me if I had any skills as he could employ me but I told him that all I could do was juggle a ball 300 times. He figured that wouldn't help much on a building site but he offered me work as an unskilled labourer. I was still quite fit so I thought that I'd do it.

But I didn't realise how hard it would be. It was back-breaking work. I was probably the worst labourer there ever was. You could make a film about the little ragtag workforce Froggy had put together. There wasn't a single moment in prison when I wondered what the hell I was doing with my life but, when I was with that workforce, there wasn't a single day that passed when I didn't wonder what the hell I was doing with them.

We had a heroin addict who used to disappear at lunchtime and when he'd come back, he didn't know who any of us were. We had to introduce ourselves to him twice a day. He employed his brother to help him out. We also had a Scottish guy called Jock who would refuse to do any work if he wasn't paid at 9 a.m. on the dot every Friday.

He held us hostage one Friday morning because he thought that he was a tenner light. He started arguing with the foreman about it and told us that none of us could move a muscle until he had his money. He had a piece of 4-by-2 in his hand. I was looking at the heroin addict and his eyes were spinning, going all over the place. That was my workforce. You've never seen anything like it.

We were doing some work on a house once and I popped out to get a sandwich and a packet of crisps. When I came back, the rest of the workforce each had a saw in their hands and they were sawing the joists. Everyone was doing it so I looked across and picked up a saw myself and started doing it too. The next thing, the door opened, and we heard the loudest scream in the world and it was Froggy: 'WHAT ARE YOU DOING? STOP IT! STOP! YOU'RE GOING TO COST ME THOUSANDS!'

He turned round to me and asked who had told me to saw the joists, so I said that I was just following the others. He then asked the same question to all of the crew and they all gave him the same answer. We found out later that the floor had collapsed.

This work was not for me, so I told Froggy that I had to pack it in. He asked me to work for his roofing company instead. I didn't have the guts to tell him that I was afraid of heights, so I was the roofer who would only work on bungalows or flat roofs.

Froggy really helped me, as he got me somewhere to stay. He took me to this building site and told me I could have the first flat that was built. Every morning, while the other flats were being built, I was woken by the sound of drilling, but he gave me the flat and I've been there nine or ten years now. He's a lovely, generous guy.

Building might not have worked out, but I then started DJing. I've always had a love of music and have always been a bit of a control freak, and being a DJ is a great way of making sure that you like the music that's being played. But, even with that, you have to be given a chance and, again, maybe because I was a footballer, a lot of the local restaurant owners gave me that opportunity. I've done it now for about ten or twelve years, but it's a hobby to me; it's not a job that brings in money.

I've always been a music fan since I bought a copy of Diana Ross and the Supremes' *Twenty Golden Greats* with the three lips on the cover. I've always thought that when something is unobtainable then you want it more, and at my mum and dad's it was very difficult for me to play music regularly because we weren't allowed to go into the front room to play the stereo. We had to creep in there and keep the music as low as possible as we didn't have headphones. I used to sneak in and do that so it was always a big thing for me to be able to play my own music as I got older, and it progressed from there. I then made sure that

I was in charge of music and entertainment at every club that I was at. The only exception was Leeds, as Wilko didn't want any music in the dressing room.

Lots of people have helped me in my life; I've given some examples and I'm really grateful. My life would have taken a different turn if I had been forced to fend for myself. As a footballer, everything gets done for you. Even when you go away, the club takes your passport and looks after it; they book flights – they do it all. In the long run, it didn't help my development as a person, and that's the truth.

I've suffered from depression. People talk about it openly now, and it seems like everyone is an expert on the subject. People think they know why I'm depressed, but it's not necessarily because I was a footballer and that's now gone. I've always had quiet moments and that's simply because of the way I was brought up. My mum and dad weren't ones for sharing emotions. I share more emotions with my mum now, and that's because my father isn't around any more.

The thing that I'm most proud about is that I don't hate myself. Although I occasionally suffer from depression, and I don't think that depression ever leaves you by the way, I can honestly say that I never hated myself. I've regretted saying and doing things, but hating yourself is the ultimate step in depression, because it leads to terrible things. I've never got to that stage and, for that, I thank my parents. I've always been introspective – I've never had a problem with my own company. I've never been influenced by people telling me that I should go out. I do what I want to do.

Bairdy, Billy and Knighty have all acknowledged in this book that I'm a lot quieter and more private than I appear. Lots of people who don't really know me think that I'm loud and outgoing. I can be after a drink or two. That side of my personality is, obviously, in me somewhere. To me, if the company that I'm in is familiar then I drink less. If I'm with people who are unfamiliar to me, then I drink more because I don't want to appear shy.

It's been a while now since I felt really low but, truthfully, without making myself sound like an alcoholic, drink gets me down. It provides euphoria, but it's false – and temporary. I think that I'm having such a great time, but I wake up the next morning and realise that my day is now wiped out because of the way that I'm feeling. You don't want to live your day hoping that terrible hangover feeling goes away. You end up lying in bed or sleeping and, by the time that it's gone, you've lost a day and a half. That triggers it because it makes me melancholy afterwards.

I found out as I got older that you can hide being drunk. Over the last four or five years I've drunk less and less. I now drink, not to get drunk, but if I want to get drunk and there's a difference. It's a choice.

However, I genuinely don't know how people can converse with strangers; I don't know how someone can sit next to a stranger and start up a conversation. I'm not someone who thinks that people are psychos if they do that and I will talk back to people I don't know, but I'll never initiate conversations, because I find that very difficult. I was like that when I was younger too.

To me, you should live your day how you want to live it. I'm not one of those that think, 'You've got to make the most of each day'. Overall, I think I'm happy. At this moment in time, I can't think of much that would make me happier. I think that I'm at an age where the shyness I used to feel around people I don't know doesn't bother me as much. It used to, but I'm happier in my skin now. I've got to the stage where I speak as I find. I don't try to fit in any more and I don't expect people to try to fit in with me either.

It's a cliché – and it's only a cliché because it's true – but life is too short. I didn't understand when I was younger when people used to say this but, as you get older, the days go so quickly. What I'm trying to do is enjoy each day. Before you know it, you're putting your head on the pillow and going to sleep. I'm not one of these people who ask what you did with your day. If you want to sit in front of the TV all day and you enjoy it, then you should do it. If you want to go out and meet people then do that. But do something with your day.

Personally, I can't understand people who keep their head on the pillow and say, 'Just five more minutes.' If you're tired, then maybe, but if you're not, then get up. You've got to squeeze as much out of the day as you can. That's why I only sleep for three hours every night. The nearest thing to being dead is being asleep.

I try to fill my days the way that I want to. I'm a major film and TV buff and I like to read what's going on in the world, whether it's sport or news. I go out and meet people when I want to and, if I don't want to, I can go two or three days without speaking to anyone. And now I try harder and harder not to take things out on people if something is bothering me. To me, the worst invention in the world is the mobile phone and, sometimes, I find that it's best just to switch your phone off. Then I take stock. It works for me.

As I say, I've never been the most outgoing person. I can't remember who said this to me but I've remembered it for many years and that is: 'A problem shared is still a problem.' I deal with the problem myself as best I can and, to do that, I need a clear head – I don't need phone calls from others. I'll switch my phone on and if I don't have a text saying that something is urgent then I switch it back off. That's what I do.

My dad dying had a really big effect on me. Truthfully, because of that, my hopes for the future are to get to my next birthday and then the one after that. It'll be the same hope again and again. I'd have said something different before my dad died, but so many people take each day for granted. So many people moan and complain these days about things that really don't matter. I've noticed it more and more as I've got older. Moaning never solved any problem.

People who moan seem to think that every little thing that happens is the end of the world, but what is actually the end of the world? Death. Not having money isn't the end of the world as much as people go on about it. The fact that they can moan proves that it's not the end of the world.

I want to say that I feel people's love for me. There wouldn't be enough pages available for me to say thank you to everyone who has helped me, particularly since I finished playing. I'd like to say thank you to Portsmouth as a city; Portsmouth has been a big plus for me. I'm a little bit ashamed as I took a lot of people's love for granted, but at least I realise that. I'm not one of life's takers. I'm not dizzy. I always appreciate people who have helped me and I do my best not to forget it.

CAREER STATISTICS

CRYSTAL PALACE

		Apps (sub)	Goals
1976–77	League	0 (3)	0
1977–78	League	26 (4)	2
	Cup	2	0
1978–79	League	25 (6)	6
	Cup	5 (1)	0
1979–80	League	42	5
	Cup	6	2
1980–81	League	31	4
	Cup	2	0
1981–82	League	33 (3)	5
	Cup	8	2
1982–83	League	42	5
	Cup	9	1
1983–84	League	40	2
	Cup	5	2
TOTAL	**League**	**239(16)**	**29**
	Cup	**37 (1)**	**7**

SAN JOSE EARTHQUAKES

		Apps (sub)	Goals
1982	League	22	1 (loan)

LUTON TOWN

		Apps (sub)	Goals
1984–85	League	5 (1)	0
	Cup	1 (1)	0

PORTSMOUTH

		Apps (sub)	Goals
1984–85	League	26	7
	Cup	2	0
1985–86	League	41	7
	Cup	9	0
1986–87	League	39 (2)	8
	Cup	5	0
1987–88	League	38	2
	Cup	6	0
TOTAL	**League**	**144(2)**	**24**
	Cup	**22**	**0**

CAREER STATISTICS

LEEDS UNITED

		Apps (sub)	Goals
1988–89	League	42	6
	Cup	7	1
1989–90	League	0 (2)	0
TOTAL	**League**	**42 (2)**	**6**
	Cup	**7**	**1**

STOKE CITY

		Apps (sub)	Goals
1989–90	League	5	1 (loan)
1990–91	League	10	2
TOTAL	**League**	**15**	**3**

EXETER CITY

		Apps (sub)	Goals
1991–92	League	24 (9)	4
	Cup	5	0

		Apps (sub)	Goals
CAREER TOTAL	**League**	**491(30)**	**67**
	Cup	**72 (2)**	**8**

Thanks to Ian King for providing Vince's Crystal Palace statistics and Colin Farmery for supplying the information covering his time at Portsmouth.

ACKNOWLEDGEMENTS

VINCE HILAIRE

I'd like to thank all of the people at Crystal Palace who helped me to become a footballer and all the supporters of the club that backed me while I was there. I'd also like to thank everyone in the city of Portsmouth who has helped me become the man that I am today.

TOM MASLONA

Thanks to Ian King and Colin Farmery for their statistical input; to Neil Everitt and Colin for the photos that have been used in this book; to Michael Calvin for the advice; to Neil Ashton and Paul Hayward; to Jon Budd of Jon Budd Design; to Kenny Sansom, Billy Gilbert, Alan Knight and Ian Baird for their contributions and to everyone at Biteback Publishing, especially James and Olivia, who guided us through this process. Sincere thanks.

Dom Fifield: we have been friends for a long time but, even so, you blew me away with your support. Nothing was ever a problem and I'm really grateful for that. Steve Mills: thank you for 'finding' Vince in the first place. The book wouldn't have happened without you. Jaime Long: thanks for the love and support throughout.

To Vince: thanks for giving me the opportunity to write this book with you. I don't think I've told you this but yours was the first autograph I ever got. I was devastated when you left Palace. I really hope that you'll be happy with the end product.

And just because I don't know if I'll ever get the chance to write this in a book again, thanks to my mum and dad for absolutely everything. I love you both.